Just the Facts

A civilian's guide to U.S. defense and security assistance to Latin America and the Caribbean

A project of the Latin America Working Group

In cooperation with the Center for International Policy

ISBN 0-9660084-1-3

Library of Congress Catalog Card Number 98-86351

Table of Contents

149 Assistance by Country

Foreword

This study arose from the Latin America Working Group's judgment that the U.S. military relationship with Latin America and the Caribbean deserves more attention, analysis and oversight. The Latin America Working Group, or LAWG, is a coalition of sixty nongovernmental organizations that coordinates educational and advocacy efforts on U.S. policy toward Latin America and the Caribbean. In a way, we are the primary audience for our own study: our work demands a better knowledge of security assistance programs, which have changed significantly since the end of the cold war. Making this information available in one place, of course, will also benefit other nongovernmental organizations, U.S. government personnel involved in the security-assistance process, and interested members of the general public throughout the hemisphere.

Past experiences with U.S. military assistance to the region make clear why this aspect of U.S. foreign policy requires a high level of knowledge and oversight. During the cold war, security assistance helped prop up often unsavory regimes against a perceived communist threat. Although the region is moving toward democracy and the human rights situation in most countries is improving, the U.S. government has continued to offer extensive aid and training to the region's security forces.

While effective oversight and understanding of aid and training programs are essential, they are very difficult to attain. Security assistance is transferred via a confusing variety of assistance programs, scattered among different pieces of funding legislation. Responsibilities for managing programs are divided over many agencies, which in turn are overseen by different congressional committees.

During the 1980s and early 1990s, most foreign policy analysts seeking to determine the level and nature of U.S. military assistance to Latin America rarely went beyond the Foreign Military Financing (FMF) account in the U.S. budget. While simplistic even then, FMF is no longer a useful indicator of assistance to the region. Though hundreds of millions of dollars were distributed to Latin America's armed forces through the FMF account in the 1980s, it is scarcely used in the region today.

Though generally in use during the 1980s, many other channels of assistance and contact have grown in importance as FMF declined. Monitoring U.S. policy in recent years made us at least dimly aware of new programs and categories, with cryptic-sounding names like "drawdowns," "deployments for training," "JCET" or "section 1004."

During the 1980s, the congressional committees which authorize and appropriate money for foreign aid programs oversaw a much larger portion of U.S. security assistance to the region. This became more complicated following the 1989 designation of the U.S. Defense Department as the "single lead agency" for detecting and monitoring narcotics entering the United States. Today, tracking the U.S. military relationship with the region also means monitoring the defense budget process.

Faced with this new complexity, we found that many others shared our lack of knowledge. In Washington, analysts with whom we consulted tended to examine specific programs or countries, but the "big picture" of the overall U.S. relationship with Latin American militaries remained beyond our grasp. At the same time, the Latin America Working Group's close collaboration with activist groups nationwide revealed that all of us shared misperceptions about U.S. security-assistance programs. In the course of our research, we found that congressional staff responsible for oversight of these programs also suffered from striking gaps in their knowledge.

This study seeks to help readers wade through this complexity by identifying, to the greatest extent possible, all U.S. defense and security assistance, education, cooperation, and interaction programs with Latin America and the Caribbean. Where possible, we have compiled this information into a country-by-country description of U.S. programs.

Though it recommends changes in oversight and transparency, this study does not intend to critique or praise U.S. military programs with Latin America. It is a base of information from which scholars, journalists, analysts, congressional staffers and activists can begin to form their own informed opinions and exercise greater public and congressional oversight of this major component of U.S. relations with the hemisphere.

To avoid confusion, we wish to present a few caveats and definitions:

- Primary-source government documents have helped us to develop the textual explanations of many programs. Readers will find that we often quote official documents to let the government "speak for itself." We do not seek to evaluate these programs' effectiveness or appropriateness.

- Our use of the term "security assistance" differs slightly from the traditional definition, which refers only to programs authorized in the Foreign Assistance Act and Arms Export Control Act. For the purpose of our analysis, we use the term "security assistance" as shorthand for all activities that have a direct impact on the U.S. relationship with Latin American security forces. In addition to traditional security-assistance programs, we include aid programs authorized within defense budget funding legislation, deployments, exercises, bases, open-ended military presences, and military-to-military contact activities.

- The text of this study frequently shortens the clause "Latin America and the Caribbean" to improve readability. When we use the term "Latin America," in no instance do we mean to exclude the Caribbean. Though technically inaccurate, the term "Latin America" should be understood to mean every country in the Western Hemisphere except Canada and Mexico.

The study begins with a "findings" section, which presents the most important observations to emerge from our research. It includes recommendations that focus chiefly on ways to improve access to information, thereby improving public and congressional oversight of U.S. military programs.

Descriptions of the programs themselves follow, grouped according to the following scheme:

- **Programs governed by the Foreign Assistance Act and Arms Export Control Act.** These military financing, arms-transfer and training programs generally correspond to the traditional definition of "security assistance," as Congress authorizes and funds them through annual foreign aid budget legislation.

- **Defense Department programs.** These activities are authorized and funded through annual defense budget legislation. They are divided into four subcategories: counternarcotics aid programs, training and education programs, training exercises and deployments, military-to-military contact programs, and humanitarian programs.

- **Bases and other overseas military presences.** This category, also funded through the defense budget, includes overseas military bases, ongoing military operations (particularly counter-drug operations), and other open-ended overseas military presences.

The next section presents this information for each country in Latin America and the Caribbean. Finally, an appendix discusses the security assistance process, explaining the conditions that make a country eligible for assistance and the reports and notifications which keep Congress and the public informed.

The individual country sections contain the numerical figures for security assistance to each country. The programs themselves are described in the "program descriptions" section. Those seeking detailed information about assistance to a particular country should first find the relevant table in the "assistance by country" section, then read the discussions of the relevant programs. These discussions may include descriptions of the program's activities in that country.

We are presenting this study in three forms. The book you are reading is also available as a web site (http://www.ciponline.org/facts/) and as a 12-page summary report.

Methodology

In carrying out this study, we sought to collect all publicly-available information about U.S. defense and security-related programs in the hemisphere. We also wanted to gauge how difficult it would be for a non-governmental group like ours to acquire information, in order to judge the ease with which oversight can be performed. From the outset, we decided to utilize only primary-source government documents or interviews carried out with U.S. government personnel.

We pursued three avenues in fulfilling these objectives. First, we collected all of the relevant budget documents submitted annually to the Congress. Some of these reports, particularly the State Department's Congressional Presentation for Foreign Operations, contain considerable information about arms transfers and State Department-funded military training and counternarcotics programs. After the budget documents we acquired other reports -- most of them required by law -- that are produced for Congress, such as the annual report on Humanitarian and Civic Assistance programs, General Accounting Office reports and documents from the Office of National Drug Control Policy.

We embarked upon our second avenue of research when we realized that the Defense Department does not provide similarly-detailed reporting, in a non-classified format, with its annual budget requests to Congress. In order to learn more, we began a round of interviews with Defense Department officials. We started with the Southern Command (Southcom), the Defense Department's "unified command" responsible for operations in the Caribbean and all of Latin America with the exception of Mexico. Southcom officials were quite helpful, both in providing information about U.S. military operations and exercises, and in making contacts with other Pentagon officials. Having learned from Southcom that some of the information we sought would only be available through the individual services, we conducted interviews with the principal Latin America personnel in the Army, Air Force, Office of the Secretary of Defense (OSD), OSD / Special Operations and Low Intensity Conflict, and the Office of the Joint Chiefs of Staff. While we were well received, these meetings produced no new written information which could be incorporated into the study.

Finally, we approached legislators who sit on committees with oversight responsibility for these programs. A number of members pursued information on our behalf. We sought, and have received, only unclassified information.

Next Stages

The information presented here is incomplete. We will continue to fill gaps in the data during the next phase of this study. To facilitate public oversight of military programs, the information presented here needs to be updated regularly. This project will continue for two more years, during which we will publish annual supplements to update this book. The web site, which doubles as the database for our published materials, will be updated constantly.

Having identified gaps in information, we are now pursuing more data about several programs, particularly the Defense Department's counternarcotics programs, foreign military interactions, special forces activities, and forward presences. We will carry out more interviews, pursue congressional inquiries and file Freedom of Information Act requests when needed.

Acknowledgments

Many thanks go to the Ford Foundation for providing the generous support that made this study possible. We are especially grateful to the Ford Foundation's Cristina Eguizábal for her interest, her advice, and her confidence in our project.

Many individuals in the U.S. government have contributed to this report by providing information or allowing us to interview them. We are very grateful for their assistance.

We also want to thank our advisory committee: Nicole Ball of the Overseas Development Council, Lilian Bobea of FLACSO – Dominican Republic, Tom Cardamone of the Council for a Livable World Education Fund, Jay Cope of the National Defense University, Rut Diamint of the University of Buenos Aires, Gen. (Ret.) Kermit Johnson, Lora Lumpe of the Federation of American Scientists, and Coletta Youngers of the Washington Office on Latin America. It was a privilege to have had access to such a brilliant group; their guidance was extremely useful at every phase of the project, from initial conceptualization to the final edits. Any errors or opinions in this study are the authors' responsibility, and not those of the advisory committee or their organizations.

We owe a great debt to the staffs of the Latin America Working Group and Center for International Policy for their unflagging support and useful advice throughout the course of the study. Special thanks go to the LAWG's Lisa Haugaard for her input throughout the course of the study and for helping us with a wonderfully thorough final edit.

Like most of the accomplishments of the Latin America Working

Group, this project could not have succeeded without the active participation of a dedicated group of interns and support staff. Our deepest thanks go out to Alison Giffen, Andrew Loomis, Nadia Martínez, Douglas Reilly, and Gail Taylor; their many contributions are evident in every section of this document.

Joy Olson   Adam Isacson

Director   Associate
Latin America Working Group   Center for International Policy

Findings and Recommendations

Findings:

- **The U.S. military presence in Latin America is substantial.** The near-disappearance of Foreign Military Financing (FMF) funding for the region -- the largest single source of security assistance during the 1980s -- should not be interpreted as signaling reduced military collaboration. For example, about 56,000 U.S. troops rotated through Latin America during 1997, most on counterdrug missions, training deployments or other foreign military interaction activities. The U.S. Southern Command (Southcom), the "unified command" of the U.S. military responsible for all of Latin America and the Caribbean except Mexico, maintains bases in Panama, Honduras, and Cuba, radar sites and special-forces trainers in many other countries, and Security Assistance Organizations attached to embassies throughout the region.

- **U.S. military training for Latin America goes far beyond the School of the Americas.** During the past few years, much public attention has been focused upon the U.S. Army's School of the Americas and its role in training Latin American military personnel. This is an important debate; however, in order to understand the broad range of U.S. training many other programs must be considered.
  1. Other institutions exist for Spanish-language training of Latin American officers. The Air Force maintains an Inter-American Air Forces Academy in Texas, and the Navy maintains a small-craft instructional school in Panama.
  2. Courses eligible to be subsidized by the International Military Education and Training (IMET) program, which 2,377 Latin Americans attended in 1997, were given at 150 U.S. institutions in 1995.
  3. Many courses are taught by Mobile Training Teams (MTTs) given by U.S. instructors sent to the region.
  4. Under the Joint Combined Exchange Training (JCET) program, U.S. Special Forces teams carry out dozens of joint training activities each year with Latin American militaries.
  5. The Department of Defense (DOD) carries out significant counternarcotics training through its own budget.

- **Primary source materials are difficult to obtain, particularly from the Pentagon.** Much information that is technically "public" could only be acquired with significant effort and, at times, through political connections. Statistics that the State Department (DOS) provides Congress for training, assistance and cooperation programs under its jurisdiction, we found, are seldom collected and reported in a similar fashion by the Defense Department (DOD). For example, the DOS <u>Congressional Pres-</u>

entation for Foreign Operations provides annual country-by-country program descriptions and spending breakdowns for the programs that it administers. The DOD provides nothing comparable in a non-classified form; most unclassified reports required of DOD are smaller documents that are submitted separately and therefore are less accessible.

Much of the most useful information about DOD programs in this study was the hardest to acquire. The difficulties we experienced in obtaining information about U.S. military programs indicate that it would be all but impossible for anyone in Latin America, on the receiving end of these programs, to do the same.

- **The State Department's reporting about its military-related programs makes it easier for Congress to exercise its oversight responsibilities.** This may seem unusual since the congressional committees responsible for authorizing assistance -- the House International Relations and Senate Foreign Relations Committees -- have been unable to pass legislation authorizing foreign assistance programs since the mid-1980s. Foreign aid, however, is a very controversial part of the budget, and the yearly process of appropriating money for aid programs is often quite contentious. To persuade Congress to approve its foreign aid request, DOS must convincingly justify the programs to be funded. As a result, significant reporting is provided in the annual budget justification documents sent to Congress. The foreign aid appropriations bills themselves contain their own mandatory notification and reporting requirements on military-related programs. The reporting that DOS provides often goes beyond legal requirements, making reporting the norm for DOS-administered programs. It is worth noting that the ratio of dollars appropriated to congressional staff responsible for oversight is much smaller with DOS-administered programs than with DOD programs.

- **On the other hand, Congress cannot adequately monitor DOD's activities in Latin America, especially counternarcotics programs, due to a lack of reporting and public information.** DOD has a very large counternarcotics program, spending about $650 million in 1998 on interdiction and counter-drug assistance -- most of it in Latin America. While it is clear that the designated congressional staff have access to more detailed classified information about DOD counternarcotics activities, readily available public information is very limited. The country-by-country breakdown of DOD counternarcotics assistance reproduced in this study, which provides little more than aggregate figures, was only acquired after a congressional inquiry was made.

The role played by congressional staff overseeing the Defense Department, according to a staffer interviewed for this study, could be called "management by exception." More detailed monitoring would be almost impossible considering the small committee staff responsible for this large budget. If a program requires an expensive weapons system, is controversial or of special interest to a member of Congress, the committee requests information from DOD and it is provided. Otherwise, the institution is largely assumed to be functioning as intended. It is not that DOD is necessarily hiding information; more often than not, no one is asking for it.

For example, most congressional staffers interviewed knew little about the "section 1004" counternarcotics program, which provided over $230 million in assistance to the region last year. Originally authorized to allow some forms of counterdrug military assistance, section 1004 of the 1991 National Defense Authorization Act (NDAA) -- while large in comparison to other U.S. programs in Latin America -- accounts for perhaps one-tenth of one percent of the yearly defense budget. Staffers' attention has instead been drawn to the newer, more controversial "section 1033" and "section 1031" DOD counternarcotics programs, which had significant oversight and reporting requirements added to them.

- **The principal authorizations for the military's involvement in counternarcotics are extremely broad and have no reporting requirements.** Very little public information is available about the authorizations provided DOD under section 1004 of the 1991 NDAA and section 124 of Title 10, U.S. Code. There is no way for policy analysts or most congressional staffers to track the execution of, or trends in, these programs in specific countries because they do not have the basic data needed to do so.

- **Oversight of counternarcotics activities and foreign military training is difficult due to multiple funding sources.** Foreign military training is now funded through both DOS and DOD, and general counternarcotics programs are funded through several departments. While this may have a certain rationale, it is problematic that no single body has oversight responsibility for all programs. Under the current arrangement, individuals responsible for oversight have only a partial picture and lack the time and mandate to concern themselves with the whole. In essence, the buck stops nowhere.

A new riverine counternarcotics program for Colombia and Peru provides an example. While this kind of activity would have been funded through DOS foreign-aid legislation in the past, the program was instead funded through the 1998 Defense Department budget authorization (section 1033). Meanwhile, the program received additional support from a Special Forfeiture Fund directed through the Office of National Drug Control Policy (ONDCP) in the White House, which ultimately channeled the money through the DOS International Narcotics and Law Enforcement

Bureau.

Greater oversight is particularly necessary because training and equipping militaries to carry out counternarcotics operations is a controversial policy choice. Critics both within and outside military establishments express concern about promoting a military role abroad that is not accepted within the United States.

- **DOD's international counternarcotics budget is almost triple that of State; the DOD and DOS budgets for counternarcotics assistance programs are roughly equal.** The State Department's International Narcotics Control budget for Latin America totaled $161 million in 1997. DOD's counternarcotics programs in Latin America during the same year were $444 million, while programs that provide assistance and training (as opposed to detection and monitoring operations carried out by U.S. personnel) totaled about $163 million. Despite the significant size of DOD counternarcotics assistance programs, most congressional debate around U.S. counternarcotics programs in Latin America still takes place within the foreign operations funding committees outside the context of the defense budget process [monitoring state, not defense].

- **Multiple funding sources, together with distinctions about what constitutes "assistance," create loopholes which could be used to skirt congressional intent.** Normally, eligibility and reporting requirements applied to a specific program through one funding mechanism, such as the foreign aid bill, do not apply to similar programs funded under a separate piece of legislation like the defense appropriations bill. Additionally, much DOD training -- such as exercises, deployments, and special-forces activities -- is not considered "security assistance" because its primary purpose is to train the U.S. forces involved. Even though foreign military training is clearly a frequent by-product, these activities are not considered training programs.

While seemingly an exercise in legalistic hair-splitting, these distinctions obviate rules dictating which militaries can receive assistance and what information must be disclosed. This erupted in controversy recently when it was reported that certain U.S. training for the Indonesian military prohibited in the foreign aid bill was carried out by U.S. special forces with DOD funding.

Where Latin America is concerned, this issue comes to light around implementation of the "Leahy amendment," a provision in the foreign aid appropriations law named after its sponsor, Sen. Patrick Leahy (D-VT). The Leahy language states that no U.S. military assistance can be provided to a foreign military unit if credible evidence exists that the unit's members committed gross human rights violations, until action is taken to prosecute those responsible. The Clinton administration said it would apply this provision to all U.S. counternarcotics programs, regardless of funding source. By force of law, however, the Leahy restriction only applies to programs funded within the foreign aid process, and not programs funded through the defense budget. The Defense Department's JCET and counternarcotics programs, for instance, have both involved Colombian Army units prohibited from receiving U.S. assistance through traditional security assistance programs.

- **The rationale for funding counternarcotics and other programs through different channels seems to depend more on which department has money available than with what is most effective, appropriate and transparent.** While foreign military training has historically been funded out of foreign aid accounts, counternarcotics foreign military training programs and the new Center for Hemispheric Defense Studies (CHDS) are funded through the much larger defense budget. The CHDS, a component of the National Defense University, works toward ends similar to those of expanded IMET, a program in the foreign aid bill. Yet if CHDS had been authorized under the expanded IMET program, it would likely have competed for funding within the program and not added to the total amount available for IMET. The same is true of DOD's counternarcotics training. This training would likely have received much greater scrutiny and competed for funds within a much more limited budget had the Administration sought to authorize it within the foreign aid bill.

- **Budgets for Humanitarian and Civic Assistance (HCA) programs in Latin America doubled between 1996 and 1997.** These programs raise jurisdictional questions. While development assistance programs are generally funded out of the foreign aid bill, under HCA schools are built, wells are dug and children are vaccinated by a program funded and carried out by the DOD. While supporting development in Latin America is a worthwhile endeavor, the funding mechanism is an odd jurisdictional decision. The State Department's Agency for International Development budget for Latin America has been slashed 60% since 1990, yet in two years the HCA program has doubled its reach. At the same time, analysts of civil-military relations have raised concerns regarding the signals these programs send to host-country militaries about proper roles, arguing that these activities may encourage military involvement in internal functions that would be unacceptable in a well-established democracy and can just as easily be carried out by civilians.

- **The end-use monitoring reports provided Congress are so old by the time they are submitted that they were of little more than historic value for this investigation.** The International Narcotics and Law Enforcement Affairs (INL) <u>End-Use Monitoring Report</u> for 1995, for instance, was released in September 1997. As of April 1998, the 1996 report remains unavailable.

"End-use monitoring" is the practice of ensuring that equipment and training transferred to other countries are used for the purpose for which they were provided. End-use monitoring procedures and requirements should be reviewed to ensure that the information provided to Congress is actually useful.

- **While there is some end-use monitoring of equipment, there is no after-training tracking of foreign military personnel who have been trained by the United States.** Without such evaluation, there is no easy way to determine whether trainees have returned to commit human rights violations, or if those trained in counternarcotics actually performed counternarcotics duties upon their return. The first is important because monitoring any correlation between U.S. training and human-rights violations is necessary to assess the value of training programs. The second matters because DOD training for Colombians and Mexicans is taking place under authorizations that only allow DOD to offer counternarcotics training. Both of these countries have significant insurgencies as well. At present, it is impossible to know if the line been counternarcotics and counterinsurgency is being crossed with U.S. assistance.

- **New attention is being given to programs focusing on civilian control of the military, defense management and human rights.** In 1997, 21 percent of Latin American IMET students took courses qualifying as expanded IMET. Furthermore, the new CHDS, which focuses on training civilians from Latin America in defense issues, is now functioning and may contribute to the civilian capacity for military oversight.

Recommendations:

- Congressional oversight and public disclosure regarding the Department of Defense's military activities with Latin America should be improved, particularly with regard to section 1004, section 124 and special-forces programs.

  Congress should require the DOD to provide a public annual report to the appropriate congressional committees on counternarcotics programs in Latin America, providing both country and functional breakdowns of expenditures.

- All foreign military training programs should be documented in a single, unified annual report to Congress, without respect to their funding authority. This report should include: the country receiving training, the number of students trained, courses attended and location of training. The report should provide this information for all other functionally-similar programs, even if they are funded out of different budget categories.

- Congress should review its end-use monitoring reports to see: a) what information is needed, b) if the information received is meeting its needs, c) whether there is sufficient funding available to carry out effective end-use monitoring, and d) how reports might be made in a timely fashion.

- There should be "after-training tracking" of foreign military personnel trained by the United States, to monitor the effectiveness of training. If soldiers are trained using section 1004 funds restricted to counternarcotics training, they should be monitored to ensure that, upon returning home, they use their acquired skills to carry out counternarcotics responsibilities. Furthermore, U.S. embassy personnel should use sources such as the reports of local and international human rights groups to monitor accusations of abuse by local militaries. If soldiers trained by the United States are credibly accused of human rights violations, the Leahy language should be implemented, regardless of the mechanism originally used to fund the training or assistance. U.S. training programs with a track record of graduating human rights abusers should be re-evaluated.

- Congress should take a closer look at Special Forces operations in Latin America. Though some of this information will be classified, an effort should be made to see that annual public reporting on Special Forces is made available, so that their role in the military relationship can be assessed.

- If Congress clearly expresses its intent to condition or restrict a program, such as training, the administration should respect that intent by applying the restriction to other functionally similar programs, even if funded from other accounts.

- Debate within the Congress on international counternarcotics issues needs to take place more actively within the Armed Services and National Security Committees, considering the significance of their role as funders of these programs.

- Since end-use monitoring is a critical oversight mechanism, Congress should consider making more resources available for defense personnel to perform end-use monitoring and reporting in a timely fashion.

- The non-governmental community must become more involved in the oversight of U.S. military programs with Latin America. Nongovernmental organizations must go beyond their traditional focus on foreign aid and begin analyzing defense programs. Foreign-policy analysts should not leave this field entirely to defense analysts, but should take a closer look at the military relationship with Latin America, a key component of U.S. foreign policy toward the region.

Programs governed by the Foreign Assistance Act (FAA) and Arms Export Control Act (AECA)

- **FMS: Foreign Military Sales**

- **DCS: Direct Commercial Sales**

- **FMF: Foreign Military Financing**

- **IMET: International Military Education and Training**

  - Expanded IMET

- **INC: International Narcotics Control**

  - ONDCP Discretionary Funding

- **EDA: Excess Defense Articles**

  - "Major Non-NATO Ally" Status

- **Emergency Drawdown Authority**

- **Leased Defense Articles**

- **ICITAP: International Criminal Investigative Training Assistance Program**

FMS: Foreign Military Sales

Program description:

FMS

The Foreign Military Sales (FMS) program manages government-to-government purchases of weapons and other defense articles, defense services, and military training. A military buying weapons through the FMS program does not deal directly with the company that makes them. The Defense Department serves as an intermediary, usually handling procurement, logistics and delivery and often providing product support and training.

DCS

FMS should be distinguished from the Direct Commercial Sales (DCS) program, which oversees sales between foreign governments and private U.S. companies, and the Foreign Military Financing (FMF) program, which provides grants and loans for FMS and DCS purchases.

FMF

Security Assistance Organizations (SAOs), military personnel stationed at U.S. embassies, promote the sale of U.S.-produced defense items and carry out most tasks associated with managing FMS "cases," or agreements to make a sale. SAOs advise foreign defense ministries on potential military purchases, often by coordinating "security assistance surveys" to assess perceived needs and occasionally by aiding the development of procurement plans.

A possible FMS case begins when a foreign government requests "price and availability data" (P&A data) on the U.S.-produced items it is interested in purchasing. The SAOs in the embassy cannot provide this data unless the State Department, through its Bureau of Political and Military Affairs, issues its approval. The Arms Control and Disarmament Agency (ACDA) may play an advisory role in the approval. Without this approval, an FMS sale will not proceed any further.

If the State Department approves, P&A data are provided to the purchasing government, which then decides whether to buy the items through the FMS program or another source, such as the DCS program or another country. An implementing agency within the Pentagon -- the U.S. Army, Navy, Air Force, or Defense Logistics Agency, depending on the type of item being considered -- negotiates the terms of the sale. If agreement is reached, both parties sign a letter of offer and acceptance (LOA), the contract which sets an FMS "case" in motion.

LOA

DSCA

Once an LOA has been signed, the Defense Security Assistance Agency (DSAA), a Defense Department agency that oversees security assistance programs, buys the item or items from U.S. manufacturers. This purchase normally goes through Defense Department procurement channels, and may not happen quickly; the time lag between an LOA and a delivery can take a year or more, particularly for complex weapons systems. The price quoted in the LOA may not match the cost of the items upon delivery, though in fact most final prices fall below the original estimate.

DSCA

The U.S. government applies a 3 percent "administrative surcharge" to all FMS sales. An additional 3.1 percent "logistics support charge" is applied on certain spare parts, equipment modifications, secondary support equipment and supplies. These surcharges recuperate some of the costs incurred while promoting and managing sales of commercially-manufactured U.S. weapons. FMS surcharges pay a significant amount of the salaries and operating costs of Security Assistance Organizations (SAOs) and other Defense Department personnel who carry out the program.

Sur-Charge

FMS versus DCS[1]

Though the Direct Commercial Sales (DCS) program tends to be speedier and less transparent, purchasing governments may choose FMS for several reasons.

- Countries desiring closer military-to-military contact with the United States will opt for an FMS sale. Contact between military officers occurs in all stages of the sale, and in many cases while providing follow-on training and support.
- FMS sales are often less expensive, particularly for more advanced items. When purchasing items from manufacturers, the Pentagon frequently combines its own orders with its requests on behalf of foreign governments. This can result in lower prices through economies of scale despite the FMS surcharges.
- FMS sales often carry guarantees of U.S. service and training.
- Countries with limited experience in negotiating complex procurement contracts find FMS convenient, as the Pentagon negotiates with the arms manufacturer and handles the paperwork.
- Because FMS sales are publicly recorded, at least to some extent, countries may opt for this channel to show they have "nothing to hide."

High-tech arms sales

As noted above, a purchase of high-tech weaponry normally goes through the FMS program. In 1997, the U.S. government lifted a twenty-year-old "ban" on sales of high-tech weapons to Latin America. Under this policy, the State Department had made clear that it would issue automatic denials to Latin American requests for price and availability data on high-tech weapons.

In March 1997, the policy was softened to allow Chile to request P&A data on fighter aircraft. In August 1997 the ban was lifted altogether. As of May 1998, Chile had not yet decided to buy U.S. fighters, and no letters of offer and acceptance (LOAs) have yet been signed for Latin American high-tech weapons purchases.

Law:

The FMS program is regulated by the Arms Export Control Act (P.L. 90-269, or the AECA), as amended. In order to purchase weapons through FMS, countries must meet all the eligibility requirements contained in the Foreign Assistance Act and the Arms Export Control Act.

Notification and congressional power to disapprove

According to section 36(b) of the AECA, Congress must be notified of U.S. government intention to offer an LOA if the items to be sold are:

- Defense articles or services valued at $50 million or more;
- Design and construction services valued at $200 million or more; or
- Major defense equipment valued at $14 million or more.

["Major defense equipment" means any item on the United States Munitions List with a research and development cost of at least $50 million or a total production cost of at least $200 million.]

This notification must specify:

1. The foreign country or international organization to which the offer is being made;
2. The dollar amount of the offer and the number of defense articles offered;
3. A description of the defense article or service being offered;
4. The U.S. agency (or branch of the armed forces) making the offer; and
5. If construction and design services are being offered, a description of the facilities to be constructed.

If the Speaker of the House, House International Relations Committee or Senate Foreign Relations Committee requests it, the President must "promptly" submit a statement with additional information. The items this statement must include are enumerated in Appendix C.

Within 30 days after receiving this notification, Congress may prohibit the sale by enacting a joint resolution.

Reports

Every February, the President must submit to Congress a report, known popularly as the "Javits report," which includes:

1. An Arms Sales Proposal listing all probable Foreign Military Sales (FMS) or Direct Commercial Sales (DCS) exports for the current calendar year that exceed:
   - $7 million for major weapons or weapons-related defense equipment; or
   - $25 million for other weapons or weapons-related defense equipment;
2. An indication of which sales or licenses are most likely to be approved during the current year;
3. An estimate of the total amount of FMS sales and DCS licenses expected to be made to each foreign country; and

4.   Other information about the status and rationale of FMS and DCS sales.

Though not classified, the Javits report has never been released to the public.

As part of a report submitted in accordance with section 655 of the Foreign Assistance Act of 1961 (P.L. 87-195, or the "FAA"), as amended, each February the President must list the dollar value and quantity of defense articles furnished under FMS in the previous fiscal year.

Section 36(a) of the AECA requires the President to submit a quarterly unclassified report to Congress:

1.   Listing all LOAs for major defense equipment exceeding $1 million;
2.   Listing all LOAs accepted during the current fiscal year, together with the total value of all sales to each country that year;
3.   Including projections of dollar amounts of expected FMS for the rest of the quarter and the rest of the year; and
4.   Providing other information about the status of FMS and DCS sales.

House Appropriations Committee report language accompanying the Foreign Operations Appropriations Act for 1998 required the Secretary of State to provide "a report detailing the security needs in Latin America and the impact of lifting the existing U.S. ban on high technology weapons sales to the region." This report, a one-time-only request, was due on February 24, 1998. By May 1998 the Committee had not yet received this report.

FMS agreements by country:

(Thousands of U.S. dollars)

Country	1996 actual[2]	1997 actual[4]	1998 estimate[4]	1999 estimate[4]
Antigua and Barbuda	174	262	110	110
Argentina	17,382	18,981	20,000	20,000
The Bahamas	0	51	2,010	2,010
Barbados	539	139	110	110
Belize	314	327	10	10
Bolivia	378	3	1,500	1,500
Bolivia, Int'l. Narcotics	10,265	9,124	4,600	4,900
Brazil	169,283	24,962	28,000	23,500
Chile	2,512	2,322	16,500	26,000
Colombia	45,822	74,987	18,000	18,000
Colombia, Int'l. Narcotics	19,425	0	10,000	10,000
Costa Rica	916	175	4,400	11,010
Dominica	182	0	110	110
Dominican Republic	418	187	2,000	2,000

FMS: Foreign Military Sales

Country	1996 actual[2]	1997 actual[4]	1998 estimate[4]	1999 estimate[4]
Ecuador	1,508	4,158	8,510	8,000
Ecuador, Int'l. Narcotics	168	1,812	3,410	1,210
El Salvador	19,173	6,703	2,100	2,100
Grenada	406	353	110	110
Guatemala	0	0	0	0
Guyana	10	70	80	80
Haiti	2,063	877	1,000	1,000
Honduras	19,173	910	1,000	950
Jamaica	2,374	50	2,000	2,000
Mexico	4,430	27,663	15,000	15,000
Nicaragua	0	0	0	0
OAS Hqs.	173	601	0	0
Panama	146	0	1,510	1,510
Paraguay	204	31	0	0
Peru	125	285	3,710	3,510
Peru, Int'l Narcotics	885	100	0	0
St. Kitts and Nevis	228	187	110	110
St. Lucia	610	0	110	110
St. Vincent and the Grenadines	1,366	66	110	110
Suriname	0	0	182	110
Trinidad and Tobago	165	185	110	110
Uruguay	1,926	1,078	2,240	2,260
Venezuela	21,332	59,421	15,000	15,000
Total	344,075	236,070	163,642	172,540

Training purchased through FMS:

Portions of the amounts listed above are for sales of training (as opposed to weapons, equipment, or construction services). The following countries purchased training through FMS. The amounts given do not include the cost of training aids and devices. **These amounts are included in, and not in addition to, the numbers in the above table.**

(Thousands of U.S. dollars)

Country	1996[2]	Training as % of all FMS agreements	1997 (as of September 1997)[2]	Training as % of all FMS agreements
Argentina			$506.029	4%
Bolivia, Int'l. Narcotics	$1,744.990	17%		
Brazil	$1,942.025	1%	$1,019.791	1%
Chile	$36.115	1%		
Colombia	$635.615	1%	$1,376.673	2%
Colombia, Int'l. Narcotics	$129.625	1%		
Dominican Republic			$78.285	2%
Ecuador, Int'l. Narcotics			$6.500	0%
El Salvador	$27.486	0%	$1,630.968	43%
Haiti	$490.502	24%		
Honduras	$253.541	1%		
Peru	$5.000	4%		
Venezuela	$167.591	1%	$252.748	1%
Total	$5,432.490	2%	$4,870.994	2%

Most FMS agreements (ranked in dollar terms):

Rank	1996	1997
1	Brazil	Colombia
2	Colombia	Venezuela
3	Venezuela	Mexico
4	El Salvador (tie)	Brazil
5	Honduras (tie)	Argentina
6	Argentina	Bolivia
7	Bolivia	El Salvador
8	Mexico	Ecuador
9	Chile	Chile
10	Jamaica	Uruguay

FMS agreements in the hemisphere

Legend:
$25 million +
$5 million - $25 million
$100,000 - $5 million

1996 (actual)   **1997 (actual)**

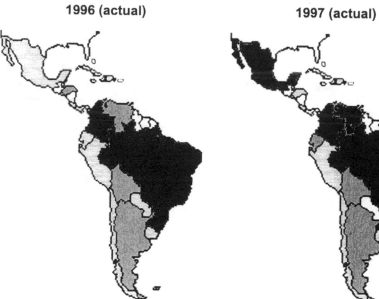

DCS: Direct Commercial Sales

Program description:

The State Department's Direct Commercial Sales (DCS) program oversees private U.S. companies' overseas sales of weapons and other defense articles, defense services, and military training. DCS should be distinguished from the Foreign Military Sales (FMS) program, which manages government-to-government sales.

A direct commercial sale requires an export license, which is issued by the Office of Defense Trade Controls at the State Department's Bureau for Political-Military Affairs. The granting of a license does not necessarily mean that items will be delivered immediately; licenses are valid for five years, during which sales may be delayed or canceled. About half of export licenses result in deliveries.

DCS versus FMS

Purchasing governments may choose DCS over FMS for several reasons:

- Unlike FMS sales, direct commercial sales are negotiated directly between the foreign government and the U.S. arms manufacturer without the Pentagon serving as an intermediary. DCS purchases avoid the surcharges for U.S. government administrative costs that are levied on FMS sales.
- FMS sales are often less expensive than DCS, though cost depends on many factors. For instance, less complex items or items produced by two or more companies are frequently cheaper when sold directly. DCS sales are usually quicker than FMS, as they avoid much "red tape" associated with the government-to-government program.
- DCS are also less transparent than FMS; some buyers are attracted to the program's relative lack of reporting requirements.
- Governments that have more experience in military procurement, and do not feel a need to have the U.S. government negotiate sales on their behalf, tend to choose DCS.

Law:

The DCS program is regulated by the Arms Export Control Act (P.L. 90-269, or the AECA), as amended. Section 38 of the AECA deals most specifically with the DCS program.

In order to purchase weapons through a direct sale, countries must meet all the eligibility requirements contained in the Arms Export Control Act and the Foreign Assistance Act of 1961 (P.L. 87-195, or the "FAA"), as amended.

Notification and congressional power to disapprove

According to section 36(c) of the AECA, Congress must be notified of a decision to issue an export license if the items to be sold are:

- Defense articles or services valued at $50 million or more; or
- Major defense equipment valued at $14 million or more.

  ["Major defense equipment" means any item on the United States Munitions List with a research and development cost of at least $50 million or a total production cost of at least $200 million.]

This notification must:

1. Specify the foreign country or international organization to which the export will be made;
2. Specify the dollar amount of the items to be exported; and
3. Describe the items to be exported.

If the Speaker of the House, House International Relations Committee or Senate Foreign Relations Committee requests it, the President must "promptly" submit a statement including:

1. A description of the capabilities of the items to be exported;
2. An estimate of the number of U.S. government personnel needed in the country in connection with the items to be exported; and
3. An analysis, prepared in consultation with the Secretary of Defense, of the export's arms-control impact.

These requirements are significantly less exacting than those for a similar statement that may be requested about a proposed FMS sale (see Appendix C).

Within 30 days after being notified, Congress may turn down a proposed export license by enacting a joint resolution.

Reports

Every February, the President must submit to Congress a report, known popularly as the "Javits report," described in the FMS section on pages 12 and 13.

As part of a report submitted in compliance with section 655 of the Foreign Assistance Act, each February the President must list the dollar value and quantity of defense articles licensed for export under DCS in the previous fiscal year.

Section 36(a) of the AECA requires the President to submit a quarterly unclassified report to Congress:

1. Listing, by country, licenses and approvals for private exports of defense articles exceeding $1 million, together with the total of licenses for the current year. This listing must detail:
   a) The items to be exported under the license;
   b) The quantity and price of each item to be furnished; and
   c) The name and address of the ultimate user of each item; and
2. Providing several other pieces of information about the status of FMS and DCS sales.

House Appropriations Committee report language accompanying the Foreign Operations Appropriations Act for 1998 (P.L. 105-118) required the Secretary of State to provide "a report detailing the security needs in Latin America and the impact of lifting the existing U.S. ban on high technology weapons sales to the region." This report, a one-time-only request, was due on February 24, 1998. By May 1998 the Committee had not yet received this report.

DCS licenses and deliveries by country:

Data about DCS licenses do not necessarily refer to final sales; they indicate only that the State Department has granted permission for a possible sale. The State Department estimates that about half of all export licenses it grants result in actual deliveries.[1] The "actual deliveries" columns in this table reflect only items delivered during the first five months of the fiscal year in question (October through early March).

(Thousands of U.S. dollars)

Country	1996		1997		1998	1999
	DCS licenses[2]	Actual deliveries (as of March 1997)[3]	DCS licenses[4]	Actual deliveries (as of March 1998)[5]	Estimated deliveries 1998[5]	Estimated deliveries 1999[5]
Antigua and Barbuda	12.363	Less than 0.5	1	0	1	1
Argentina	81,579.458	741	198,780	3,283	25,626	99,423
Aruba	190.871	2	62	5	25	31
The Bahamas	59.680	0	9	6	7	5
Barbados	45.993	9	96	8	14	47
Belize	1,411.548	14	95	6	152	706
Bermuda	1,071.319	10	68	6	114	536
Bolivia	2,158.361	249	1,666	94	384	1,087
Brazil	75,941.338	945	191,334	4,029	22,584	91,261
British Virgin Islands	0.346	Less than 0.5	4	4	Less than 0.5	Less than 0.5
Cayman Islands	0	0	7	0	4	14
Chile	44,527.076	417	32,564	1,028	5,737	12,271
Colombia	27,934.542	5,536	39,077	6,223	5,217	19,617

DCS: Direct Commercial Sales

Country	1996		1997		1998	1999
	DCS licenses[2]	Actual deliveries (as of March 1997)[3]	DCS licenses[4]	Actual deliveries (as of March 1998)[5]	Estimated deliveries 1998[5]	Estimated deliveries 1999[5]
Costa Rica	6,614.808	172	1,653	215	327	810
Dominica	6.400	0	0	0	1	3
Dominican Republic	2,714.978	5	7,319	254	1,003	1,358
Ecuador	23,694.504	1,506	7,540	2,720	2,040	6,302
El Salvador	7,978.534	324	8,244	52	1,631	4,032
French Guiana*	125,439.680	1,732	5,538	4,710	13,098	62,720
Grenada	0	0	68	10	7	0
Guatemala	3,011.536	272	2,211	303	512	1,517
Guyana	185.974	10	108	22	29	93
Haiti	157.487	46	61	0	22	79
Honduras	5,089.128	123	3,696	70	878	2,545
Jamaica	430.818	5	335	97	77	215
Martinique	0	0	0		6	
Mexico	146,617.738	991	22,153	12,642	11,665	47,225
Montserrat	3.340	0	3			
Netherlands Antilles	1,353.602	2	136	32	28	72
Nicaragua	21.685	10	80	77	10	11
Panama	9,148.361	89	11,941	219	2,110	4,574
Paraguay	102.712	13	42	0	14	51
Peru	31,293.666	180	5,367	95	2,170	8,146
St. Kitts and Nevis	5.824	3	5	2	1	3
St. Lucia	26.771	9	44	8	7	13
St. Vincent and the Grenadines	5.169	Less than 0.5	4	1	1	3
Suriname	135.761	11	139	5	27	68
Trinidad and Tobago	332.302	25	809	55	97	166
Turks and Caicos Islands	0	0	1	0	0	0
Uruguay	5,101.998	121	14,723	111	1,995	2,615
Venezuela	711,891.676	1,103	342,929	2,101	71,945	188,237
Total	1,316,297.35	14,677	828,912	38,493	169,566	555,857

---

* French Guiana's large amount of DCS licenses owes to the colony's use as a base of operations for the European Space Agency. Satellite and rocketry equipment account for the vast majority of these licenses.

Most DCS licenses (ranked in dollar terms):

Rank	1996	1997
1	Venezuela	Venezuela
2	Mexico	Argentina
3	French Guiana*	Brazil
4	Argentina	Colombia
5	Brazil	Chile
6	Chile	Mexico
7	Peru	Uruguay
8	Colombia	Panama
9	Ecuador	El Salvador
10	Panama	Ecuador

DCS licenses in the hemisphere

Legend:
$100 million +
$10 million - $100 million
$1 - $10 million

1996 (actual)   **1997 (actual)**

FMF: Foreign Military Financing

Program description:

The Foreign Military Financing (FMF) program provides grants and loans to help countries purchase U.S.-produced weapons, defense equipment, defense services and military training. FMF funds purchases made through the Foreign Military Sales (FMS) program, which manages government-to-government purchases. On a less frequent basis, FMF also funds purchases made through the Direct Commercial Sales (DCS) program, which oversees sales between foreign governments and private U.S. companies. FMF does not provide cash grants; it generally pays for sales of specific goods or services through FMS or DCS.

The State Department's Bureau of Political-Military Affairs sets policy for the FMF program, while the Defense Security Assistance Agency (DSAA), within the Defense Department, manages it on a day-to-day basis. Security Assistance Organizations (SAOs), military personnel in U.S. embassies overseas, play a key role in managing FMF within recipient countries. Some FMF pays for SAO salaries and operational costs. Congress appropriates funds for FMF through the yearly Foreign Operations Appropriations Act.

Until recently, FMF was one of the largest sources of military assistance to Latin America. In 1998, however, the only new FMF for the region is $3 million for a Caribbean regional fund.

Law:

The FMF program is authorized by sections 23 and 24 of the Arms Export Control Act (P.L. 90-269, or the AECA), as amended. In order to receive assistance through FMF, countries must meet all the eligibility requirements contained in the Foreign Assistance Act and the Arms Export Control Act.

Reports

Section 634 of the Foreign Assistance Act of 1961 (P.L. 87-195, or the "FAA"), as amended, requires that yearly congressional presentation documents provide amounts of FMF:

1. Obligated to each country in the past fiscal year;
2. Planned for the current fiscal year; and
3. Proposed for the following fiscal year.

"Pipeline" FMF and Colombia's decertification

Once appropriated for a country, FMF remains available until spent; in some cases, unspent FMF grant money can remain "in the pipeline" for years. Previously-appropriated yet unspent FMF from previous years remains available for many countries in Latin America and the Caribbean.

Colombia was decertified by the U.S. government in 1996 and 1997 for perceived lack of progress in counternarcotics. This measure prohibited Colombia's military and police from receiving FMF, even though FMF funds that were appropriated before 1996 had not yet been spent. Colombia's grant FMF was "frozen in the pipeline" from March 1996 until August 1997, when it was freed by a special presidential action known as a "section 614 waiver" after the relevant provision of the Foreign Assistance Act.

Defense Department officials cited in a February 1998 General Accounting Office (GAO) report stated that the decertification delayed up to $30 million in grant FMF. The aid paid for "items such as spare parts for vehicles, fixed-wing aircraft, and helicopters; explosives and ammunition; publications; and individual clothing items."[1]

The State Department's response to the GAO report cautioned that "the $30 million figure is an 'up to' figure, not an absolute. It should also be noted that it is difficult to tell how much of the FMF was 'delayed,' as the money is only spent gradually, usually over a period of several years."[2]

FMF recipients by country[3]:

(Thousands of U.S. dollars)

Country	1996 actual	1997 actual	1998 estimate	1999 requested
Caribbean regional	$2,000	$2,000	$3,000	$3,000

FMF "in the pipeline" from previous years[4]:

This table, dated September 15, 1997, details unspent FMF funds appropriated in previous years, yet still eligible for expenditure.

(Thousands of U.S. dollars)

Country	MAP[†]	1992 and earlier	1993	1994	1995	1996	Subtotal FMF	Total uncommitted
Bahamas						64	64	64
Belize	11						0	11
Bolivia	10	21					21	31
Bolivia (AntiNarc)	2	4	29		203		236	238
Colombia	70						0	70
Colombia (AntiNarc)		883	433		5,885		7,201*	7,201*
Costa Rica	3						0	3
Dominican Republic	56	60	25	5			90	146
Ecuador	24	194					194	218
Ecuador (AntiNarc)		133		57			190	190
El Salvador	1,655	51	8				59	1,714
Guatemala	2,274	303					303	2,577
Guyana						52	52	52
Haiti	40	1					1	41
Honduras	227	1,015					1,015	1,242
Jamaica	5					1	1	6
Nicaragua		28					28	28
Panama	247	166					166	413
Paraguay		8					8	8
Peru (AntiNarc)		335					335	335
St. Lucia	8						0	8
Trinidad and Tobago		16					16	16
Uruguay	123						0	123
Total	**4,755**	**3,218**	**495**	**62**	**6,088**	**117**	**9,980**	**14,735**

[†] Left over from the Military Assistance Program (MAP, now inactive).

* A special presidential waiver in August 1997 (known as a "section 614" waiver) released unspent FMF to Colombia valued at up to $30,000,000.

IMET: International Military Education and Training

Program description:

International Military Education and Training (IMET) is a financing mechanism through which the United States pays for the training or education of foreign military and a limited number of civilian personnel. IMET grants are given to foreign governments, which choose the courses their personnel will attend.

IMET is used to send students to approximately 150 U.S. military training institutions throughout the United States. A wide variety of courses for U.S. personnel -- some 2,000, including topics ranging from counterintelligence to helicopter repair to military justice systems -- qualify for IMET funding. On occasion, IMET- funded programs are conducted in the recipient country by mobile education and training teams, U.S. instructors who go to foreign countries to teach courses to groups of students in their native language.

Created in 1976, the IMET program is funded through the foreign aid appropriations and authorizations process. It is overseen by the Department of State, but actually implemented by the Defense Department.

About 20 percent of IMET funding goes to "expanded IMET (E-IMET)," a program which funds a set of noncombat courses that are available to some foreign civilians as well as to military personnel.

Law:

Chapter 5 of Part II of the Foreign Assistance Act of 1961 (P.L. 87-195), as amended, authorizes the IMET program to provide military education and training to foreign military and civilian personnel.

According to Section 541 of the FAA, IMET-funded training is intended:

- To encourage effective and mutually beneficial relations and increased understanding between the United States and foreign countries in furtherance of the goals of international peace and security;
- To improve the ability of participating foreign countries to utilize their resources, including defense articles and defense services obtained by them from the United States, with maximum effectiveness, thereby contributing to greater self-

reliance by such countries; and
- To increase the awareness of nationals of foreign countries participating in such activities of basic issues involving internationally recognized human rights.

Colombia and Guatemala:

Due to concerns about the military's involvement in several human rights abuses, Guatemala was prohibited from receiving any IMET assistance in 1996 and has not received regular IMET since 1995. The 1998 Foreign Operations Appropriations Act limits Guatemala to Expanded IMET only.

About $1.4 million in planned IMET assistance for Colombian police and military units involved in counternarcotics operations was canceled by Colombia's narcotics decertifications in 1996 and 1997. The General Accounting Office (GAO) explains:

> This includes approximately $800,000 in fiscal year 1996 funds that were canceled due to decertification. The $600,000 in fiscal year 1997 funds had to be canceled [despite being released in August 1997 by a presidential waiver] because the funding was released too late in the fiscal year for Colombia to adequately meet its training needs. ... The canceled training for Colombian police and military officials in U.S. schools was in a variety of areas, including human rights.[1]

IMET by country:

(Thousands of U.S. dollars)

Country	1996 actual[2]		1997 actual[3]		1998 estimate[3]		1999 request[3]	
	Total allocation	Students trained	Total allocation	Students trained	Total allocation	Students trained	Total allocation	Students trained
Antigua and Barbuda	$100	11	$93	13	$115	16	$115	16
Argentina	$542	186	$603	179	$600	178	$600	178
Bahamas	$100	19	$107	12	$100	11	$100	11
Barbados	$100	12	$103	9	$92	8	$90	8
Belize	$250	81	$208	49	$250	59	$250	59
Bolivia	$535	133	$509	163	$550	176	$550	176
Brazil	$200	38	$222	41	$225	42	$225	42
Chile	$366	187	$395	167	$450	190	$450	190
Colombia	$147	32	$0	0	$900	100	$800	89
Costa Rica	$198	69	$200	92	$200	92	$200	92
Dominica	$40	6	$32	5	$38	6	$40	7
Dominican Republic	$500	70	$622	70	$500	56	$500	56
Ecuador	$500	135	$425	118	$500	139	$500	139
El Salvador	$541	207	$455	234	$500	257	$500	257

Country	1996 actual[2]		1997 actual[3]		1998 estimate[3]		1999 request[3]	
	Total allocation	Students trained	Total allocation	Students trained	Total allocation	Students trained	Total allocation	Students trained
Grenada	$40	9	$49	7	$49	7	$50	7
Guatemala	$0	0	$205	122	$225	134	$225	134
Guyana	$214	31	$178	72	$175	71	$175	71
Haiti	$250	9	$275	125	$300	136	$300	136
Honduras	$500	213	$425	164	$500	193	$500	193
Jamaica	$450	73	$487	66	$500	68	$500	68
Mexico	$1,000	221	$1,008	192	$1,000	190	$1,000	190
Nicaragua	$0	0	$57	4	$200	14	$200	14
Panama	$0	0	$0	0	$0	0	$100	7
"Panama Canal Area Military School"	$500		$520		$550		$550	
Paraguay	$182	10	$284	42	$200	30	$200	30
Peru	$400	75	$483	133	$450	124	$450	124
St. Kitts and Nevis	$48	11	$56	10	$55	9	$55	9
St. Lucia	$46	9	$42.5	5	$47	5	$50	7
St. Vincent and the Grenadines	$46	10	$44	6	$54	8	$50	7
Suriname	$79	138	$149	100	$100	67	$100	67
Trinidad and Tobago	$57	8	$95	12	$125	16	$125	16
Uruguay	$330	85	$332	65	$300	59	$300	59
Venezuela	$430	114	$388	100	$400	103	$400	103
Total	$8,691	2,202	$9,052	2,377	$10,250	2,564	$10,250	2,562

Top recipients of IMET funding:

Rank	1996	1997 Actual
1	Mexico	Mexico
2	Argentina	Dominican Republic
3	El Salvador	Argentina
4	Bolivia	Bolivia
5	Dominican Republic	Jamaica
6	Ecuador	Peru
7	Honduras	El Salvador
8	Jamaica	Ecuador
9	Venezuela	Honduras
10	Peru	Chile

IMET funding in the hemisphere

Legend:
$500,000+
$300,000 - $500,000
$100,000 - $300,000

1996 (actual)   **1997 (actual)**

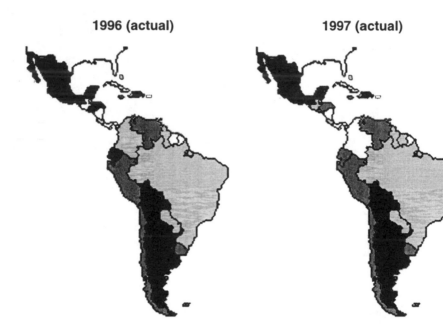

Expanded IMET

Program description:

Expanded IMET, a subset of the International Military Education and Training (IMET) program, was first mandated by Congress in 1991. Unlike traditional military training, courses funded by E-IMET do not teach combat or technical skills. E-IMET courses are most focused on strengthening defense management and human rights practices. This category of education is available to foreign civilians as well as military personnel.

According to the Defense Security Assistance Agency's E-IMET Handbook, the program's purpose is:

> to educate U.S. friends and allies in the proper management of their defense resources, improving their systems of military justice in accordance with internationally recognized principles of human rights and fostering a greater respect for, and understanding of, the principle of civilian control of the military.[1]

In 1997, E-IMET represented 22% of the overall IMET program for Latin America. About 30% of E-IMET students were civilians.

Law:

The law governing E-IMET is contained within the overall authorization for IMET, section 541 of the Foreign Assistance Act of 1961 (P.L. 87-195, or the FAA), as amended.

Civilians authorized to participate in E-IMET-funded courses include personnel with defense responsibilities in government ministries, legislators and non-governmental actors. For civilian participants, such training and education must:

1. Contribute to responsible defense resource management;
2. Foster greater respect for and understanding of the principle of civilian control of the military;
3. Contribute to cooperation between military and law enforcement personnel on counternarcotics law enforcement efforts; or
4. Improve military justice systems and procedures in accordance with internationally-recognized human rights.

Report language accompanying the Foreign Assistance Appropriations Act for 1998 (P.L. 105-118) states that "every effort" should be made to ensure that 30 percent of IMET funds for Latin America be dedicated to E-IMET courses. It also called on the secretaries of State and Defense to ensure that "approximately 25 percent of the total number of individuals from Latin American countries attending United States supported IMET programs and the Center for Hemispheric Defense Studies at the National Defense University are civilians."

Section 584(c) of the appropriations bill required that the Secretary of Defense submit a report to the congressional oversight committees "on the progress made to improve military training of Latin American participants in the areas of human rights and civilian control of the military ... [and to] include in the report plans for implementing additional expanded IMET programs for Latin America during the next three fiscal years." This report is due November 26, 1998.

While IMET expenditures by country are documented in the State Department's yearly Congressional Presentation for Foreign Operations, the law does not require the State Department and Pentagon to report on expanded IMET outlays.

E-IMET by country:

(Thousands of U.S. dollars)								
	1996 actual				1997 actual			
Country	Total used for E-IMET[2,3]	E-IMET as a percentage of total IMET	No. of E-IMET students[2,3]	No. of civilians trained by E-IMET[3]	Total used for E-IMET[2,3]	E-IMET as a percentage of total IMET	No. of E-IMET students[2,3]	No. of civilians trained by E-IMET[3]
Antigua and Barbuda	$6.091	6%	1	0	$4.958	3%	1	0
Argentina	$213.259	39%	140	78	$141.724	24%	55	28
Bahamas	$11.429	11%	1	0	$15.430	14%	2	0
Barbados	$3.705	4%	2	0	$0	0%	0	0
Belize	$43.980	18%	6	1	$14.634	7%	2	0
Bolivia	$170.557	32%	42	0	$125.707	25%	44	25
Brazil	$0.555	0%	1	0	$0	0%	0	0
Chile	$77.803	21	13	9	$40.985	10%	8	6
Colombia	$50.679	34%	3	0	$0	0%	0	0
Costa Rica	$43.236	22%	13	0	$67.244	33%	19	0
Dominica	$6.357	16%	1	0	$2.671	9%	1	0
Dominican Republic	$118.828	24%	7	0	$135.787	17%	11	0
Ecuador	$46.621	9%	13	1	$56.477	13%	15	2
El Salvador	$212.271	39%	97	40	$235.110	52%	222	114
Grenada	$7.008	18%	1	0	$0	0%	0	0
Guatemala	$0.000	0%	0	0	$156.826	77%	87	21
Guyana	$39.264	18%	3	0	$37.119	20%	50	2
Haiti	$23.867	6%	4	2	$66.781	22%	2	0
Honduras	$140.495	28%	168	87	$46.119	12%	59	3
Jamaica	$3.232	1%	2	1	$17.523	4%	2	0

Country	1996 actual				1997 actual			
	Total used for E-IMET[2,3]	E-IMET as a percentage of total IMET	No. of E-IMET students[2,3]	No. of civilians trained by E-IMET[3]	Total used for E-IMET[2,3]	E-IMET as a percentage of total IMET	No. of E-IMET students[2,3]	No. of civilians trained by E-IMET[3]
Mexico	$96.366	10%	26	0	$108.489	11%	21	0
Nicaragua	$0.000	0%	0	0	$52.796	44%	4	0
Panama	$0.000	0%	0	0	$0	0%	0	0
Panama Canal Area Military School	$0.000	0%	0	0	$0	0%	0	0
Paraguay	$36.151	20%	3	0	$45.692	16%	7	0
Peru	$73.732	18%	78	16	$125.126	28%	16	2
St. Kitts and Nevis	$0.000	0%	0	0	$0	0%	0	0
St. Lucia	$7.075	15%	1	0	$7.010	17%	1	0
St. Vincent and the Grenadines	$7.316	16%	1	0	$0	0%	0	0
Suriname	$27.514	35%	88	28	$38.417	26%	33	4
Trinidad and Tobago	$0	0%	0	0	$9.370	10%	1	0
Uruguay	$141.043	43%	7	0	$71.470	21%	10	0
Venezuela	$236.729	35%	60	9	$143.321	37%	13	0
Total	$1,845.163	20%	782	272	$1,766.786	21%	686	207

Top recipients of expanded IMET funding:

Ranked by dollar amount:			Ranked as a percentage of total IMET outlay:		
Rank	1996	1997	Rank	1996	1997
1	Venezuela	El Salvador	1	Uruguay	Guatemala
2	Argentina	Guatemala	2	El Salvador	El Salvador
3	El Salvador	Venezuela	3	Argentina	Nicaragua
4	Bolivia	Argentina	4	Venezuela	Venezuela
5	Uruguay	Dominican Republic	5	Suriname	Costa Rica
6	Honduras	Bolivia	6	Colombia	Peru
7	Dominican Republic	Peru	7	Bolivia	Suriname
8	Mexico	Mexico	8	Honduras	Bolivia
9	Chile	Uruguay	9	Dominican Republic	Argentina
10	Peru	Costa Rica	10	Costa Rica	Haiti

Expanded IMET funding in the hemisphere

Legend:
35 percent+ of all IMET
20 percent - 35 percent of all IMET
5 percent – 20 percent of all IMET

1996 (actual)   **1997 (actual)**

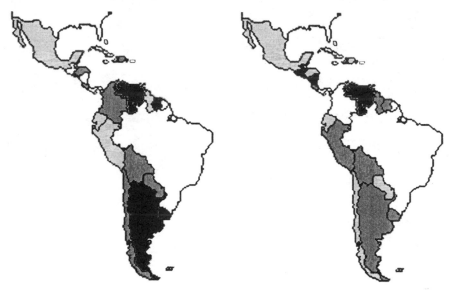

INC: International Narcotics Control

Program description:

The State Department is the "lead agency" for international drug control policy. Its Bureau for International Narcotics and Law Enforcement Affairs (INL) designs and carries out international counternarcotics policy, while coordinating all other U.S. agencies' overseas anti-drug activities.

The INL bureau funds and manages the International Narcotics Control (INC) program, through which the State Department provides aid and training to the governments and security forces of countries in which drugs are produced or transported. Several U.S. embassies in Latin America and the Caribbean have a "narcotics affairs section" (or "NAS") which manages the INC program in the host country.

According to its 1999 *Congressional Presentation,* the INC program has the following strategic objectives:

1. Reduce drug crop cultivation through a combination of eradication and alternative development programs;
2. Strengthen the ability of law enforcement and judicial institutions to investigate and prosecute major drug trafficking organizations, seize and block their assets; and
3. Improve the capacity of host nation police and military forces to attack narcotics production and trafficking centers.[1]

The INC program combines economic and security assistance, aiding civilian and military agencies with counternarcotics responsibilities. Types of assistance include (but are not limited to) training, technical assistance, equipment and arms transfers, development assistance (particularly to encourage cultivation of legal crops), and aid to administration of justice and domestic drug demand-reduction programs. State Department INL officials themselves may manage assistance programs, or INC funds may be transferred to other government agencies.

The INC program's budget, $230 million in 1998, is spent overwhelmingly on programs in Latin America and the Caribbean. Of these, programs in the three main drug source countries -- Bolivia, Colombia and Peru -- account for the largest share of funding. Specific programs exist in seven other Latin American and Caribbean countries, while INC manages smaller initiatives elsewhere under a "Latin American Regional" account.

INC funds and manages several other programs which are not earmarked for specific countries. These include the following.

- The Interregional Aviation Support program maintains an "air wing" of U.S.-owned planes which carry out drug eradication and support interdiction activities in Latin America.
- Funding for International Organizations supports the United Nations Drug Control Program (UNDCP) and the OAS Inter-American Council Against Drug Abuse (CICAD).
- Law Enforcement Training pays for training programs carried out by the DEA, Customs Service, and Coast Guard. This program operates both within and outside Latin America.
- Demand Reduction programs seek to help other countries reduce their own domestic demand for illegal drugs. This program also operates globally.
- The Systems Support and Upgrades account funds aircraft used for counternarcotics operations in Latin America.
- The Program Development and Support account covers personnel and administrative costs.

In 1996, the INC program began providing counternarcotics aid that had previously come from the Foreign Military Financing (FMF) program and USAID development assistance.[2]

The "end use" of counternarcotics aid is a common concern of observers both within and outside the U.S. government. Without sufficient oversight, U.S.-supplied equipment or training can be misused for purposes unrelated to narcotics, including the abuse of human rights.

The General Accounting Office (GAO) reported in February 1998 that end-use monitoring continues to be problematic:

> The Departments of State and Defense were not coordinating their efforts with each other and did not have complete oversight over U.S. counternarcotics programs because they had not developed an adequate end-use monitoring system to ensure that U.S.-provided counternarcotics assistance was being used as intended.[3]

Law:

The INC program is authorized by section 481 of the Foreign Assistance Act of 1961 (P.L. 87-195, or the "FAA"), as amended. Section 481 authorizes the President "to furnish assistance to any country or international organization, on such terms and conditions as he may determine, for the control of narcotic and psychotropic drugs and other controlled substances, or for other anticrime purposes." The law makes the Secretary of State responsible for coordinating this assistance.

Non-binding language in the conference committee report accompanying the 1998 Foreign Operations Appropriations Act (P.L. 105-118) called on the State Department to use $36 million of the 1998 INC account to buy three UH-60 Blackhawk helicopters for Colombia's National Police. The State Department has indicated that it does not view the helicopters as a good use of limited resources; as of mid-May 1998, it remains unclear whether the Blackhawks will indeed be delivered.

Limitations

The 1997 Foreign Operations Appropriations Act (P.L. 104-208) contained a provision known popularly as the "Leahy Amendment" after its sponsor, Sen. Patrick Leahy (D-VT). The Leahy Amendment prohibits a unit of a foreign security force from receiving INC assistance if:

1. Credible evidence exists that the unit's members have committed gross violations of human rights; and
2. Effective measures are not being taken to bring the responsible members of the unit to justice.

The 1997 version of the Leahy Amendment applied only to the INC program. The 1998 Foreign Operations Appropriations Act (P.L. 105-118) expanded the Leahy Amendment to encompass all security assistance programs authorized by the Foreign Assistance Act and the Arms Export Control Act.

Reports

The laws which authorize the INC program require regular reporting to Congress about its activities. The most extensive of these reports is the International Narcotics Control Strategy Report (INCSR) required by section 489 of the Foreign Assistance Act. The INCSR discusses certification decisions, narcotics activity, and U.S. programs in each drug source or transit country. It must be submitted every March 1 to the Speaker of the House and the Senate Foreign Relations Committee.

The 1998 Foreign Operations Appropriations Act (P.L. 105-118) also included two reports that must be submitted one time only:

1. A financial plan for the INC program, to be provided to the House and Senate Appropriations Committees as soon as possible. Ten percent of INC funds were withheld pending the plan's submission; and
2. A report on international narcotics and law enforcement activities, to be submitted to the House and Senate Appropriations Committees by January 25, 1998, 60 days after enactment of the foreign operations appropriations law.

Notification

The Foreign Assistance Act (FAA) also requires that Congress be notified if certain actions are taken within the INC program.

According to section 482(b) of the FAA, INC can only supply weapons or ammunition if they are to be used:

- For the defensive arming of aircraft that are used for counternarcotics purposes; or
- For defensive purposes by State Department employees or contract personnel engaged in counternarcotics activities.

These transfers cannot take place until fifteen days after the President notifies the House and Senate Appropriations Committees, the House International Relations Committee, and the Senate Foreign Relations Committee.

Section 484(a) of the FAA specifies that aircraft provided to foreign countries through the INC program must be either leased or loaned. The President may grant aircraft through INC, however, by determining that a lease or loan would be "contrary to the national interest of the United States."

The aircraft cannot be transferred until fifteen days after the President notifies the same congressional committees.

According to section 488 of the FAA, INC funds cannot be obligated for construction until fifteen days after the President notifies the congressional committees.

Bolivia:

Since Bolivia is a significant drug source country, the INC program in La Paz "focuses on eradication, interdiction and alternative development."[4] Narcotics law enforcement efforts are divided into four subprojects which, according to the 1999 INL Congressional Presentation, "assist the various police units that conduct counternarcotics law enforcement operations and the military units that complement them."[5]

The INC Bolivia program's Ground Operations Support subprogram funds several police and military units, among them[6]:

- The Special Force for the Fight Against Narcotics Trafficking (FELCN), a police unit charged with leading Bolivia's anti-drug efforts. The FELCN were completely reorganized in February 1996 "from a combined military/police organization to a primarily police based organization." An active duty police officer, instead of a retired senior military officer, now serves as the unit's Director General. The new Director General of the FELCN, with help from U.S. advisors, is reorienting the unit toward "more traditional investigative functions."[7]
- The Rural Mobile Police Patrol Units (UMOPAR), the uniformed interdiction force of the FELCN. UMOPAR detachments are active in the Chapare, Trinidad and the Yungas.[8]
- The Bolivian Army's Green Devil Task Force, which transports police personnel, fuel and commodities.

- The urban narcotics police, which performs investigations.
- Special Prosecutors of Controlled Substances assigned to police units.
- Other investigative and intelligence-gathering units.

U.S. government personnel provide advice and training to the FELCN. U.S. goals for the unit include helping it "to develop an operational-level planning capability," improving its command and control over UMOPAR and the three military task forces it supervises, and increasing coordination with counternarcotics agencies elsewhere in the Andean region.

The three Bolivian military counternarcotics task forces that receive aid under the INC program are the air force's Red Devils Task Force (RDTF), the navy's Blue Devils Task Force (BDTF), and the army's Green Devils Task Force (GDTF). All are charged with providing transport and logistics support to the police, and are ostensibly under police command. The FELCN, the police unit leading Bolivian counternarcotics efforts, is still struggling to assert full command over Bolivia's counternarcotics forces, however; the General Accounting Office (GAO) has noted that "coordination between the counternarcotics police and military units continues to be a problem."[9]

The Red Devils' eradication and transportation activities are supported by the INC Bolivia program's *Air Operations Support subprogram*. According to the 1999 INL Congressional Presentation, this subprogram "consists of Bolivian Air Force units operating UH-1H helicopters used in eradication and enforcement operations, and C-130 aircraft used to transport police, heavy equipment, and pre-stage fuel in areas not reachable by road, or made impassable through much of the year by heavy rains."[10] The chief of Bolivia's air force recently revised the chain of command to make counternarcotics the Red Devils' only responsibility.[11]

Red Devil pilots fly U.S.-owned aircraft maintained in Bolivia through INL's interregional aviation program (described below). State Department-owned aircraft in Bolivia include sixteen UH-1H utility helicopters, one C-55 Beech Baron airplane, and five Cessna fixed-wing planes. Most of these are located in Santa Cruz, Chimore, Trinidad and La Paz.[12]

The U.S.-owned UH-1H helicopter fleet was reduced from 22 to 16 in November 1997. In June of that year, the Senate Appropriations Committee had recommended that INL reevaluate the need to keep helicopters in Bolivia.

[T]he Committee notes that currently there are 22 United States owned UH-1 helicopters stationed in Bolivia for interdiction efforts, with total estimated costs at $3,400,000. According to an onsite staff evaluation by the Senate Caucus on International Narcotics Control, the helicopters have limited interdiction use, serving primarily logistics and transport functions. With Bolivian eradication efforts mostly focused on land operations, the Committee is concerned that costs associated with the upkeep of the helicopters are unjustified. The Committee recommends the Department of State evaluate the costs associated with airborne operations in Bolivia, and report back no later than March 1, 1998, on whether funds are being properly utilized.[13]

The *Riverine Operations Support subprogram* has helped the Bolivian Navy to develop, equip and train four task groups, the "Blue Devils," which are located in Trinidad, Puerto Villaroel, Riberalta, and Guayaramerin. The subprogram has developed a training academy for naval and police personnel, which "will broaden its scope to include more students from neighboring countries."[14] The Blue Devils provide logistical support to the police, and monitor and interdict riverine traffic in drugs and precursor chemicals. In December 1997, the unit was granted law enforcement authority by the Bolivian government, which means its members have the power to arrest suspects.[15]

A June 1997 Senate Appropriations Committee report was quite critical of U.S. support for the Blue Devils, alleging that the unit has not performed well:

> While the Committee supports the administration's request for counternarcotics efforts in Bolivia, it is concerned about the effectiveness of some of the components of this effort. In particular, the Committee notes the continued support of the blue devil task force, a Bolivian Navy river interdiction unit, which has consumed $20,000,000 in United States funds with few returns. In 56 operations in 1996, the blue devils enjoyed limited success. There are no indications that outcome-based performance standards are used to judge the effectiveness of the program or justify its cost. The Committee strongly urges the Department of State to seriously review the costs associated with the blue devil task force and recommends a general phase-out of the program unless significant eradication or interdiction goals are met.[16]

The 1999 INC <u>Congressional Presentation</u> defends the decision to continue support for the Blue Devils, citing the recent decision to grant them law enforcement authority. "The BDTF," it adds, "has the capacity to conduct its own training, maintain standards of performance and carry out its mission with minimal USG [U.S. government] advisory assistance."[17]

Due to cutbacks in INC support for Bolivia, the Riverine Operations Support Subprogram might not receive funds in 1998. "Permanent" U.S. Coast Guard advisor support in Trinidad and a senior Coast Guard advisor position in La Paz have been eliminated.[18]

The *Field Support and Bolivian Government Infrastructure subprogram* pays for the administrative and operating expenses of Bolivian counternarcotics agencies that do not fall within the other subprograms. It also covers many personnel and administrative costs for four field offices of the U.S. embassy's Narcotics Affairs Section (NAS), which provide logistical support for counternarcotics activities.[19]

Due in part to a large one-year increase in INC funding for Colombia, Bolivia's 1998 State Department counternarcotics aid has been cut back dramatically. Bolivia's 1997 funding levels are to be restored in 1999.

Colombia:

Colombia is currently the largest recipient of aid through the INC program. The Colombian government will receive INC assistance valued at more than $80 million in 1998, more than one-third of the program's world-wide budget.

Police and military aid

Most of this assistance will support Colombian National Police (CNP) and military units involved in drug interdiction and eradication. A much smaller amount goes to Colombian government agencies that enforce money-laundering and asset-forfeiture laws and investigate drug-trafficking organizations.

The CNP has primary responsibility for Colombia's interdiction and eradication programs. Its Anti-Narcotics Directorate (DANTI) carries out most anti-narcotics missions. The INC program's "major thrust" is to support the DANTI's aerial drug eradication (fumigation) efforts, disruption of drug-trafficking organizations and interdiction of precursor chemicals and cocaine laboratories.

Colombia's armed forces frequently support the police on counter-narcotics missions. However, according to the State Department's March 1998 International Narcotics Control Strategy Report (INCSR), military-police counterdrug cooperation "was, for the most part, dependent on CNP requests for assistance and military ability to meet those requests. In most cases cooperation took the form of multi-day deployments in areas where police felt under a significant guerrilla threat."[20]

The military, the INCSR points out, carries out some counterdrug operations with no police involvement. The armed forces "undertook independent counternarcotics operations in 1997 in order to deprive their primary target, the guerrilla forces, of a source of financing." Meanwhile Colombia's Air Force "continues to attempt, with limited success, to track and force down trafficker aircraft."[21]

Much of the INC program's assistance for the DANTI seeks to improve the police unit's air capability. The program paid for the training of 153 police anti-narcotics aviators, mechanics and logisticians in 1997 (81 for ground training, 41 pilots and 31 technicians). INC also provided parts and fuel, as well as instructor pilots and technical advisors, for the 56 helicopters and 17 fixed-wing aircraft of the police force's anti-narcotics air wing. The INC interregional aviation program (described below) employed an additional 27 U.S.-owned aircraft (10 T-65 spray planes, 5 OV-10 Bronco spray planes, and 12 helicopters) for narcotics eradication missions in Colombia.[22]

The DANTI will continue to be the principal recipient of INC assistance to Colombia in 1999. The INC project "will provide aviation parts in support of the CNP Air Wing, augmentation of base facilities, training and advisory services, and fund many operational costs."[23]

"Assistance to military units," reads the 1999 INC Congressional Presentation,

> will be directed to those activities that support the CNP's counternarcotics efforts. The Colombian Air Force will receive maintenance assistance and training for its helicopter fleet and fixed-wing C-130, OV-10, and A-37 units, as warranted, to advance the overall counternarcotics effort. The Colombian Navy and its Marine branch is expected to manage a counternarcotics campaign on the rivers and the coast. Equipment, training, and technical assistance will be provided to Colombian riverine and coast guard harbor patrol programs.[24]

Blackhawks and equipment upgrades

Of the $80 million or more in INC funds destined for Colombia, at least $50 million will buy, repair or upgrade aircraft for the CNP. The committee report which accompanied the 1998 Foreign Operations Appropriations Act (P.L. 105-118) instructs that $36 million of the 1998 INC account be used to buy three UH-60 Blackhawk helicopters for Colombia's National Police. An additional $14 million will be spent to upgrade ten to twelve UH-1H Huey utility helicopters, and Colombia will share a $4 million region-wide account for repairs to C-26 aircraft. The remaining $30 million will pay for the regular INC program in Colombia, including the police and military aid described in the previous section.

State Department officials interviewed by the General Accounting Office (GAO) indicated that the Blackhawk purchase may displace other activities:

> State may not have adequate funding support for all its programs in Colombia in fiscal year 1998 because State will spend about $50 million to help the Colombians purchase three new Blackhawk helicopters and upgrade UH-1H helicopters, in addition to the regular INC Program. State officials told us the fiscal year 1998 INC Program for Colombia is currently under review.[25]

Indeed, R. Rand Beers, the acting secretary of state for INL, warned a congressional committee in March 1998 that "INL would be hamstrung by the $36 million directed in report language ... to be spent on 3 Black Hawk helicopters."[26] In fact, Beers predicted that the $30 million originally estimated for the regular 1998 INC program in Colombia will be increased significantly. "We estimate these program increases at $21 million," he told the committee, "and that is a conservative estimate."[27]

The "Huey upgrades" and "C-26 Support" accounts will pay for improvements and repairs to helicopters and planes transferred to Colombia by special presidential drawdown authority in September 1996. This equipment is either out of service or lacking key capabilities.

Interregional Aviation and the cost of eradication

As indicated above, the INC interregional aviation program maintains 27 U.S.-owned aircraft (10 T-65 spray planes, 5 OV-10 Bronco spray planes, and 12 helicopters) in Colombia. They are mainly used for narcotics eradication, though "resources are also being used for interdiction missions." Colombia continues to receive "a high level of support" for "flight operations and instruction, maintenance, quality control and spare parts."[28]

"In October 1996," the GAO reports, "the State Department, through its Bureau of International Narcotics and Law Enforcement Affairs, decided to significantly increase the level of U.S. support for and participation in Colombia's aerial eradication of coca and opium poppy."[29] Aircraft on drug-crop eradication missions are flown by U.S. contract personnel escorted by police aircraft. This is a risky task, as most of the areas being fumigated are controlled by Colombia's FARC and ELN guerrillas. "Spray operations are increasingly hazardous," notes the March 1998 INCSR, "due to the need to fly at low altitude coupled with the threat of hostile ground fire. A total of 94 aircraft were hit by hostile fire in 1997, 51 of them while involved in or supporting spray operations."[30]

The interregional aviation program grew rapidly during 1997, while becoming increasingly dependent on contract personnel. A February 1998 GAO report documents the increased size and role of private contractors in the drug eradication effort:

> During fiscal year 1997, State increased the number of aircraft and U.S. contractor personnel involved in the aerial eradication program. As of July 1997, 112 contractor personnel - 9 management and administrative staff, 56 pilots and operations staff, and 47 maintenance staff - were in Colombia. The contractor personnel's role also changed from being primarily responsible for training Colombian pilots and mechanics to directly maintaining aircraft and actively participating in planning and conducting eradication operations. The State Department estimates that the direct costs of supporting the

contractor in Colombia increased from about $6.6 million in fiscal year 1996 to $14 million in fiscal year 1997.[31]

Citing poor coordination within the State Department and a failure to account for unforeseen costs, the GAO contends that eradication efforts have gone well over budget and taken resources from other INC assistance to Colombia.

In July 1997, the Embassy's Narcotics Affairs Section informed the State Department that because of the expanded aerial eradication effort, it had to reallocate $11 million from other planned counternarcotics programs. The Section went on to report that it could not fully support programs for Colombian police interdiction units, demand reduction, and efforts to strengthen Colombian law enforcement institutions. The Section also reported its concerns about adequate funding for these activities in fiscal years 1998 and 1999.[32]

Meanwhile, critics of the program's reliance on fumigation contend that this practice frequently destroys legal crops, may cause health and environmental problems, causes displacement of local populations, and has little effect on the amount of land under illicit cultivation.

Effect of decertification

Colombia's narcotics decertification in 1996 and 1997 had little effect on INC aid to Colombia, as counternarcotics assistance is usually exempt from the aid cutoff that accompanies a decertification. Decertification did, however, end up delaying or canceling about $35 million in U.S. counternarcotics aid through several programs, including $1.1 million in INC funding that was delayed for eight months in 1996.

After the first decertification in March 1996, the State Department and other executive-branch agencies, citing "interagency legal concerns as well as differences within the State Department," took about eight months to decide what aid could and could not be provided to Colombia. "During this period," the GAO reports, "the United States did not provide Colombia with some aviation spare parts, vehicles, or ammunition and funding to repair a Colombian counternarcotics aircraft."[33]

The end result:

- Up to $30 million in counternarcotics Foreign Military Financing (FMF) was delayed until August 1997, when it was released by a special presidential waiver.
- About $1.4 million in International Military Education and Training (IMET) funds were delayed until August 1997, when they were released by the same presidential waiver. This funding was then canceled, because it could not be spent by the end of fiscal year 1997 (the government's fiscal years end on September

30).

- $2.5 million in counternarcotics Foreign Military Sales (FMS) were freed in November 1996 when the State Department determined that the decertification did not stop the sales from going forward.

- $1.1 million in INC funding was freed in November 1996 when the State Department determined that the decertification did not stop the grant from going forward.

Thanks to increased INC funding, however, overall counter-drug aid to Colombia's security forces underwent a substantial net increase during the country's two years of decertification. In its response to a GAO report on the matter, the State Department stated that it sharply increased 1997 INC in part as a response to decertification: "Due recognition should be given to the fact that the primary alternative funding source was the State Department's INC funds. Our funding for Colombia more than doubled in 1997, in part to make up for shortfalls caused by the cutoff of FMF."[34].

End-use monitoring agreement and status of aid to the Colombian Army

As the human rights crisis in Colombia escalates, assistance to the Colombian Army has become increasingly controversial. As noted earlier, a provision in the 1997 and 1998 foreign aid appropriations bills, known popularly as the "Leahy Amendment" after its sponsor, Sen. Patrick Leahy (D-VT), prohibited the obligation of INC and other aid to units of a country's security forces when there is credible evidence that a unit is committing gross human rights violations with impunity.

The State Department decided to enforce the law by requiring Colombia to sign an end-use monitoring agreement to ensure that aid does not go to units with questionable human rights records. The Colombian police were cleared to receive aid in February 1997. The Colombian Defense Ministry signed an end-use monitoring agreement in August 1997, and the Colombian Navy and Air Force were certified to receive aid soon afterward. The Colombian Army, however, has not yet complied fully with the terms of the end-use monitoring agreement; as of May 1998 only two army units have been identified as eligible to receive U.S. assistance, and these have not been certified. As it is funded through a different appropriations law, however, the Defense Department has trained Colombian army units through its counternarcotics and Joint Combined Exchange Training (JCET) programs.

Mexico:

In 1996, the U.S. Embassy in Mexico City raised counternarcotics to its list of top-level policy priorities, alongside business and trade, and increased counternarcotics assistance accordingly. A U.S.-Mexico High Level

Contact Group was established that year to guide both countries' counternarcotics cooperation. The Contact Group developed a comprehensive binational drug strategy, which was issued in February 1998.

The United States has provided varying levels of counternarcotics law-enforcement assistance to Mexico since 1973. Between 1993 and 1995, the Mexican government declined U.S. anti-drug aid in an effort to fund its own counternarcotics activities. The 1994-95 peso crisis, combined with a large increase in the trafficking of drugs through Mexican territory, forced Mexico to reverse this policy and resume accepting U.S. assistance.[35]

According to its 1999 Congressional Presentation, the International Narcotics Control (INC) program in Mexico "draws heavily on the support of other USG [U.S. Government] agencies, particularly the Department of Justice."[36] It focuses in particular on the strengthening of law-enforcement and judicial institutions. This largely means improving investigative capabilities while offering training in law-enforcement and drug-interdiction methods.

The chief civilian beneficiaries of INC aid to Mexico are:

1. The Mexican Attorney General's Office (PGR).
2. The Special Prosecutor for Crimes Against Health (FEADS), within the PGR. This office was created to replace the Mexican National Counternarcotics Institute (INCD) after the INCD's director, Gen. Jesus Gutiérrez Rebollo, was arrested and charged with maintaining links to drug traffickers. According to the INCSR, personnel assigned to this office must pass "a rigorous suitability examination."[37]
   Two special units within the FEADS receive significant amounts of assistance:
   a) The Organized Crime Unit, a 300-member force which conducts "investigations and prosecutions aimed at criminal organizations, including drug trafficking activities"; and
   b) Bilateral Task Forces, charged with "investigating and dismantling the most significant drug-trafficking organizations along the U.S.-Mexican border." These task forces, established by a 1996 Memorandum of Understanding between the United States and Mexico, have a combined strength of 70 members.[38]
3. The PGR's Division of Air Services, which provides aviation support for over 160 aircraft, including 27 U.S.-owned UH-1H helicopters, used in the PGR's operations.
4. The Northern Border Response Force (NBRF), a joint civilian/military interdiction program that began in 1990 as "a cooperative U.S.-Mexican air interdiction program aimed at stopping cocaine shipments from South America into Mexico, but has since expanded to include ground and maritime components." Mexican Air Force intercept aircraft are integrated into the NBRF.[39]
5. The national legal training academy (INACIPE).
6. The counternarcotics planning center (CENDRO).
7. The Mexican Federal Judicial Police (MFJP).
8. Personnel from the treasury ministry (Hacienda).

The INC program has provided these units with equipment and training, and has developed "an extensive project to upgrade data processing and communications systems for drug enforcement elements of the PGR." Training and technical assistance ranges "from highly-technical investigative techniques down to new approaches to administration and personnel system management."[40]

The INC program provides field support funding to the Northern Border Response Force. "While the GOM [government of Mexico] has assumed most of the program's support costs," the 1999 Congressional Presentation states, "INL will continue to provide periodic assistance, particularly with specialized equipment and pilot activities to further enhance the GOM's interdiction capabilities, in addition to logistical, communications, computer and other support."[41]

Until the early 1990s, the INC Air Support subproject funded the maintenance of the entire PGR Division of Air Services, including its U.S.-owned aircraft. The Mexican government's "Mexicanization" policy has reduced this assistance to communications upgrades, specialized field support equipment, test equipment, and training. INC assistance may fund maintenance of sensor equipment aboard Mexican Citation tracker aircraft; this equipment can only be repaired by cleared U.S. personnel.[42]

The INC program has provided only limited support to the Mexican military in the past, such as aerial surveillance equipment to detect drug cultivations. While no military aid through the INC program is foreseen this year, the personnel of the Narcotics Affairs Station at the U.S. Embassy, which carries out the INC program in Mexico, will help deliver military aid from other U.S. assistance programs.[43] These programs include:

- Drawdowns;
- Grants and sales of excess defense articles;
- Foreign military sales (FMS) and direct commercial sales (DCS);
- Training through the International Military Training and Education (IMET) program; and
- Training and equipment provided through accounts authorized by section 1004 of the 1991 defense authorization law and section 1031 of the 1997 defense authorization law.

Peru:

The INC program in Peru combines police and military assistance; support for intelligence-gathering and air and riverine interdiction; law-enforcement, customs and judiciary training; and demand reduction, development and alternative agriculture programs. The $50 million request for Peru in 1999 would represent a 100 percent increase over 1997 spending levels.

According to the State Department's 1999 Congressional Presentation, the Peru INC program's *Counternarcotics Law Enforcement project* is "structured around a mobile-basing concept which allows police and helicopters to conduct operations against major trafficking facilities from a variety of secure locations." The "mobile basing" strategy allows U.S.-owned helicopters to transport Peruvian police, along with U.S. law-enforcement advisors, "on counternarcotics operations throughout eastern Peru."[44] The project's main logistical and maintenance area is located in the town of Pucallpa, in Ucayali department.[45]

The Counternarcotics Law Enforcement project has a Narcotics Field Support subproject, which "provides essentially all costs," except salaries, associated with training, equipping, and operating the Anti-Drug Directorate (DIRANDRO) of the Peruvian National Police (PNP).[46] DIRANDRO is Peru's lead counternarcotics law-enforcement agency.

A second project, *Counternarcotics Aviation Support*, pays for operation and maintenance of the Peruvian police force's air wing, the National Police Aviation Division (DIPA). As the 1999 Congressional Presentation indicates, this project:

Provides pilots, aircrews, and support personnel for approximately 17 Department of State-owned UH-1H helicopters and 11-14 Peruvian [Russian-made] Mi-17 helicopters which support coca eradication and law enforcement actions in the field. Aviation support funds the counternarcotics operations of the State-owned helicopters, providing fuel, maintenance, hangars and warehousing, aircraft rental when needed, and operational support for DIPA personnel.[47]

In Peru, the INC interregional aviation program (discussed below) supports the use of helicopters in crop eradication. Unlike Colombia, where U.S. contractors fly the program's U.S.-owned planes, "all missions are flown by pilots in the Peruvian National Police (PNP)."[48]

The *Military Counternarcotics Support project* is the INC program's main source of assistance to the Peruvian military. It provides Peru's air force and navy with training and limited logistical support, including "training for pilots and mechanics, facility improvements, spare parts for aircraft, boats and resources required to implement riverine commerce control on inland waterways and container shipping ports."[49]

While the military is charged with supporting police anti-drug efforts, the two institutions often work separately. In 1997, the General Accounting Office found that "coordination between the counternarcotics police and military units continues to be a problem" in Peru.[50]

The INC *Narcotics Intelligence project* supports a national narcotics intelligence center, which collects and analyzes information on narcotrafficking in Peru. A Customs Narcotics Interdiction project supports Peruvian Customs Service cooperation with the U.S. Drug Enforcement Administration (DEA) through such limited logistic support as "vehicles, investigative and communications equipment, training, and operational support."[51]

Interregional Aviation Support:

INL carries out an "air wing" program in Central and South America, which maintains U.S.-owned aircraft used for drug eradication and interdiction. These planes and helicopters are used for transportation of counterdrug forces, interdiction of drug smugglers, surveillance of drug cultivation, and eradication (fumigation) of illicit crops.

The Interregional Aviation program is most active in Bolivia, Colombia and Peru, with a significant presence in Belize, Guatemala, Panama, and Venezuela. Helicopter operations receive the most emphasis in Peru and Bolivia, while airplane-based eradication programs are the focus elsewhere. The interregional aviation program also "responds to aerial eradication requests" from other countries.[52]

INL has hired Dyncorp, a private defense contractor, to provide "logistical, operational and training support," which includes maintaining and, in some cases, flying the planes and helicopters.[53]

INC by country / program:

INC is a particularly fast-growing program; 1999 funding is expected to be 80 percent above 1996 levels. According to the Office of National Drug Control Policy (ONDCP)'s 1998 National Drug Control Strategy, the $45 million increase requested for 1999 includes "funds to build on FY 1998 support for Andean Ridge nations involved in interdiction and counterdrug law-enforcement operations. This effort will expand crop eradication and alternative-development programs to reduce illicit coca cultivation."[54]

The INC amounts for 1998 presented here represent the State Department's estimates as of March 1998. Due to a number of issues, particularly the uncertain status of the Blackhawk helicopters for Colombia, actual aid amounts may differ greatly from these estimates by the end of fiscal year 1998.

(Thousands of U.S. dollars)

Program	1996 actual[55]	1997 actual[56]	1998 estimate[56]	1999 request[56]
Narcotics programs				
The Bahamas	700	800	500	1,000
Bolivia	30,000	45,500	12,000	45,000
Brazil	290	700	500	1,200
Colombia	16,000	33,450	30,000	45,000
Blackhawks			36,000	
Ecuador	500	600	500	1,500
Guatemala	2,000	2,000	3,000	4,000
Jamaica	700	650	600	800
Mexico	2,200	5,000	5,000	8,000
Peru	18,500	25,750	31,000	50,000
Venezuela	500	600	600	700
Latin American regional programs	3,708	5,100	4,000	9,000
Latin America Subtotal	75,098	120,150	123,700	166,200
(Asia/Africa/Europe)	12,892	9,050	8,700	13,000
Interregional Aviation Support	25,755	31,500	38,000	41,000
Total Country Programs	113,745	160,700	170,400	220,200
International Organizations	7,710	12,000	4,000	8,000
Law Enforcement Training and Demand Reduction	7,000	9,000	9,000	8,000
Systems Support and Upgrades • C-26 Support • Huey Upgrades – Colombia			4,000 14,000	
Total	0	3,500	18,000	10,000
Program Development and Support	6,500	7,800	8,600	8,800
Total Narcotics Programs (INC)	$134,955	$193,000	$210,000	$255,000
Anticrime programs carried out by INL	$18,200	$20,000	$20,000	$20,000
All programs carried out by INL	$153,155	$213,000	$230,000	$275,000
Total for Latin America and the Caribbean[55]	(n/a)	$161,150	$181,700	$221,200

INL budget by function, worldwide:

(Thousands of U.S. dollars)

Function	1996 actual[58]	% of total	1997 actual[59]	% of total	1998 estimate[59]	% of total	1999 request[59]	% of total
Law Enforcement Assistance and Institution Development	59,185	43.9	55,904	29.0	83,109	39.6	94,785	37.2
Economic Incentive / Eradication	42,521	31.5	95,275	49.4	90,126	42.9	120,920	47.4
International Organizations	7,710	5.7	12,000	6.2	4,000	1.9	8,000	3.1
Drug Awareness / Demand Reduction	3,610	2.7	5,535	2.9	4,865	2.3	4,950	1.9
Law Enforcement Training	5,300	3.9	6,700	3.5	6,700	3.2	6,200	2.4
Program Development and Support	16,629	12.3	17,586	9.1	21,200	10.1	20,145	7.9
Total Narcotics Programs	134,955	100	193,000	100	210,000	100	255,000	100
Anti-crime Programs	18,200		20,000		20,000		20,000	
Total Program Plan	153,155		213,000		230,000		275,000	

INC funding in the hemisphere

Legend:
$5,000,000+
$750,000 - $5,000,000
$250,000 - $750,000

1996 (actual)

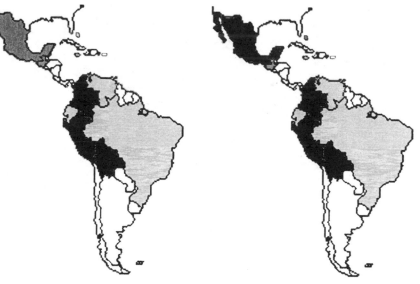

1997 (actual)

Office of National Drug Control Policy Discretionary Funding

Program description:

The Office of National Drug Control Policy, otherwise known as the office of the White House's "Drug Czar," designs anti-drug strategies and coordinates U.S. government counternarcotics efforts.

ONDCP receives some "discretionary funding," money that is not directed for a specific purpose, through a Special Forfeiture Fund. This fund gets its resources from the Justice and Treasury Departments, which maintain Assets Forfeiture Funds from the seized assets of convicted drug offenders. ONDCP's Special Forfeiture Fund may also receive resources through specific congressional appropriations.

ONDCP did not receive discretionary funding from the Special Forfeiture Fund in 1996. In 1997, however, it received $112.9 million, $60.9 million of which was made available to the office's director to distribute to other agencies.

Of this amount, $11.5 million went to international programs, all of them in Latin America. These included the following.

1. **A one-time transfer of $9.8 million to the State Department's Bureau of International Narcotics and Law Enforcement Affairs (INL).** INL used this funding to provide aid to Peru through its International Narcotics Control (INC) program, which budgeted $25.75 million of its own funds for Peru in 1997.

   According to a June 1997 press release from ONDCP, "U.S. funding will be used to support the A-37 aircraft which are employed in patrolling the 'airbridge' between Peru and Colombia. Specifically, the funds will support engine overhauls, maintenance, parts and materials. Additionally, the resources will augment counternarcotics operational support for Peru's National Anti-Drug Directorate, Navy and Coast Guard."[1]

   A February 1998 ONDCP memo states that $4.5 million of the transfer went to the refurbishment of "Peruvian Air Force aircraft flying source country interdiction and crop eradication missions." The remaining $5.3 million funded riverine drug

---

 Although ONDCP discretionary funding is not governed by the Foreign Assistance Act or the Arms Export Control Act, it is included in this section because it has mostly been used to transfer funds to the International Narcotics Control (INC) program.

interdiction assistance to the Peruvian National Police, Navy, and Coast Guard, supporting "operational and tactical missions in coca-producing areas and a capability for small riverine patrol craft operations in Peruvian waterways."[2]

2. **A one-time transfer of $500,000 to the Narcotics Affairs Section at the U.S. Embassy in Colombia for "Colombian aviation support."** This funding went "to replenish stockpiles of helicopter spare parts and purchase fuel for helicopters and spray planes."[3]

3. **A one-time transfer of $1.2 million to the Defense Department for "source country operations."** This funding supported "a variety of DoD [Department of Defense] counterdrug operational, support and intelligence programs in South America, including Peru."[4]

ONDCP will not receive discretionary funding in 1998; it has requested $26 million from this source for 1999. The destination of that money has not yet been determined.

Law:

The ONDCP Special Forfeiture Fund is governed by section 1509 of Title 21, U.S. Code. It was enacted as part of the Anti-Drug Abuse Act of 1988.

The Fund's purpose is to provide supplementary resources for the head of ONDCP for drug control efforts. Within four months of the end of a fiscal year, the President must submit to Congress a detailed report on the Fund's deposits and expenditures.

Funding:

Country	Receiving Department	1997
Peru – Aviation Refurbishment	State Department	$4.5 million
Peru – Riverine Program	State Department	$5.3 million
Colombia – Aviation Support	State Department / Narcotics Affairs Station - Bogotá	$500,000
Source Country Operations	Defense Department	$1.2 million
Total		**$11.5 million**

EDA: Excess Defense Articles

Program description:

Under section 516 of the Foreign Assistance Act of 1961 (P.L. 87-195, or the "FAA"), as amended, the U.S. government has the authority to transfer surplus military equipment to foreign security forces.

Defense articles no longer needed by the U.S. armed forces and eligible for transfer range from rations and uniforms to used vehicles, cargo aircraft, and ships. Between 1990 and 1995, the United States transferred excess military equipment worldwide valued at $7 billion, most of it to developing countries.

Although most transfers of surplus U.S. stocks are given away at no cost, they may also be sold, loaned, or leased to the recipient country. All EDA transactions, like Foreign Military Sales (FMS) purchases, are coordinated by Security Assistance Organizations (SAOs) at U.S. embassies, individual armed services, and the Defense Security Assistance Agency (DSAA).

The armed service overseeing a transfer determines the current value of EDA, which normally ranges between 5 and 50 percent of the articles' original value. The General Accounting Office has found values assigned by the services to be "generally unreliable," since they tend to be undervalued.

The maximum amount of EDA that a foreign government may acquire during any given fiscal year is $350 million, measured by current value (although exceptions can be made for high-cost items).

Law:

Section 516 authorizes the President to transfer excess defense articles on a grant basis to countries which the State Department defines as eligible. The list of eligible countries must be included in the State Department's annual Congressional Presentation for Foreign Operations.

Limitations

Section 516 places the following restrictions on the President's power to transfer EDA to Latin America and the Caribbean:

1. The items must be drawn from existing Defense Department stocks;
2. The Defense Department cannot buy the items for the sole purpose of transfer-

ring them;
3. Giving up the defense articles must not harm the U.S. armed forces' level of readiness;
4. Transfers on a sales basis are preferred, after taking into account the potential proceeds from such sales and comparative foreign policy benefits of a grant; and
5. The transfer must not harm the U.S. technological and industrial base, and must not compete with the sale of a new or used article.

Under section 516, priority in delivery of EDA is given to NATO member countries and "major non-NATO allies" (as of May 1998, Argentina is the United States' only major non-NATO ally in the Western Hemisphere).

Transportation costs and any costs associated with refurbishing and repairing the transferred items must be paid by the recipient. The President can waive EDA transportation charges if:

1. He or she determines that to do so is in the U.S. national interest;
2. The recipient is a developing country receiving less than $10 million in other military assistance during the current fiscal year;
3. The total weight of the transfer does not exceed 25,000 pounds; and
4. The transportation is carried out on a "space available" basis.

Notification

If the original value of a proposed EDA transfer exceeds $7 million, section 516 requires that the President provide 30 days' advance notice to the Senate Foreign Relations Committee, the House International Relations Committee, and the Senate and House Appropriations Committees. This notification must include the following information:

1. A statement outlining the purposes for which the article is being provided, indicating whether the article has been provided to that country in the past;
2. An assessment of the transfer's impact on U.S. military readiness;
3. An assessment of the transfer's impact on the U.S. technological and industrial base, and of possible competition with sales of new or used equipment to that country; and
4. A statement of the article's current value and original value.

Reporting

Section 516 requires that the annual <u>Congressional Presentation</u> include amounts of EDA transferred to every country in the past fiscal year, separating sales and grants.

An accounting of EDA transfers to every country, broken down by category, is included in a report on arms sales required by section 655 of the FAA.

The Defense Department also maintains EDA information on an on-line computer "bulletin board," which can be accessed by dialing (703) 604-

6470, or by using the telnet internet protocol (telnet://134.152.212.131). A free sign-up is required for first-time users. This resource, however, is only sporadically maintained and is frequently out of service.

EDA grants by country:

An offer of EDA does not necessarily mean that the articles will be transferred. The articles' delivery may be delayed, or recipient countries may turn down EDA offers.

(Thousands of U.S. dollars)

Country	Offered, 1996[1]		Delivered, 1996 (as of March 1997)[1]		Offered, 1997[2]		Delivered, 1997 (as of March 1998)[2]	
	Original value	Current value	Original value	Current value	Original value	Current value	Original value	Current value
Argentina	$83,805.5	$17,879.8	$0	$0	$66,233	$23,352	$8,393	$460
Belize					$208	$42	$0	$0
Bolivia	$90	$4.5	$90	$4.5				
Chile	$4,401.3	$486.7	$99	$40				
Costa Rica	$2.8	$0.1	$0	$0				
Dominican Republic	$341	$17	$341	$17	$1,874	$232	$1,874	$232
Ecuador	$282	$14	$282	$14	$375	$77	$375	$77
Jamaica	$4,163.0	$618.7	$0	$0				
Mexico	$16,242	$2,372	$11,269	$1,122	$18,454	$3,023	$18,454	$3,023
Paraguay	$76	$4	$76	$4				
Peru	$4,993.9	$1,249.2	$0.0	$0.0				
Uruguay	$16,839	$2,794	$0	$0				
Venezuela	$522	$208	$522	$208				
Regional Total	$131,759	$25,648	$12,679	$1,410	$87,144	$26,726	$29,096	$3,792

EDA sales by country:

(Thousands of U.S. dollars)

Country	Offered, 1996[2]		Delivered, 1996 (as of March 1997)[3]		Offered, 1997[4]		Delivered, 1997 (as of March 1998)[4]	
	Original value	Current value	Original value	Current value	Original value	Current value	Original value	Current value
Mexico	$61,880	$6,863	$0	$0				
Venezuela	$6,459	$1,058	$0	$0				
Chile					$941	$47	$941	$47
Regional total	$68,339	$7,921	$0	$0	$941	$47	$941	$47

"Major Non-NATO Ally" (MNNA) Status

The notion of "major non-NATO ally" (MNNA) status first surfaced in 1989, with the addition of section 2350a ("Cooperative agreements with allies") to Title 10 of the U.S. Code. For several years, this status was limited to Australia, Egypt, Israel, Japan, and South Korea.

The benefits of MNNA status are largely symbolic, implying a close working relationship with a country's defense forces. MNNAs do not enjoy the same mutual defense and security guarantees afforded to members of the North Atlantic Treaty Organization.

The granting of MNNA status, however, does carry some advantages in the foreign assistance process. Major non-NATO allies are eligible for:

- Priority delivery of excess defense articles (EDA);
- Stockpiling of U.S. defense articles;
- Purchase of depleted uranium anti-tank rounds;
- Participation in cooperative research and development programs; and
- (For countries that were MNNAs as of March 31, 1995) participation in the Defense Export Loan Guarantee (DELG) program, which backs up private loans for commercial defense exports.

For now, the list of MNNAs in the Western Hemisphere is limited to one country. President Bill Clinton designated Argentina as the first Latin American major non-NATO ally in a determination signed on January 6, 1998.

Public Law 104-164, enacted in July 1996, added a new section 517 to the Foreign Assistance Act of 1961 (P.L. 87-195) governing the designation of major non-NATO allies. The new section granted the President the authority to name new countries to be MNNAs. The President's designations of new MNNAs take effect thirty days after Congress is notified in writing.

Emergency Drawdown Authority

Program description:

If an "unforeseen emergency" should arise overseas, two sections of the Foreign Assistance Act of 1961 (P.L. 87-195, or the "FAA"), as amended, empower the President to "draw down" articles and services from existing U.S. government holdings, budgets or arsenals.

A "drawdown" is a transfer of weapons, parts, equipment, services or training that are not considered "excess." Drawdown provisions give the President a limited ability to shift resources from other agencies' budgets and inventories into security assistance.

Section 506 of the FAA contains two provisions which, taken together, allow the President to carry out drawdowns valued at up to $250 million per year. Of this amount, up to $100 million may be drawn down from the Defense Department for unspecified emergencies that require immediate military assistance. This provision -- known as subsection 506(a)(1) -- has not been used recently to transfer arms to the Western Hemisphere.

Subsection 506(a)(2), on the other hand, has been invoked quite frequently to provide anti-drug assistance to security forces in Latin America and the Caribbean. This provision authorizes yearly drawdowns of up to $150 million for four purposes:

- International narcotics control;
- International disaster assistance;
- Migration and refugee assistance; or
- Efforts to locate U.S. personnel unaccounted for from the Vietnam War.

This $150 million can come from any U.S. government agency. The law specifies, however, that no more than $75 million per year may come from Defense Department inventories. Counternarcotics cannot be used to justify more than $75 million per year in drawdowns under this subsection.

Section 552 of the FAA authorizes drawdowns for international peacekeeping activities, allowing the transfer of up to $25 million per year. Haiti is the only Western Hemisphere country to have received a drawdown under section 552 in the past few years. Haiti's new civilian security forces have been the main beneficiaries.

Law:

Notification

Before carrying out a drawdown, the President must notify the House International Relations Committee, the Senate Foreign Relations Committee, and both appropriations committees. This notification must specify the nature and purpose of the drawdown, as well as the country or countries involved. If the drawdown is for international narcotics control assistance under section 506(a)(2), the committees must receive at least 15 days' notice.

The Foreign Operations Appropriations Act for 1998 (PL 105-118) amended section 506 to add a new notification requirement. Once a drawdown is completed, the President must now provide a report detailing all defense articles, services, education and training that were transferred.

Before a drawdown for peacekeeping under section 552, the President must determine that a "peacekeeping emergency" exists.

All drawdown notifications are published in the Federal Register. These notifications, however, normally do not specify the items that are to be provided. This information is included in justification documents sent to the congressional committees.

Reporting

Section 655 of the FAA requires a yearly report on arms-transfer programs. This report includes breakdowns, by country and by category, of defense articles supplied through drawdowns.

Colombia:

The Clinton Administration ordered a $40.5 million drawdown for Colombia's security forces on September 30, 1996, the last day of that fiscal year. The drawdown, according to a February 1998 report by the General Accounting Office (GAO), "was justified on the basis that important programs would grind to a halt without the aid and that past investments in counternarcotics programs would suffer due to the deterioration of equipment, training skills, and goodwill on the part of those Colombians who daily put their lives at risk."[1]

The drawdown package, however, "was hastily developed and did not include sufficient information on specific Colombian requirements, the ability of the host country to operate and maintain the equipment, or the funding necessary from the United States or Colombia to support it." Officials from the State Department, Defense Department, and the U.S. Embassy told GAO they had spent little time consulting on the items to be included in the package. Some items, like five C-26 aircraft, were added at the last minute, and several were inoperable.[2]

The State Department's response to the GAO alleges that the Department did the best it could under the circumstances:

> Extensive interagency consultation took place. ... The final content of the 506 package for Colombia was heavily dependent on the availability from existing stocks, as determined by the Defense Department. We acknowledge that [section] 506 is a blunt instrument, but it was the only one available to us.[3]

Officials expressed concern about the U.S. government's heavy reliance on drawdowns to provide counternarcotics assistance to Colombia. They told GAO that "such assistance was a poor substitute for a well-thought out counternarcotics assistance program and could be harmful if complementary funding was not provided" to help maintain the articles being transferred.[4]

As of May 1998, drawdown aid to the Colombian Army has yet to be delivered. No army unit has been certified as in compliance with the Leahy Amendment (see the Colombia description in the INC section and the Leahy Amendment discussion in Appendix A).

Mexico:

53 UH-1H helicopters and three C-26 aircraft were delivered to the Mexican military during 1996 and 1997, along with 20 more UH-1H helicopters transferred through the Excess Defense Articles (EDA) program.[5]

The helicopters are intended to support the counterdrug operations of the Mexican military's Air-Mobile Special Forces Groups (GAFEs), elite counternarcotics units which are receiving extensive U.S. training. "These air mobility assets [helicopters and planes]," the White House's Office of National Drug Control Policy (ONDCP) reports, "mark a significant improvement in Mexico's counterdrug capabilities. They are employed in conjunction with the GAFE as well as in reconnaissance, eradication, and interdiction operations."[6]

The GAO has uncovered several logistical problems associated with this drawdown. In 1997, the U.S. Embassy in Mexico City reported that the helicopters are "of little utility above 5,000 feet, where most of the opium poppy is cultivated."[7] Due to delays in delivering spare parts, the GAO reports, the helicopters' operational rates have declined to between 35 and 54 percent.[8] The C-26s, which were intended to perform surveillance of drug cultivations, were delivered without surveillance capabilities, which could cost an extra $3 million per plane.[9]

Observers have expressed some concern about the "end use" of equipment and training transferred to Mexico through drawdowns and other programs. Much of this concern was inspired by the misuse of U.S.-provided counternarcotics helicopters to transport troops during the 1994 Chiapas uprising.[10] In March 1998 testimony, the GAO indicated that

> oversight and accountability of counternarcotics assistance continues to be a problem. We found that embassy records on UH-1H helicopter usage for the civilian law enforcement agencies were incomplete. Additionally, we found that the U.S. military's ability to provide adequate oversight is limited by the end-use monitoring agreement signed by the governments of the United States and Mexico.[11]

A 1996 GAO report notes that "the Mexican government ... has objected to direct oversight of U.S.-provided assistance and, in some instances, has refused to accept assistance that was contingent upon signing such an agreement. ... According to U.S. officials," the report goes on, "the U.S. Embassy relies heavily on biweekly reports that the Mexican government submits. Unless they request specific operational records, U.S. personnel have little knowledge of whether helicopters are being properly used for counternarcotics activities."[12]

Drawdowns by country:

Fiscal Year 1997:

Country	Date	Authorization	Amount
Colombia[13]	9/30/97	506(a)(2) / Counter-narcotics	$14,200,000
Eastern Caribbean[13]	9/30/97	506(a)(2) / Counter-narcotics	$1,500,000
Mexico[14]	12/2/96	506(a)(2) / Counter-narcotics	$37,000,000
Peru[13]	9/30/97	506(a)(2) / Counter-narcotics	$2,300,000
Venezuela[13]	9/30/97	506(a)(2) / Counter-narcotics	$1,000,000
Transportation costs[15]	9/30/97	506(a)(2) / Counter-narcotics	$1,000,000
Total			$57,000,000

Items transferred through drawdowns in 1997 include the following:

- **Colombian National Police:** field gear, airstrip cratering charges, minigun ammunition, flight equipment, UH-1H helicopter spare parts[13]

- **Colombian Armed Forces:** communications equipment, M-16A1 rifles, M-60 machine guns[13]
- **Eastern Caribbean:** field gear, M-16A1 rifles, .45-caliber pistols, C-26 air support, coast guard support[13]
- **Mexican military "counternarcotics special forces":** UH-1H helicopters, spare parts and support equipment; C-26 aircraft[14]
- **Peruvian National Police:** field gear[13]
- **Peruvian Air Force:** flight equipment[13]
- **Venezuelan security forces:** field radios, canine training, coast guard support[13]

Fiscal Year 1996:

Country	Date	Authorization	Amount
Colombia[16]	9/30/96	506(a)(2) / Counter-narcotics	$40,500,000
Eastern Caribbean[16]	9/30/96	506(a)(2) / Counter-narcotics	$8,500,000
Haiti[17]	9/12/96	552(c)(2) / Peacekeeping	$3,000,000
Peru[16]	9/30/96	506(a)(2) / Counter-narcotics	$13,750,000
Venezuela[16]	9/30/96	506(a)(2) / Counter-narcotics	$12,250,000
Total			$78,000,000

Items transferred through drawdowns in 1996 include the following:

- **Colombian National Police:** C-26 aircraft, UH-1H helicopters, rations and commodities, ammunition, communications equipment[18]
- **Colombian Armed Forces:** C-26 aircraft, UH-1H helicopters, aircraft spare parts, utility landing craft, river patrol craft, communications equipment, field gear, training, utility vehicles[18]
- **Eastern Caribbean:** ocean patrol boats, training, communications equipment, C-26 aircraft and flight equipment for Barbados[18]
- **Peruvian security forces:** C-26 aircraft, communications equipment, river patrol craft[18]
- **Venezuelan Armed Forces and National Guard:** coastal patrol boats, river patrol craft, utility landing craft, communications gear, training, spares, C-26 aircraft[18]

Fiscal Year 1995:

Country	Date	Authorization	Amount
Haiti[18]	6/23/95	552(c)(2) / Peacekeeping	$7,000,000

Leased Defense Articles

Program description:

At times a country only desires defense materials for a short period; leasing allows an article to be used for up to 5 years at the lowest possible cost. The government can lease defense articles to foreign countries or international organizations for national security reasons. The articles must not be needed by the United States at the time. The government is also required to justify the articles' lease, as opposed to a sale.

The foreign country or organization must agree to pay a rental fee, which covers all costs incurred by the United States Government, including depreciation. The lessee must also agree to pay a replacement or restoration fee should leased articles be destroyed or broken.

The lease resembles a grant if the President exercises his right to waive the rental fee. This can be done for items that are past three-quarters of their service life, or items that are to be used in a cooperative research and development effort determined to be "in the national security interest" of the United States.

The lease agreement, including all renewals, can not be longer than 5 years. The U.S. government can end a lease at any time.

Law:

Chapter 6 of the Arms Export Control Act (P.L. 90-269, or the AECA), as amended, authorizes the President to lease defense articles to a foreign country or international organization, in accordance with several requirements and limitations.

Limitations

In order to lease weapons or equipment to a country, the following eligibility requirements must be met:

1. The President must determine that there are foreign policy or national security reasons for the lease;
2. The President must justify why the articles in question must be leased, rather than sold;
3. The articles must not be needed by the United States at the time;
4. The country or organization reimburses the United States for all incurred costs and the depreciation value, and
5. The recipient country or organization can not be barred from receiving aid by

other sections of the Foreign Assistance Act and Arms Export Control Act.

The law also limits the terms under which the lease can be negotiated:

1. The recipient country or international organization must pay all costs related to the articles during the time they are leased, as well as their depreciation value;
2. The recipient party is responsible for fixing or replacing damaged or lost goods;
3. Foreign Military Financing (FMF) funds cannot be used for the rental payment; and
4. The lease cannot be more than five years in duration, including renewals.

Notification

The Speaker of the House of Representatives and the chairmen of the Senate Foreign Relations Committee and the Senate Armed Services Committee must be notified within 30 days of an agreement or renewal if:

- A lease will be for one year or more; or
- A renewal period is for at least one year.

Within the notification period, Congress may prohibit a lease by passing a joint resolution, but only if:

- The value of major defense equipment (replacement cost not including depreciation) is $14,000,000 or more; or
- The value of the defense articles to be leased is $50,000,000 or more.

  ["Major defense equipment" means any item on the United States Munitions List with a research and development cost of at least $50 million or a total production cost of at least $200 million.]

Exceptions and waivers

The President can waive rental fees if:

- It is determined that the lease is in the U.S. national-security interest;
- The articles are past three-quarters of their expected useful life; or
- The President determines, through a written certification to Congress, that an emergency situation exists.

Leases by country, 1996[1]

(Thousands of U.S. dollars)

Country	Replacement value	Total rental value
Brazil	14,176	0
Chile	6,364	1,004
Venezuela	501	29
Regional total	21,041	1,033

Leases by country, 1997[2]

(Thousands of U.S. dollars)

Country	Replacement value	Total rental value
Chile	5,303	1,148
Venezuela	3,351	88
Regional total	8,654	1,236

ICITAP: International Criminal Investigative Training Assistance Program

Program description:

Through the International Criminal Investigative Training Assistance Program (ICITAP), the Department of Justice provides law enforcement and judicial training to Western Hemisphere democracies.

ICITAP works in tandem with OPDAT (Overseas Prosecutorial Development Assistance and Training), a Justice Department program offering administration of justice assistance.

ICITAP seeks to:

1. Enhance prosecutorial and judicial capabilities;
2. Enhance investigative and forensic capabilities;
3. Assist in development of training curricula for law enforcement personnel;
4. Improve administrative capabilities of law enforcement agencies; and
5. Improve penal institutions and the rehabilitation process.

ICITAP is not a military training program; it is a program for training civilian police and judicial functionaries. The program has, however, trained some police forces within, or under the authority of, defense ministries.

Law:

ICITAP is authorized by section 534(b)(3) of the Foreign Assistance Act of 1961 (P.L. 87-195, or the "FAA"), as amended. This section permits the executive to create programs in Latin America and the Caribbean to assist in administration of justice.

Section 534(b)(3) is a legal exception to the general ban on police assistance enacted in section 660 of the FAA.

The Anti-Drug Abuse Act of 1988 and the International Narcotics Control Act of 1990 expanded ICITAP's legal mandate to include specialized assistance to Bolivia, Peru and Colombia. The Urgent Assistance for Democracy in Panama Act of 1990 provided authority and funding for large-scale civilian law enforcement assistance (otherwise outlawed by Section 660 above) in Panama. Section 122 of Public Law 102-166 extended this coverage to El Salvador.

ICITAP by country[1]:

(Thousands of U.S. dollars)

Country	1996 (or multi-year)	1997
Bolivia	700	1,000
Caribbean	6,000 (1986-1995)	
Colombia	8,700 (1989-1994)	
Costa Rica	500	223
Dominican Republic	500	230
El Salvador	33,150(1990-1996)	2,200
Guatemala	2,500(1994-1996)	3,500
Haiti Administration of Justice Program	414	1,092
Haiti Police Development Project	50,800 (1991-1996)	6,500
Honduras	1,500	1,000
Panama	32,153 (1990-1996)	500

Note: The March 1998 State Department International Narcotics Control Strategy Report (INCSR) states that "[T]he International Criminal Investigative Training Assistance Program (ICITAP), the first ever in Nicaragua, is aimed at improving the investigative techniques of police, prosecutors, and judges."[2]

Defense Department Programs

Counternarcotics Authorizations

- "Section 1004" and "Section 124" Counterdrug Assistance

- "Section 1031" Counterdrug Assistance to Mexico

- "Section 1033" Counterdrug Assistance to Colombia and Peru

Training and Education

- School of the Americas

- Inter-American Air Forces Academy

- Naval Small Craft Instruction and Technical Training School

- Center for Hemispheric Defense Studies

- Foreign Student Program at U.S. Service Academies

Deployments

- Exercises

  - Tentative Exercise Calendar

- Humanitarian and Civic Assistance

- Deployments for Training

- Special Operations Forces (SOF) Training

Foreign Military Interaction

Non-Lethal Excess Property Transfers

"Section 1004" and "Section 124"
Counterdrug Assistance

Program description:

With the 1989 inclusion of section 124 in Title 10, U.S. Code, the Department of Defense became the lead U.S. agency responsible for detecting and monitoring illegal drugs entering the United States by air or sea.

Section 124 does not authorize the provision of assistance. It permits the use of funds for drug-interdiction operations, such as radar sites, surveillance flights and intelligence-gathering, carried out by U.S. military personnel stationed in Latin America and the Caribbean.

Section 1004 of the 1991 National Defense Authorization Act (P.L. 101-510) detailed further the Pentagon's role in counternarcotics. This provision allows the military to provide specific types of support to domestic U.S. law-enforcement agencies, and -- unlike section 124 -- permits some assistance and training for foreign security forces.

Section 1004 authorizes U.S. military training of foreign police forces, an activity that the Foreign Assistance Act -- a separate law governing most security assistance programs -- does not authorize for counternarcotics purposes.

Types of support allowed under section 1004 include the following:

1. Maintenance, repair and upgrading of equipment;
2. Transport of U.S. and foreign personnel and supplies;
3. Establishment and operation of bases of operation and training;
4. Training of foreign law enforcement personnel;
5. Detection and monitoring;
6. Construction to block drug smuggling across U.S. borders;
7. Communication networks;
8. Linguistic and intelligence services; and
9. Aerial and ground reconnaissance.

Though this provision authorizes a wide variety of activities, it has received little scrutiny on the part of congressional oversight bodies. While large when compared with many other programs that provide assistance to Latin American security forces, section 1004 activities in the region make up about one-tenth of one percent of the Defense Department's overall budget.

Law:

Programs authorized by sections 124 and 1004 apply only to the

Defense Department's involvement in counternarcotics. Activities authorized by section 1004 must fulfill a counternarcotics mission.

Section 124 establishes that the Defense Department is "the single lead agency of the Federal Government for the detection and monitoring of aerial and maritime transit of illegal drugs into the United States." Defense Department personnel may operate equipment necessary to intercept vessels or aircraft suspected of smuggling drugs outside the land area of the United States. Section 124 does not authorize the provision of assistance.

Unlike section 124, which is part of Title 10, U.S. Code, section 1004 of the 1991 National Defense Authorization Act (NDAA) is not a permanent authorization. Originally authorized for four years, through 1995, section 1004 was reauthorized until fiscal year 1999. Unless reauthorized again, this provision of law will expire in 1999.

No legal conditions prohibit a country from receiving assistance under section 1004. In fact, the law states that "the Secretary of Defense may not limit the requirements for which support may be provided ... only to critical, emergent, or unanticipated requirements."

Section 1004 funds are appropriated within the Defense Department's counternarcotics "central transfer account." The authorization includes no reporting requirements.

[The House and Senate versions of the 1999 NDAA are currently before Congress. Both contain provisions that would extend section 1004 beyond 1999. The House version (section 1021 of H.R. 3616) would extend it through the year 2000. The Senate version (section 332 of S. 2057) would extend it through the year 2004.]

Mexico:

Counternarcotics cooperation has made the U.S.-Mexican military-to-military relationship closer today than at any time in memory. After an October 1995 visit to Mexico by U.S. Secretary of Defense William Perry, the Mexican military agreed to accept U.S. counternarcotics assistance for the first time in several years. Earlier that year, Mexican President Ernesto Zedillo had ordered a temporary expansion of the Mexican armed forces' role in anti-drug operations, a role that has continued to expand.

Beginning in 1996, the Defense Department established what the White House's Office of National Drug Control Policy (ONDCP) describes as a "training and equipment program for the development of an airmobile, rapid-reaction, counterdrug capability to support drug interdiction efforts in Mexico."[1] In 1997, the ONDCP reports, cooperation between the U.S. and Mexican militaries "continued on an unprecedented scale. DoD [The Department of Defense] established extremely successful training and equipment counter-drug programs with the Mexican military."[2] Most of this equipment came to Mexico via a drawdown ordered in December 1996, foreign military sales (FMS) and direct commercial sales (DCS), a special one-time Defense Department authorization ("section 1031"), and transfers of excess defense articles. Some training was funded through the International Military Education and Training (IMET) program.

Additional equipment and far more training, however, was provided through Defense Department accounts authorized by section 1004 of the 1991 National Defense Authorization Act. "Section 1004" funding for Mexico totaled $28,905,000 in 1997 and is estimated at $20,079,000 for 1998. Much of this paid for training: $10.8 million in 1997 and an estimated $13.0 million in 1998.

Section 1004 funded the training of 829 Mexican military personnel in 1997, including 281 from the Mexican Navy -- a significant increase over the 300 who received Defense Department counterdrug training in 1996. Together, these troops completed 1,500 counterdrug training courses.[3] Course topics included "aircraft maintenance, communications, intelligence, pilot training, special-forces skills instruction, cadre development, and maritime counterdrug operations."[4] A similar list of courses from ONDCP also includes UH-1H helicopter pilot training.[5]

Many of the Mexican military counternarcotics personnel receiving training are members of Air-Mobile Special Forces Groups (*Grupos Aeromóviles de Fuerzas Especiales,* or "GAFEs"). ONDCP describes the GAFE training program:

> GAFEs are elite Mexican Army units that have received Special Forces and air assault training for use in counterdrug interdiction operations. The training program was designed to rapidly improve the capabilities of GAFE units and UH-1H [helicopter] squadrons that support their operations. The training will also establish a cadre of Mexican instructors to sustain these counterdrug capabilities. Training of GAFEs is scheduled to continue through FY 99. All GAFE training includes a strong human rights component.[6]

Section 1004 also paid for a maritime training program with Mexican naval forces. This program, supported by the U.S. Coast Guard, accounts for $1.95 million of the $10.8 million in 1004 funds spent on training in 1997. More than 600 Mexican Navy personnel participating in the program received training for "operations in a marine/coastal and riverine environment."[7] The Defense Department is also providing training to help Mexico operate two decommissioned Knox-class frigates it purchased through the Foreign Military Sales (FMS) program.[8] These ships, however, are currently inoperable.

Colombia and Peru:

Activities in Colombia and Peru authorized by section 1004 and section 124 include intelligence support, operational planning assistance, construction, and training. The Office of National Drug Control Policy's January 1998 National Drug Control Strategy offers the following view of these activities:

> During FY 1997, source nation counterdrug forces achieved impressive interdiction successes in Colombia and Peru. These successes were the result of: enhanced DoD [Department of Defense] intelligence support, ground-based and airborne detection and monitoring platforms, augmentation of teams assigned to provide operational planning assistance to U.S. country teams and foreign law enforcement agencies, and additional specialized training across the spectrum of tasks associated with drug law enforcement....

> U.S.-provided training has also enabled Peru and Colombia to improve their fledgling river interdiction capability. DoD support in FY 1997 also expanded host nation capability to seize remote jungle drug processing laboratories through helicopter pilot and maintenance technician training, and the design and construction of improvements to forward operating base infrastructure.

> DoD deployed personnel throughout the cocaine source region to conduct comprehensive training on river patrolling tactics, vessel boarding procedures, riverine operations planning, safety, and small boat maintenance. DoD also funded infrastructure development and upgrades in Colombia and Peru, as well as extensive training for law enforcement personnel to enhance ground-based endgame operations.[9]

The Defense Department's 1998 counternarcotics program in Colombia, according to Pentagon spokesman Kenneth Bacon, will fund 18 separate deployments involving 252 U.S. military instructors.[10]

Venezuela:

The U.S. State Department's 1998 International Narcotics Control Strategy Report includes the following description of Defense Department counterdrug activity in Venezuela:

> [T]he US armed forces have conducted 16 joint exercises for training (JCET) with the Venezuelan armed forces focused on improving capabilities for planning, coordinating and conducting counternarcotics operations. Riverine forces in particular are better prepared, organized and focused to conduct interdiction operations.

> Other law enforcement agencies, including metropolitan and state police and the Technical Judicial Police, receive more limited resources for counternarcotics-related activities.[11]

It is worth noting that this description of the JCET program's use for counter-narcotics training conflicts with Pentagon spokesman Bacon's May 1998 assertion that "the counter-narcotics program is under another program. It's separate from the JCET program."[12]

Funding by country:

No functional breakdowns by country are available for sections 124 and 1004, so it is impossible to know how much of the funds obligated through these accounts went to equipment upgrades, foreign military training, reconnaissance or other authorized activities.

While section 1004 expands the Defense Department's overseas anti-drug role, several of the activities it authorizes (such as "aerial and ground reconnaissance") fit within the original mandate of section 124. As a result of this overlap, the Defense Department's accounting of assistance provided through sections 1004 and 124 divides it into three categories:

- The **"Section 124"** category refers to assistance that, according to the Defense Department's interpretation, is allowed under section 124 but not section 1004.
- The **"Section 1004"** category refers to assistance that, according to the Defense Department's interpretation, is allowed under section 1004 but not section 124.
- The **"Section 1004 / 124"** category refers to assistance that, according to the Defense Department's interpretation, is authorized both by section 124 and section 1004.

(Thousands of U.S. dollars)

Section 124[13]:

Region	1997 actual	1998 estimate
Caribbean regional	$124,163	$129,774
Latin America regional	$65,246	$87,870
Total	**$189,409**	**$217,644**

Section 1004[13]:

Country or Region	1997 actual	1998 estimate
Antigua and Barbuda	$18	$0
Argentina	$274	$261
Bahamas	$507	$150
Barbados	$151	$391
Belize	$224	$219
Bolivia	$2,147	$2,052
Brazil	$3,096	$3,632
Caribbean regional	$8,601	$10,566
Chile	$112	$68
Colombia	$7,411	$7,341
Costa Rica	$133	$127

Country or Region	1997 actual	1998 estimate
Dominica	$101	$0
Dominican Republic	$436	$54
Ecuador	$3,014	$2,365
El Salvador	$279	$271
Guatemala	$806	$774
Honduras	$418	$404
Jamaica	$137	$6
Latin America regional	$40,213	$50,936
Latin America and Caribbean regional	$25,963	$22,958
Mexico	$28,905	$20,079
Panama	$2,799	$2,234
Paraguay	$522	$539
Peru	$27,086	$25,235
Puerto Rico	$208	$1,733
St. Kitts and Nevis	$2	$64
St. Vincent and the Grenadines	$49	$51
Trinidad and Tobago	$188	$504
Uruguay	$21	$19
Venezuela	$9,005	$10,250
Total	**$162,826**	**$163,283**

Sections 1004 / 124[13]:

Country or Region	1997 Actual	1998 Estimate
Bolivia	$70	$51
Caribbean regional	$21,701	$22,639
Colombia	$25,472	$14,687
Honduras	$400	$400
Latin America regional	$25,531	$26,795
Mexico	$3,172	$3,126
Total	**$76,346**	**$67,698**

Combined totals, sections 124 and 1004:

1997: $428.581 million / 1998: $448.625 million

Top recipients of section 1004/124 funding:

Rank	1997	1998
1	Colombia	Peru
2	Mexico	Mexico
3	Peru	Colombia
4	Venezuela	Venezuela
5	Brazil	Brazil
6	Ecuador	Ecuador
7	Panama	Panama
8	Bolivia	Bolivia
9	Honduras	Puerto Rico
10	Guatemala	Honduras

Section 1004/124 funding in the hemisphere

Legend:
$10 million +
$1 million - $10 million
$1 - $1 million

1997 (actual)   **1998 (estimate)**

"Section 1031" Counterdrug Assistance to Mexico

Program description:

Section 1031 of the 1997 National Defense Authorization Act (P.L. 104-201) permitted the Secretary of Defense to provide the Government of Mexico with limited support for counter-drug activities.

The types of support authorized included:

1. Nonlethal protective and utility personnel equipment;
2. Nonlethal specialized equipment such as night vision systems, navigation, communications, photo, and radar equipment;
3. Nonlethal components, accessories, attachments, parts, firmware, and software for aircraft or patrol boats, and related repair equipment; and
4. Maintenance and repair of equipment used for counter-drug activities.

Section 1031 did not authorize transfers of aircraft.

The amount authorized was not to exceed $8 million, to be spent during Fiscal Year 1997. When the Defense Department failed to deliver the full $8 million of support by the end of FY 1997, Congress granted an extension, but authorized no new money, for FY 1998.

The White House's Office of National Drug Control Policy (ONDCP) reported in September 1997 that the $8 million financed a Foreign Military Sales (FMS) purchase of spare parts and components for UH-1H helicopters. Seventy-three of these helicopters were transferred to Mexico in 1996 and 1997 through a drawdown and through the excess defense articles (EDA) program.[1]

Law:

While limiting the Defense Department to the types of support listed above, section 1031 carried several other restrictions and reporting requirements.

Congress would not release funds until 15 days after the Secretary of Defense submitted to the Senate Armed Services Committee, the Senate Foreign Relations Committee, the House National Security Committee and the House International Relations Committee a written certification that:

1. Providing the equipment would not affect the preparedness of the U.S. armed forces;

2. The equipment would be used only by Mexican government officials and employees who had undergone a Mexican government background check; and

3. The Mexican government had certified that none of the equipment would be transferred to any other person or entity not authorized by the United States, and that the equipment would be used only for the purposes intended by the U.S. government.

The law required that the Mexican government maintain a thorough inventory of the equipment provided, and allow U.S. government personnel access to any of this equipment or to any records having to do with it. The Mexican government had to guarantee the equipment's security to a degree deemed satisfactory by the U.S. government, and to permit continuous review by U.S. government personnel of the equipment's use.

Funding:

	1997-1998
Mexico	$8 million

"Section 1033" Counterdrug Assistance to Colombia and Peru

Program description:

Section 1033 of the 1998 National Defense Authorization Act (P.L. 105-85) allows the Department of Defense to provide Colombia and Peru with specific types of counter-drug assistance during fiscal years 1998 through 2002. The Defense Department must consult with the State Department about assistance provided under this section.

This authorization is often referred to as the "riverine program," as much of the assistance it permits is designed to strengthen the ability of the Colombian and Peruvian security forces to interdict drug trafficking via rivers. According to the White House's Office of National Drug Control Policy (ONDCP), section 1033 will allow the Defense Department to provide "the necessary equipment to establish an effective river interdiction capability in Peru and also to enhance the existing river interdiction capability of the government of Colombia."[1]

Section 1033 authorizes the following types of support:

1. Riverine patrol boats;
2. Nonlethal protective and utility personnel equipment;
3. Nonlethal specialized equipment such as night vision systems, navigation, communications, photo, and radar equipment;
4. Nonlethal components, accessories, attachments, parts, firmware, and software for aircraft or patrol boats, and related repair equipment; and
5. Maintenance and repair of equipment that is used for counter-drug activities.

The amount to be obligated under this section out of the Defense Department's counter-drug account is not to exceed $9 million during fiscal year 1998 and $20 million during each of the fiscal years 1999 through 2002.

"Key elements of the Colombia plan," according to March 1998 congressional testimony by U.S. Southern Command commander-in-chief Gen. Charles Wilhelm, "include improving infrastructure, providing spare parts, upgrading existing communications and navigation equipment, enhancing personnel protective equipment, sourcing additional riverine patrol craft and improving the quality and depth of training."[2]

"Key elements of the Peru plan," Gen. Wilhelm continued, "include establishing a Joint Riverine Training Center in Iquitos; training and equipping twelve operational Riverine Interdiction Units; and procuring and outfitting three Floating Support Bases. The training center will commence operations this summer with the first operational unit coming online during the 4th quarter of FY98."[3]

In 1997, riverine support for Peru's security forces was augmented by $5.3 million from another source of funding: a one-time grant from an ONDCP discretionary account (see page 51).

Law:

While limiting types of support to those listed above, section 1033 also specifies several restrictions and reporting requirements.

Certification

Congress would not release funds for this assistance until 15 days after the Secretary of Defense submitted to the Senate Armed Services Committee, the Senate Foreign Relations Committee, the House National Security Committee, and the House International Relations Committee a written certification that:

1. Providing the assistance would not affect the preparedness of the U.S. armed forces;
2. The equipment would be used only by government officials and employees who undergo background investigations by the recipient governments and who are approved for the performance of counter-drug activities; and
3. The recipient governments have certified that none of the equipment will be transferred to any other person or entity not authorized by the United States and that the equipment will be used only for the purposes intended by the U.S government.

The certification also had to specify that recipient governments will maintain a thorough inventory of the equipment provided, and will allow U.S. government personnel access to any of this equipment or to any records having to do with it. The recipient government must guarantee the equipment's security to a degree deemed satisfactory by the U.S. government, and must permit continuous U.S. government review of the equipment's use.

Riverine counter-drug plan

During the first fiscal year, funds cannot be spent until 60 days after the Secretary of Defense submits a riverine counter-drug plan to the above-mentioned congressional committees. Any revisions to this plan must be submitted in subsequent years.

The riverine counter-drug plan is to be prepared (and revised in subsequent fiscal years) by the Secretary of Defense in consultation with the Secretary of State. It must include the following:

1. A detailed security assessment, including a discussion of the threat posed by illicit drug traffickers in the recipient countries;
2. An evaluation of the recipient government's previous and ongoing riverine counter-drug operations;
3. An assessment of how past and current assistance provided under this section is being monitored to ensure that it is used appropriately;
4. A description of the coordination among Federal agencies involved in the plan's development and implementation;
5. A description of the roles, missions, and coordination of each U.S. agency involved in the plan's development and implementation;
6. A description of the resources that the Defense and State Departments will contribute during each fiscal year covered by the plan, and the manner in which they will be utilized;
7. For the first fiscal year in which support is to be provided, a schedule for establishing a riverine counter-drug program that the recipient government can sustain within five years, and for subsequent fiscal years, a description of the progress made in establishing and carrying out the program;
8. A reporting system to measure the riverine counter-drug program's effectiveness; and
9. A detailed discussion of how the riverine counter-drug program supports the U.S. national drug control strategy.

Funding:

Country	Authorized amount, 1998[4]	Authorized amount, 1999-2002
Colombia (estimated)	$1 million	
Peru (estimated)	$8 million	
Colombia and Peru (shared)	**$9 million**	**$20 million per year**

School of the Americas

Description:

The U.S. Army School of the Americas (SOA) is the Army's Spanish-language training facility for Latin American military personnel. Established in 1946, the school has a long and controversial history.

The SOA currently trains about 900 students per year. Historically, the national origin of the attendees has tended to reflect perceived U.S. security interests. During the mid-1980s many Central Americans studied at the SOA. In 1997, 33 percent of the students were Mexican and another 27 percent were Colombian and Chilean.

The school's fixed costs are paid by the Army's operations and maintenance account. Student tuition costs are covered mainly by grants through the International Military Education and Training (IMET) and International Narcotics Control (INC) programs, or sales of training through the Foreign Military Sales (FMS) program. In 1996, the last year for which this study has acquired a breakdown of funding, the majority of the training was funded by IMET, with INC running a close second.

In recent years, the SOA has been a highly questioned institution, with opponents pushing for the school's closure. The fundamental source of controversy is the human rights record of some of the school's graduates. A number of former SOA students have committed serious human rights violations after having studied at the school. The school's defenders argue that the actions taken by those graduates were not taught at the school and the school should not be held accountable for them. However, questions persist about the school's curriculum, instructors and oversight.

Helicopter School Battalion, U.S. Army Aviation Center, Fort Rucker, Alabama

According to its web page, since 1984 the Spanish Helicopter School Battalion (SHSB) at Fort Rucker has trained "its Latin American allies in their fight against communism, subversion, insurgency, and narco-terrorism through initial and advance aviation training."[1] This bilingual military aviation school has trained almost 1,300 aviation maintenance and logistics personnel.

In 1991 the SHSB became the Helicopter School Battalion, School of the Americas (HSB, SOA), combining all of the U.S. Army's Spanish aviation training within the curriculum of the School of the Americas. Although its name changed in October 1994 to the "Spanish Helicopter School Battalion, Aviation Training Brigade," the battalion still maintains its relationship with the School of the Americas. Courses taught at the HSB are included in the School of the Americas' course listings.

Law:

The SOA's operation is authorized by section 4415 of Title 10, U.S. Code. This law defines the school's purpose as "providing military education and training to military personnel of Central and South American countries and Caribbean countries."

During the congressional appropriations process for fiscal year 1998, the following restriction was placed on student grants to the SOA. No funds were to be disbursed to the school until:

1. The Secretary of Defense certified that the instruction and training provided by the school was consistent with training and doctrine, particularly on human rights, provided by the Defense Department to U.S. students elsewhere;
2. The Secretary of Defense certified that specific guidelines governing the selection and screening of candidates for instruction at the school had been developed and issued in coordination with the Secretary of State; and
3. The Secretary of Defense submitted to the Committee on Appropriations a report detailing the SOA's training activities and a general assessment of its graduates' performance during 1996.

A certification report addressing these issues was sent to Congress in January 1998, and the school's funding was released shortly thereafter.

Operating budget:

Source	1995[1]	1996[2]
Army operations and maintenance funds	$ 2.6 million	$ 2,701,000
Security assistance funds	$ 1.2 million	$ 1,214,700
- IMET		$640,500
- FMS		$140,900
- International Narcotics Control (INC) funds		$433,300
JCS funds for exercise support		$27,800
Total	$ 3.8 million	$ 3,943,500

Students:

	1996[3]		1997[4]	
	No. of students	% of total	No. of students	% of total
Argentina	14	1.5	18	2.0
Bolivia	55	5.9	42	4.6

School of the Americas

	1996[3]		1997[4]	
	No. of students	% of total	No. of students	% of total
Brazil	2	0.2	1	0.1
Chile	150	16.0	145	16.0
Colombia	139	14.8	99	10.9
Costa Rica	17	1.8	22	2.4
Dominican Republic	39	4.2	26	2.9
Ecuador	28	3.0	9	1.0
El Salvador	55	5.9	14	1.5
Guatemala			1	0.1
Honduras	123	13.1	33	3.6
Mexico	149	15.9	305	33.6
Paraguay	4	0.4	11	1.2
Peru	91	9.7	98	10.8
United States	22	2.3	54	5.9
Uruguay	3	0.3	8	0.9
Venezuela	47	5.0	22	2.4
Total	938	100	908	100

Top attendance:

Rank	1996	1997
1	Chile	Mexico
2	Mexico	Chile
3	Colombia	Colombia
4	Honduras	Peru
5	Peru	United States
6	Bolivia	Bolivia
7	El Salvador	Honduras
8	Venezuela	Dominican Republic
9	Dominican Republic	Venezuela
10	Ecuador	Costa Rica

SOA attendance

Legend:
75+
25-75
1-25

1996 (actual)   **1997 (actual)**

Inter-American Air Forces Academy

Description:[1]

The Inter-American Air Forces Academy (IAAFA), currently located at Lackland Air Force Base, Texas, was founded in 1945 to offer Spanish-language training and education to Latin American air force personnel. The IAAFA is presently integrated into the U.S. Air Force's training regimen, under the authority of the Air Force Education and Training Command.

According to its web page, the IAAFA was founded at the request of the government of Peru and operated initially out of the Panama Canal Zone. The student body and curriculum grew in the 1950s, expanding more rapidly during the 1960s "Alliance for Progress" era. At that time the Academy introduced a guest instructor program and formed Mobile Training Teams (MTTs) to bring the IAAFA's courses directly to Latin American nations. Matriculation declined in the 1970s but grew again in the 1980s, when the school averaged 850 students annually. In 1989, the Academy left Panama and moved to Homestead Air Force Base south of Miami. In 1992, after Hurricane Andrew heavily damaged the area, the IAAFA moved to its current home in Texas.

Aircraft flown at the academy include the C-130 cargo plane, T-53 jet trainer, F-5 fighter, and UH-1H "Huey" helicopter. Courses cover all aspects of aircraft maintenance and operation, including such topics as avionics, armaments, instruments and communications. Courses are also provided in logistics, supply, information systems, air intelligence, security and military justice. In 1998, the projected matriculation is 1,047 students.

The fixed cost of running the Academy comes out of the Air Force's operation and maintenance budget and is not considered part of "security assistance." Countries can pay student tuition through the Foreign Military Sales (FMS) program, or can have it subsidized through one of three sources:

- The International Military Education and Training (IMET) program;
- The International Narcotics Control (INC) program; or
- Funds authorized by section 1004 of the 1991 National Defense Authorization Act.

Law:

Legal authority for the Academy is located in Section 9415 of Title 10, U.S. Code. Under the law, the Academy may provide education and training to Latin American nations that are eligible to receive assistance under the Foreign Assistance Act of 1961 (P.L. 87-195, or the "FAA"), as amended.

Students:

	1996		1997	
	No. of students	% of total	No. of students	% of total
Argentina	7	1.1%	19	3.0%
Belize	0	0%	2	2.1%
Bolivia	61	9.7%	91	10.3%
Brazil	2	0.32%	24	2.7%
Chile	5	.79%	3	0.3%
Colombia	92	14.6%	128	14.5%
Costa Rica	21	3.3%	32	3.6%
Dominican Republic	15	2.4%	27	3.1%
Ecuador	65	10.3%	69	7.8%
El Salvador	85	13.4%	31	3.5%
Guatemala	0	0%	4	0.5%
Honduras	29	4.6%	18	2.0%
Mexico	141	22.3%	260	29.4%
Panama	24	3.8%	13	1.5%
Paraguay	1	0.16%	10	1.1%
Peru	22	3.5%	61	6.9%
Uruguay	17	2.7%	40	4.5%
United States	2	0.32%	3	0.3%
Venezuela	43	6.8%	49	5.5%
Total	632	100%	884	100%

1998: 1,047 students expected.
No country breakdown is yet available.

Top attendance:

Rank	1996	1997
1	Mexico	Mexico
2	Colombia	Colombia
3	El Salvador	Bolivia
4	Ecuador	Ecuador
5	Bolivia	Peru
6	Venezuela	Venezuela
7	Honduras	Uruguay

Rank	1996	1997
8	Panama	Costa Rica
9	Peru	El Salvador
10	Costa Rica	Dominican Republic

IAAFA attendance

Legend:
75+
25-75
1-25

1996 (actual)   **1997 (actual)**

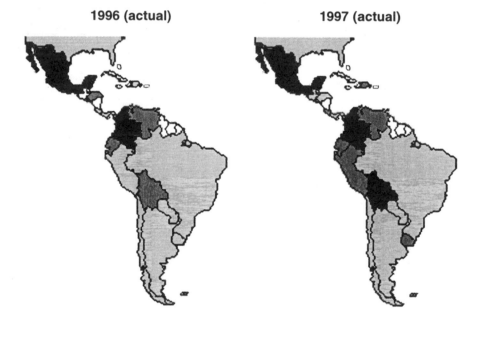

Naval Small Craft Instruction and Technical Training School (NAVSCIATTS)

Rodman Naval Station
Panama

The U.S. Navy Small Craft Instruction and Technical Training School (NAVSCIATTS) trains navies and coast guards from Latin American countries in methods of countering international terrorism, narcotics trafficking, and smuggling.

NAVSCIATTS offers Spanish-language courses in topics ranging from patrol boat navigation and tactics to small craft mechanics. Patrol boat exercises are conducted on Panama's Chagres River, where simulated counter-drug patrols teach anti-narcotics riverine operations. Funding for the training school is provided partly through IMET, which provides about US$550,000 a year for students to attend.

Center for Hemispheric Defense Studies

National Defense University
Fort Lesley J. McNair, Washington, D.C.

Program description:

The Center for Hemispheric Defense Studies (CHDS) is a new institution which began functioning in 1998 at the National Defense University, a Defense Department educational institution. Its mission is "to develop civilian specialists in defense and military matters by providing graduate level programs in defense planning and management, executive leadership, civilian-military relations and interagency operation."[1]

The school originated from discussions held at the first Defense Ministerial of the Americas (July 1995, in Williamsburg, VA). According to materials distributed at the Center's inaugural, "participating defense leaders from Latin America and the Caribbean asked the United States for assistance in improving civilians' competence in defense and military matters."[2]

The CHDS is located at Fort McNair, in Washington, DC, but will also offer seminars in Latin America and the Caribbean. Its first group of fellows began a three-week course in March 1998. The center's student body is roughly half government civilians, one-quarter nongovernmental civilians, and one-quarter military personnel. Initially, an estimated five students per country per year are expected to attend the school.

The CHDS will conduct the following programs:

- A three-week defense planning and resource management seminar offered in Washington four times per year;
- Short seminars conducted at sites in Latin America and the Caribbean, which "focus on themes identified in collaboration with counterpart institutions;
- An annual meeting for legislators and senior government officials with defense responsibilities; and
- An annual conference on defense education.[3]

The establishment of the CHDS coincides with increased interest in the issue of civilian control of the military and, along with Expanded IMET courses, is intended to enhance civilian capacity for oversight and analysis of defense issues.

Students:[4]

March 1998:	May 1998:
• 33 fellows • All 10 South American countries represented • 4 females (12%) • 8 military personnel (24%) (Army and Navy) • 25 civilians (76%) • 17 government civilians (52%) • 8 non-government civilians (24%)	• 33 fellows • All Central American countries, plus Dominican Republic, Bolivia, Canada and the United States • 6 females (18%) • 8 military personnel (24%) (Lt. Col., Col., Capt.) • 25 civilians (76%) • 16 government civilians (49%) • 9 non-government civilians (27%)

Funding:

The Center's operating budget in 1997 was $2 million, all of it used to establish the school. With the arrival of its first students in 1998, the CHDS outlay will rise to $3.2 million.[5]

Foreign Student Program at U.S. Service Academies

Program description:

The United States invites democratic countries in Latin America and the Caribbean to nominate students to compete for entrance into U.S. military academies (the Army's U.S. Military Academy at West Point, NY; the U.S. Naval Academy at Annapolis, MD; and the U.S. Air Force Academy at Colorado Springs, CO). The students are selected according to "the same criteria applied to U.S. students."[1]

Foreign cadets' tuition is waived for countries designated as "low income" or "middle income" in the World Bank's annual World Development Indicators report. All Latin American and Caribbean countries qualify by this measure, as per capita income in each is below the $8,626 threshold necessary to be considered a "high income" country.

The cost of educating students from these countries is paid by the armed services' operation and maintenance accounts. The annual attendance cost at the academies is $69,147 per student.[2]

Students from Latin America and the Philippines have been attending the service academies at no charge since before World War II. In 1983, the law was changed to give the program worldwide reach, authorizing a maximum of 40 foreign students per academy. As of 1997, 115 foreign students were in attendance at the three academies.[3]

In 1997, the following countries from Latin America and the Caribbean had students at U.S. service academies[4]:

- Barbados
- Colombia
- Costa Rica
- Ecuador
- El Salvador
- Guatemala
- Guyana
- Honduras
- Nicaragua
- Peru
- Trinidad and Tobago

Law:

Three similar sections in Title 10, U.S. Code -- one each for the Army (section 4346), Navy (section 6957) and Air Force (section 9344) -- govern the practice of funding foreign students at U.S. service academies.

All three sections limit the number of foreign students to 40 per academy. Foreign students, of course, are not required to serve in the U.S. military after graduation.

Exercises

Description:

Exercises are high-profile, short-term events in which U.S. military personnel are deployed for training, often through simulations of scenarios or conditions they might face as part of their operational duties. Exercises are generally the largest, in terms of cost and personnel, of the many types of U.S. military "deployments for training" that take place in Latin America and the Caribbean.

Though an exercise's primary officially-defined purpose is to train U.S. forces, foreign militaries often receive training as well. The U.S. Southern Command (Southcom), the Defense Department's "unified command" responsible for Latin America and the Caribbean, makes interaction with foreign militaries a high priority; as a result, its exercises in the region frequently include other armed forces in some capacity, whether as co-participants, observers, or perimeter guards. Other militaries' participation results in some transfer of skills and knowledge, making foreign military training a key secondary outcome of exercises.

Other objectives of U.S. military exercises in the region, according to a National Defense University (NDU) publication, include:

1. Fostering interoperability between U.S. forces and potential military partners; *["Interoperability" means "the ability of systems, units or forces to provide services to and accept services from other systems, units or forces, and to use the services so exchanged to enable them to operate effectively together."* [1]*]*
2. Building interpersonal contacts and force collaboration;
3. Serving as confidence-building measures among neighboring states; and
4. When an exercise involves construction, providing "a tangible example of U.S. commitment to a country" and facilitating "subsequent U.S. deployments in response to regional crises."[2]

Exercises, the NDU notes, "tend to be expensive and often, because of their strategic importance, drain funding intended for other defense programs."

Within its area of operation, Southcom divides its exercises among three categories: operational, multinational and engineer exercises.

1. Operational exercises are carried out with specific threats or scenarios in mind. Participants -- which may or may not include foreign units -- follow action plans devised for dealing with these scenarios. A key purpose of operational exercises is to gauge a plan's effectiveness and the participants' ability to carry it out.

In Latin America and the Caribbean, according to a May 1997 Southcom document, operational exercise scenarios might include:

- Defense of the Panama Canal;
- Combating terrorism;
- Noncombatant evacuation operations;
- Peace enforcement operations;
- Peacekeeping operations;
- Counterdrug;
- Counterterrorism;
- Haiti;
- Cuba;
- Humanitarian assistance / disaster relief; or
- Migrant operations.[3]

Examples of recent operational exercises include:

- Blue Advance

In January 1997, the U.S. Southern Command began Blue Advance, a "multi-phased" exercise, in Panama and at remote locations. The exercise sought to ensure that the Atlantic Command and Southern Command are able "to provide strategic and operational direction" over the Caribbean, which switched from Atlantic Command to Southern Command control in mid-1997. They did so by simulating a wave of migrants from the Caribbean to the United States.

- Ellipse Echo
- Defense Forces / Fuerzas de Defensa (Panama Canal Defense)
- Rescue Forces / Fuerzas de Rescate
- Non-Combatant Evacuation (NEO) Forces / Fuerzas de Evacuación[4]

2. Multinational exercises, also referred to as "Foreign Military Interaction (FMI)" exercises, are carried out jointly with other militaries, normally several at a time. Southcom is seeking to phase out bilateral exercises within this category, pushing instead "for integrated and coordinated regional approaches to regional challenges."[5]

Southcom states that it uses multinational exercises to build skills for non-traditional "military operations other than war," such as peacekeeping, humanitarian assistance, disaster relief, counter-drug efforts, and medical assistance.

The Distinguished Visitor Program, a component of most Southcom multinational exercises, invites host-region government, business and military leaders "to observe an exercise, sit as panel members in special exercise seminars and participate in exercise After Action Reviews."[6]

Examples of multinational exercises include:

1. Peacekeeping
    - Fuerzas Aliadas Peacekeeping
    - Fuerzas Unidas Peacekeeping
    - Fuerzas Unidas Cabanas

    Civilian and military participants in the Fuerzas Aliadas / Fuerzas Unidas Peacekeeping Operation (PKO) series of exercises learn skills relevant to United Nations-style peacekeeping missions. The exercises use scenarios in fictitious countries to simulate how armed forces, international organizations like the United Nations, non-governmental organizations like the Red Cross, or other interested groups should interact in peace operations. When the exercise takes place in Central America, it is called Fuerzas Aliadas (Allied Forces); in South America it goes by the name Fuerzas Unidas (United Forces).

2. Humanitarian
    - Fuerzas Aliadas Humanitarian

3. Counterdrug
    - Fuerzas Unidas Counterdrug
    - Fuerzas Aliadas Riverine
    - Tradewinds
    - Fairwinds

4. Other
    - UNITAS

    UNITAS is a yearly, multinational naval deployment exercise. Every year since 1960, several United States Navy vessels have circumnavigated the South American continent, participating in maneuvers with local navies. This circumnavigation alternates each year between counterclockwise and clockwise.

    3. Engineer exercises involve construction of basic infrastructure and provision of medical, dental and veterinary services. As U.S. law forbids the military from carrying out most civilian construction or health missions on U.S. soil, engineer exercises give U.S. forces a chance to learn and practice these skills on foreign soil without similar restrictions.

    By providing basic services to populations in developing countries, these exercises also include a major humanitarian and civic assistance component. Participating military personnel normally leave behind new or renovated schools, wells, clinics, roads or bridges, while offering medical, dental or veterinary care at no cost to civilian populations.

    Critics of these exercises express concern that they encourage military involvement in activities that are non-military in nature, inviting an expansion of military roles beyond that normally seen in well-established democracies.

Engineer exercises can be performed with or without host-nation military participation. In most cases, host-country security forces either participate or provide security around the perimeter of the exercise area.

Examples of engineer exercises include:

1. Humanitarian and civic assistance exercises
   - New Horizons / Nuevos Horizontes
   - Medical / dental / veterinary support

2. Skills exchange exercises

Law:

Report

Section 2010 of Title 10, U.S. Code mandates that, by March 1 of each year, the Secretary of Defense submit a report containing the following information about the past fiscal year:

1. A list of the developing countries which the United States reimbursed for incremental expenses incurred while participating in a military exercise; and
2. The amount each country was reimbursed.

"Incremental expenses," according to section 2010, means "the reasonable and proper cost of the goods and services that are consumed by a developing country as a direct result of that country's participation in a bilateral or multilateral military exercise with the United States." These may include rations, fuel, training ammunition and transportation. Incremental expenses do not include pay, allowances, and other normal costs.

Operational Tempo (number of exercises to be carried out)[7]

FY 1996: 15 exercises	FY 1997: 20 exercises	FY 1998 (projected): 25 exercises
5 Operational exercises • Ellipse Echo • Noncombatant Evacuation Operations (NEO) • Defense Forces (FD) • Rescue Forces • Eligible Receiver	4 Operational exercises • Ellipse Echo • "Fuerzas de Evacuación" Noncombatant Evacuation Operations (NEO) • Defense Forces (FD) • Blue Advance	4 Operational Exercises • Ellipse Echo • Noncombatant Evacuation Operations (NEO) • Defense Forces (FD) • Blue Advance
6 Foreign Military Interaction (FMI) Command Post exercises (CPXs) *[A "Command Post Exercise," which often relies on a computer simulation, guides decisionmakers through a hypothetical scenario. A CPX normally takes place in one central location, such as a military headquarters.]*	5 Foreign Military Interaction (FMI) Command Post exercises (CPXs)	4 Foreign Military Interaction (FMI) Command Post exercises (CPXs)
1 Foreign Military Interaction (FMI) Field Training exercise (FTX) *[A "Field Training Exercise" simulates actual operations "in the field," focusing more on improvement of skills than on the making of command decisions.]* • UNITAS	2 Foreign Military Interaction (FMI) Field Training exercises (FTXs) • Cabanas • UNITAS	3 Foreign Military Interaction (FMI) Field Training exercises (FTXs) • Cabanas • UNITAS • Tradewinds
3 Engineer exercises	4 Engineer exercises	10 *Nuevos Horizontes* Engineer exercises
	2 Skills Exchanges	4 *Nuevos Horizontes* MED Skills Exchanges
	3 "Caribbean EX"	

Tentative Exercise Calendar[1]

Date	Name	Type	Component	Location	Participating countries
October 1996	Fuerzas Unidas Cabanas 97	Multinational Peacekeeping	U.S. Special Operations Command South (SOCSOUTH)	Puerto Rico	U.S., Argentina, Bolivia, Paraguay, Uruguay
February 1997	Blue Advance	Operational (validation of command plan)	Atlantic Fleet (LANTFLT)	Panama	U.S.
January-June 1997, October 1997-?	New Horizons Haiti "Fairwinds"	Humanitarian civic assistance (HCA)	Atlantic Command (ACOM)	Caribbean	U.S.
February-May 1997	New Horizons 97	Engineer / Humanitarian civic assistance (HCA)	U.S. Army South (USARSO)	Panama	U.S.
February-May 1997	New Horizons 97	Engineer / Humanitarian civic assistance (HCA)	U.S. Army South (USARSO)	Belize	U.S.
February 1997	Fuerzas Aliadas Humanitarian 97	Disaster relief	U.S. Army South (USARSO)	El Salvador	U.S., Belize, Costa Rica, El Salvador, Guatemala, Honduras, Nicaragua
March-April 1997	Skills Exchange package	Engineer / Humanitarian civic assistance (HCA)	U.S. Southern Air Force (US-SOUTHAF)	Chile	U.S., Argentina, Brazil, Chile
March 1997	Ellipse Echo	"Contingency" command and control exercise	U.S. Special Operations Command South (SOCSOUTH)	Panama	U.S.
March-April 1997	Tradewinds	Disaster relief	Atlantic Command (ACOM)	Caribbean	U.S.
March-August 1997	New Horizons Caribbean	Humanitarian civic assistance (HCA)	Atlantic Command (ACOM)	Caribbean	U.S.
May 1997	Fuerzas Aliadas Centam Peacekeeping 97	Peacekeeping	U.S. Army South (USARSO)	El Salvador	U.S., Belize, El Salvador, Guatemala, Honduras, Nicaragua
May-June 1997	Skills Exchange package	Engineer / Humanitarian civic assistance (HCA)	Atlantic Fleet (LANTFLT)	El Salvador	U.S., El Salvador, Guatemala, Honduras
July-November 1997	UNITAS 97	Operational, naval	Atlantic Fleet (LANTFLT)	Puerto Rico, Venezuela, Colombia, Ecuador, Peru, Paraguay, Chile, Argentina, Uruguay, Brazil	U.S., Argentina, Brazil, Chile, Colombia, Ecuador, Paraguay, Peru, Uruguay, Venezuela
July 1997	Fuerzas Unidas Chile	Operational	U.S. Army South (USARSO)	Ft. Leavenworth (U.S.)	U.S., Chile
July-August 1997	Skills Exchange package	Engineer / Humanitarian civic assistance (HCA)	U.S. Southern Air Force (US-SOUTHAF)	Brazil	U.S., Argentina, Brazil, Chile
July-September 1997	New Horizons	Engineer / Humanitarian civic assistance (HCA)	U.S. Southern Air Force (US-SOUTHAF)	Guyana	U.S.

Exercises – Tentative Calendar

Date	Name	Type	Component	Location	Participating countries
August 1997	Fuerzas Unidas Southam Peacekeeping 97	Peacekeeping	U.S. Army South (USARSO)	Brazil	U.S., Argentina, Brazil, Bolivia, Paraguay, Uruguay
August 1997	Fuerzas Unidas Counterdrug 97	Counterdrug	Marine Forces South (MAR-FORSOUTH)	Either Panama or Camp Lejeune (U.S.)	U.S., Argentina, Brazil, Colombia, Ecuador, Guyana, Suriname, Venezuela
July 1997	Fuerzas Aliadas Riverine 97	Counterdrug	Marine Forces South (MAR-FORSOUTH)	Honduras, El Salvador	U.S. El Salvador, Honduras
January-February 1998	Skills Exchange Package	Medical / Humanitarian civic assistance (HCA)	U.S. Southern Air Force (US-SOUTHAF)	TBD	U.S, TBD
January-June 1998	New Horizons 98	Engineer / Humanitarian civic assistance (HCA)	U.S. Army South (USARSO)	Honduras	U.S., Honduras
February-April 1998	New Horizons 98	Engineer / Humanitarian civic assistance (HCA)	TBD	Ecuador	U.S., Ecuador
February-March 1998	Skills Exchange Package	Medical / Humanitarian civic assistance (HCA)	Atlantic Fleet (LANTFLT)	El Salvador	U.S., El Salvador, Guatemala, Honduras
February-April 1998	New Horizons 98	Engineer / Humanitarian civic assistance (HCA)	U.S. Army South (USARSO)	El Salvador	U.S., El Salvador
February-March 1998	Skills Exchange Package	Medical / Humanitarian civic assistance (HCA)	Marine Forces South (MAR-FORSOUTH)	Bolivia	U.S., Bolivia, Colombia, Ecuador, Peru
January-February 1998	Fuerzas Aliadas Humanitarian 98	Disaster relief	U.S. Army South (USARSO)	Guatemala	U.S., Belize, El Salvador, Guatemala, Honduras, Nicaragua
March-August 1998	New Horizons Caribbean 98	Humanitarian civic assistance (HCA)	U.S. Army South (USARSO)	Caribbean	U.S.
March-June 1998	Tradewinds	Disaster relief	U.S. Army South (USARSO)	Caribbean	U.S.
May 1998	Fuerzas Aliadas Centam Peacekeeping 98	Peacekeeping	U.S. Army South (USARSO)	Guatemala	U.S., Belize, El Salvador, Guatemala, Honduras, Nicaragua
June-December 1998	UNITAS 98	Operational, naval	Atlantic Fleet (LANTFLT)	South America	U.S, countries visited
July-August 1998	Skills Exchange Package	Medical / Humanitarian civic assistance (HCA)	U.S. Southern Air Force (US-SOUTHAF)	Haiti	U.S., Argentina, Brazil, Uruguay
July-September 1998	Cabanas 98	Peacekeeping	U.S. Special Operations Command South (SOCSOUTH)	Puerto Rico	U.S. Argentina, Bolivia, Chile, Paraguay, Uruguay
July 1998	Fuerzas Unidas Southam 98	Peacekeeping	U.S. Army South (USARSO)	Paraguay	U.S., Paraguay
October 1998-September 1999	New Horizons 99	Humanitarian civic assistance (HCA)	U.S. Army South (USARSO)	Haiti	
August 1999	Cabanas 99	Peacekeeping Operation (PKO)	U.S. Special Operations Command South (SOCSOUTH)	Puerto Rico	

Exercises – Tentative Calendar

Date	Name	Type	Component	Location	Participating countries
November 2-16, 1998	Fuerzas Aliadas Humanitarian	Disaster Relief	U.S. Army South (USARSO)	Headquarters-JTF-B Honduras	
December 1998	Ellipse Echo	Contingency	U.S. Special Command South (SOCSO)	Miami	
January 17-February 28, 1999	Skills Exchange Package	Medical/ Humanitarian civic assistance (HCA)	TBD	TBD	
January 18 - June 7, 1999	New Horizons	Engineer exercise	TBD	Colombia	
February 1- April 12, 1999	New Horizons	Engineer exercise	TBD	Bolivia	
February 1-March 28, 1999	Skills Exchange Package	Medical/ Humanitarian civic assistance (HCA)	TBD	TBD	
February 7-March 28, 1999	Skills Exchange Package	Medical/ Humanitarian civic assistance (HCA)	TBD	TBD	
February 11- 23, 1999	Blue Advance	Operational (validation of command plan)	Atlantic Fleet (LANTFLT)	Miami	
March 1- September 30, 1999	New Horizons Caribbean series	Emergency/ humanitarian civic assistance (HCA)	U.S. Army South (USARSO)	Caribbean	
March 20- June 26, 1999	Tradewinds	Disaster relief	U.S. Army South (USARSO)	Caribbean	
April 21- May 4, 1999	Fuerzas Aliadas Centam Peacekeeping 99	Peacekeeping	U.S. Army South (USARSO)	TBD	
June 1-9, 1999	Fuerzas Defensas	Operational exercise	U.S. Army South (USARSO)	Miami	
June 25- December 15, 1999	UNITAS 99	Operational, naval	Atlantic Fleet (LANTFLT)	South America	
July 5- August 30, 1999	New Horizons	Engineer exercise	TBD	Nicaragua	
July 6- 18, 1999	Fuerzas Evacuación	Non- Combatant Evacuation Forces-- NEO	Atlantic Fleet (LANTFLT)	Miami	
July 18- August 29, 1999	Skills Exchange Package	Medical/ Humanitarian civic assistance (HCA)	TBD	TBD	
July 25- September 12, 1999	Skills Exchange Package	Medical/ Humanitarian civic assistance (HCA)	TBD	TBD	
August 1- 14, 1999	Fuerzas Unidas Southam	Peacekeeping	U.S. Army South (USARSO)	Argentina	
August 15- 29, 1999	Fuerzas Aliadas Counterdrug	Counterdrug	Marine Forces (MARFOR)	Miami	

Humanitarian and Civic Assistance

(Also known as "civic action")

Program description:

Humanitarian and Civic Assistance (HCA) is the Defense Department's term for relief and development activities that take place in the context of an overseas military exercise. Under the HCA program U.S. military personnel participating in overseas deployments carry out humanitarian activities like building schools, vaccinating children and animals, and digging wells. HCA programs are often executed with the involvement of host-country civilian and military personnel. Many involve National Guard or reserve units.

HCA programs cannot be carried out for solely humanitarian purposes. The deployment's primary purpose must be training of U.S. forces, readiness exercises or military operations. The HCA activity is considered "incidental" to the deployment. As a result, most costs associated with HCA activities, such as school construction, are considered incidental expenses.

According to the Defense Department, "these exercises enhance U.S. military operational readiness by providing unique training opportunities in remote and austere environments. During these deployments, U.S. forces practice command and control procedures, logistical operations, and sustainment over extended distances."[1]

It is important to note that the U.S. military carries out these programs overseas in part because, as the Defense Department states, "such training cannot be conducted in the U.S. because the military is not permitted to compete with private industry."[2]

Between 1996 and 1997 the number of HCA programs in Latin America doubled. In 1996 there were 111 HCA projects executed in 12 Latin American countries, while in 1997 there were 237 in 19 countries.

Law:

Section 401 of Title 10, U.S. Code authorizes the Humanitarian and Civic Assistance program and applies a number of specific definitions and restrictions to the program. It defines HCA as:

1. Medical, dental, and veterinary care provided in rural areas of a country;
2. Construction of rudimentary surface transportation systems;

3. Well drilling and construction of basic sanitation facilities;
4. Rudimentary construction and repair of public facilities; and
5. Detection and clearance of land mines.

The Secretary of State must approve all HCA activities, and the Secretary of Defense must determine that the activity will promote:

1. The security interests of both the United States and the country in which the activities are to be carried out; and
2. The specific operational readiness skills of the members of the armed forces who participate in the activities.

By definition, HCA must complement -- and not duplicate -- any other form of social or economic assistance that the United States is providing to the host country. HCA cannot be provided to any "individual, group or organization engaged in military or paramilitary activity." The cost of equipment, services and supplies provided worldwide through HCA may not exceed $5,000,000 in any fiscal year.

Report

Section 401 of Title 10, U.S. Code requires the Secretary of Defense to submit a report by March 1 of each year including:

1. A list of countries in which humanitarian and civic assistance activities were carried out during the preceding fiscal year;
2. The type and description of such activities carried out in each country during the preceding fiscal year; and
3. The amount spent carrying out each activity in each country during the preceding fiscal year.

Funding:

The budget for Humanitarian Civic Assistance projects is presented in a yearly Defense Department report. The amounts indicate "incidental expenses" – the cost of materials, supplies, and some services. However, the funding listed below does not include costs for transportation, personnel expenses, oil, petroleum, or the repair of equipment. Expenses reported as HCA are only those components of a deployment which are directly related to the project at hand. Thus the dollar amounts categorized as "HCA" are very small when compared with the activity's actual expense.

Country	1996[3]			1997[4]		
	Engineer	Medical	Total	Engineer	Medical	Total
Belize	$189,664.38	$74,195.15	$263,859.53	$341,185	$47,956	$389,141
Bolivia	$0	$21,300.92	$21,300.92	$54,249	$94,600	$148,849
Costa Rica	$38,520.41	$15,531.88	$54,052.29	$39,038	$18,000	$57,038
Dominica				$50,000	$15,000	$65,000
Dominican Republic				$60,000	$15,000	$75,000
Ecuador	$205,553.99	$143,950.39	$349,504.38	$164,496	$184,894	$349,390
El Salvador	$471,488.76	$80,187.31	$551,676.07	$0	$122,220	$122,220
Grenada				$66,675	$14,300	$80,975

Country	1996[3]			1997[4]		
	Engineer	Medical	Total	Engineer	Medical	Total
Guatemala	$0	$49,844.99	$49,844.99	$0	$117,851	$117,851
Guyana	$0	$18,200.00	$18,200.00	$313,579	$110,962	$424,541
Haiti				$476,737	$60,000	$536,737
Honduras	$408,429.86	$84,797.99	$493,227.85	$0	$84,643	$84,643
Jamaica				$69,511	$14,798	$84,309
Nicaragua	$0	$21,941.64	$21,941.64	$0	$24,787	$24,787
Panama	$659,946.73	$88,448.54	$748,395.27	$456,500	$79,861	$536,361
Paraguay	$0	$25,043.10	$25,043.10	$0	$31,570	$31,570
Peru	$0	$92,045.10	$92,045.10	$0	$82,451	$82,451
Trinidad and Tobago				$70,000	$10,178	$80,178
Total	$1,973,604	$715,487	$2,689,091	$2,161,970	$1,129,071	$3,291,041

Projects[5]:

Country	Bridges		Clinics		MED-RETES*		Schools		Wells		Other		Totals	
	96	97	96	97	96	97	96	97	96	97	96	97	96	97
Argentina						1							0	1
Belize		3	1		3	7	2	14				3	6	27
Bolivia				2	1	7		3		14		2	1	28
Brazil						1							0	1
Chile													0	0
Colombia													0	0
Costa Rica				1	1	3	4	9				2	5	15
Ecuador				2	6	8	3	3		3			9	16
El Salvador			1	10	3	4	9	12	6	8			19	34
Guatemala					2	4							2	4
Guyana				3	2	7		4				1	2	15
Honduras		1	2	1	23	24	11	8	4				40	34
Nicaragua					1	1							1	1
Panama			3	8	5	3	5	12	8	10			21	33
Paraguay					1	2							1	2
Peru				2	4	9		4					4	15
Suriname				3		4		1				1	0	9
Uruguay													0	0
Venezuela													0	0
Total	0	4	7	32	52	85	34	70	18	35	0	9	111	235

* Medical readiness training exercises.

Deployments for Training (DFTs)

Description:

"Deployment for Training" (DFT) is a broad term used to describe the practice of sending U.S. military personnel -- an individual, a group, even an entire unit -- overseas on a short-term basis for training. In most cases, the primary purpose of DFTs is to train the U.S. personnel themselves, though training host-country military personnel is usually a secondary result. DFTs are funded through the Department of Defense's Operations and Mainte-nance (O&M) account.

This study has so far been unable to ascertain the number of DFTs that take place in a typical year. As the table indicates, the U.S. Southern Command (Southcom) deploys some 56,000 military personnel, many of them members of Reserve and National Guard units, to Latin American and Caribbean countries each year. Not all of these deployments are for training purposes; many are sent down to relieve active-duty personnel or to provide other operational support. According to a 1997 Southcom publication, about 17,000 of those temporarily sent to the region are on counter-drug missions -- about half performed detection and monitoring tasks, and many of the rest were deployed for counter-drug training.[1]

	1994[2]	1995[2]	1996[2]
Number of deployments	3,858	3,135	3,000 (est.)
Personnel involved (about 40% reserves)	55,776	56,744	56,000+

Types of DFTs:

The list in this section, much of it taken from a May 1997 Southcom document, is by no means comprehensive, and includes some deployments whose purpose would more accurately be described as "operational support" rather than training.[3] The list includes some deployments whose primary purpose is to train foreign personnel, not U.S. forces, and some that are not funded through the Defense Department's O&M account. It nonetheless il-lustrates the variety of military deployments that rotate through Latin America and the Caribbean.

- **Mobile Training Team (MTT)**
  Mobile Training Teams are made up of Defense Department personnel "on temporary duty in a foreign country for the purpose of training foreign personnel in the operation, maintenance, or other support of weapon systems and support equipment, as well as training for general military operations." A country may purchase a course taught by an MTT through the Foreign Military Sales (FMS)

program, or the MTT may be subsidized through the International Military Education and Training (IMET) program.[4] As they are not funded through the Pentagon's O&M account, MTTs are not technically considered deployments for training.

- **Mobile Education Team (MET)**

    Mobile Education Teams are made up of Defense Department personnel on temporary duty in a foreign country to educate foreign personnel in defense resource management. METs, according to a Defense Department publication, "are normally funded from Expanded IMET program funds."[5] As they are not funded through the Pentagon's O&M account, METs are not technically considered deployments for training.

- **Logistics Training Team (LTT)**

    Logistics Training Teams are made up of Defense Department personnel on temporary duty in a foreign country to educate foreign personnel in defense logistics. A Defense Department manual defines "logistics" as "the science of planning and carrying out the movement and maintenance of forces."[6]

- **Riverine Training Team (RTT)**

    Riverine Training Teams are made up of Defense Department (usually Navy or Coast Guard) personnel on temporary duty in a foreign country to educate foreign personnel in operations that take place on rivers. An RTT normally teaches riverine counter-drug interdiction skills.

- **International Maritime Law Enforcement Training (IMLET)**

    IMLET programs are carried out by the U.S. Coast Guard. Coast Guard personnel help partner countries develop their own maritime law enforcement programs, improve port security, and improve institutional capabilities. The Coast Guard may also be a part of training programs that involve many U.S. agencies, if their particular area of expertise is needed.

- **Joint Combined Exchange Training (JCET)**

    JCETs are small special forces teams sent overseas to work with, or to train with, foreign militaries. The average JCET group is comprised of 10 to 40 troops, though groups can include as many as 100. The law dictates that the training of U.S. special forces must be these activities' primary purpose. The program, according to a Defense Department spokesman, "is not designed to train the forces of other countries. It's designed to train our special forces in how forces of other countries operate."[7] The JCET program operated in 101 countries in 1997, and will be in about 95 countries worldwide in 1998.

- **Tactical Analysis Team (TAT)**

    Tactical Analysis Teams do not have a training mission. TATs are Defense Department groups deployed to a country to gather, analyze and share intelligence on narcotics traffickers. Intelligence on key drug traffickers is assembled into "tactical-information portfolios." According to a 1994 General Accounting Office (GAO) report, TATs "use a sophisticated communications system that can securely transmit and receive classified documents, photographs, text, or radar images on a real-time basis to and from U.S. counter-narcotics personnel in the Western Hemisphere."[8]

- **Security Assistance Survey Team**

    Security Assistance Survey Teams do not have a training mission. A "security assistance survey," as defined by the Arms Export Control Act (P.L. 90-269, or the "AECA"), is "any survey or study conducted in a foreign country by United States Government personnel for the purpose of assessing the needs of that country for security assistance," including "defense requirement surveys, site surveys, general surveys or studies, and engineering assessment surveys." The Security Assistance Survey team's study, available upon request to the Speaker of the House and the Chairman of the Senate Foreign Relations Committee, often forms the basis for future arms sales to the country in question. Security Assistance Surveys are part of the security assistance process, and are normally not considered to be DFTs.

- **Joint Planning Assistance Team / Planning Assistance Team (JPAT / PAT)**

    Joint Planning Assistance Teams do not have a training mission. Their role, according to a National Defense University (NDU) publication, is to "assist foreign forces in developing operational plans around intelligence collection activities."[9]

- **Subject Matter Expert Exchange (SMEE)**

    Subject Matter Expert Exchanges are short visits by three or four U.S. military experts who exchange information with host-nation counterparts on a mutually-agreed topic. Topics may include "personnel, intelligence, operations, logistics, civil affairs, information processing, and others that may be of interest." Usually, both countries' subject-matter experts brief each other on their methods and procedures for dealing with the topic.[10]

- **Humanitarian and Civic Assistance (HCA)**

    Under the Humanitarian and Civic Assistance program, U.S. military personnel, while deployed overseas, carry out activities like building schools, vaccinating children and animals, and digging wells. HCA programs are often executed with the involvement of host country civilian and military personnel. Many HCA activities involve National Guard or reserve units. The deployment's primary purpose must be training of U.S. forces, readiness exercises or military operations.

- **Engineer Readiness Training Exercise (ENRETE)**

    Participants in an ENRETE practice building basic infrastructure like schools, roads, bridges, and wells. There is significant overlap between ENRETEs and HCA.

- **Medical Readiness Training Exercise (MEDRETE)**
- **Veterinary Readiness Training Exercise (VETRETE)**

    MEDRETEs and VETRETEs practice medical and veterinary skills by providing these services to civilians and their livestock. There is significant overlap between these deployments and HCA.

- **Extended Training Service Specialist (ETSS)**

    Extended Training Service Specialists are Defense Department personnel, both military and civilian, who are "technically qualified to provide advice, instruction, and training in the installation, operation, and maintenance of weapons, equipment, and systems." ETSS may be deployed for up to a year; they are attached, but not formally assigned, to the Security Assistance Organizations (SAOs) stationed at U.S. embassies. As they participate in security assistance, ETSS are not considered to be deployments for training.

- **Military Information Support Team (MIST)**

    A MIST is deployed from the U.S. Army's Civil Affairs and Psychological Operations Command. They provide information in an effort to influence host-country opinion in a way that benefits U.S. interests.

Special Operations Forces (SOF)

Program description:

Special operations forces (SOF, or "special forces") are specialized military units designed to confront a wide spectrum of situations, from peace to open warfare. They are frequently employed in three settings, as the Secretary of Defense's 1998 Report to the President and Congress explains:

1. In "crises and conflicts below the threshold of war, such as terrorism, insurgency, and sabotage";
2. In major conflicts, where they serve as "force multipliers ... increasing the effectiveness and efficiency of the U.S. military effort";
3. In "situations requiring regional orientation and cultural and political sensitivity, including military-to-military contacts and noncombatant missions like humanitarian assistance, security assistance, and peacekeeping operations."[1]

Special operations forces units from the Army, Navy and Air Force are coordinated by several "commands": Special Operations Commands within each military service, the U.S. Special Operations Command (USSOCOM) at MacDill Air Force Base in Florida, and individual Special Operations Commands (SOCs) within regional military commands. The U.S. Southern Command (Southcom) is the regional military command responsible for Latin America and the Caribbean (except Mexico). Special Operations Command South (SOCSOUTH), based at Fort Clayton in Panama, is the relevant Special Operations Command within the U.S. Southern Command. As a result, SOCSOUTH coordinates most special-forces activity in Latin America and the Caribbean.

Special operations policymaking and resource allocation are the responsibility of the Assistant Secretary of Defense for Special Operations and Low-Intensity Conflict (SO/LIC). The Assistant Secretary for SO/LIC is "the principal civilian advisor to the Secretary of Defense" on SOF policy.[2] Special operations forces have a separate program and budget, known as "Major Force Program 11," to fund activities that are unique to their mission.

Over 46,000 people, both active-duty and reserve personnel, are members of SOF units, which include Army Green Berets, Rangers, Special Operations Aviation, psychological operations and civil affairs units; Navy Sea-Air-Land forces (SEALs) and special boat units; and Air Force special operations squadrons.[3]

Special forces' main roles include counterproliferation, counterterrorism, reconnaissance, direct action (small-scale strikes), psychological operations (influencing public opinion), civil affairs (relations between military forces and civilian authorities), foreign internal defense (organizing, training, advising and assisting host-nation military and paramilitary forces), and "unconventional" warfare (military or paramilitary operations in enemy-held territory in support of forces resisting a standing government). SOF also take part in what the Secretary of Defense's 1998 Report to the President and Congress calls "collateral activities," in which they "share responsibility with other forces, as directed by the geographic combatant commanders" such as the head of Southcom. Four of these collateral activities take place with some frequency in Latin America and the Caribbean:

- **Humanitarian Assistance.** Limited assistance "to supplement or complement the efforts of host nation civil authorities or agencies to relieve or reduce the results of natural or man-made disasters."
- **Security Assistance.** "Provide training assistance in support of legislated programs which provide U.S. defense articles, military training, and other defense related services."
- **Humanitarian Demining Operations.** "Reduce or eliminate the threat to noncombatants posed by mines and other explosive devices by training host nation personnel in their recognition, identification, marking, and safe destruction. Provide instruction in program management, medical, and mine awareness activities."
- **Counterdrug Activities.** "Train host nation counterdrug forces to detect, monitor, and counter the production, trafficking, and use of illegal drugs."[4]

Included in many of these roles is the subsidiary task of maintaining military-to-military contact. By training with foreign military forces and interacting with foreign military leaders, explains Joint Chiefs Chairman Gen. Henry Shelton (formerly of the U.S. Special Operations Command), SOF "establish special enduring relationships with their host nation military counterparts." This is valuable, Shelton contends, because "[i]n many parts of the world, the military is often the most cohesive institution and wields significant power and thus can influence the outcome of events during a crisis and affairs of the government."[5]

Special forces were deployed to "over 140 countries" in 1996 and to 144 countries in 1997. In 1997, an average of 4,760 SOF personnel per week were deployed on a total of 3,061 overseas missions – "a threefold increase in missions since 1991."[6] Missions in 1997 worldwide included 17 crisis-response operations (such as evacuation of noncombatants), 194 counterdrug missions, demining activities in 14 countries, and 224 combined training exercises with foreign forces in 91 countries.[7]

It is impossible to get a specific picture of SOF activity in Latin America and the Caribbean, because their operations are normally kept secret. As the Secretary of Defense's 1998 Report explains, "The sensitivity of special operations precludes a detailed discussion of many current operations in this report." Some examples of activities in the region, however, include the following.

- In Haiti, special operations civil-affairs forces provide "Ministerial Advisory

Teams" to the Haitian government.

- SOF run the U.S. portion of the "Military Observer Mission Ecuador-Peru (MOMEP)" peacekeeping force monitoring the two countries' border dispute.
- SOF support counterdrug operations by training and providing "expert advice to host nation armed forces and police dedicated to the counterdrug mission, primarily through exercises, joint combined exchange training programs, planning, assistance, and training teams."[8]

Counternarcotics

Counter-drug missions account for much SOF activity in Latin America and the Caribbean today. Army special forces, according to a Southern Command publication, are well represented on "an interconnecting network of military teams" that provide "intelligence, planning and training to countries actively engaged in countering cocaine cartels." This article notes that "Company C, 3rd Battalion, 7th Special Forces Group, based in Panama, recently received its second Superior Unit Award for service in Colombia and elsewhere in Latin America."[9] Much special-forces counternarcotics activity is funded through accounts authorized by section 1004 of the 1991 National Defense Authorization Act.

The 7th Special Forces Group is heavily involved in training Mexican Air-Mobile Special Forces Groups (GAFEs), "elite Mexican Army units that have received Special Forces and air assault training for use in counterdrug interdiction operations." Mexican naval forces are also receiving maritime counternarcotics training with assistance from SOF units.[10]

Navy special forces are training Peruvian counterparts, as a Southcom publication describes:

> In the combat training arena, men from Special Warfare Unit 8 (SEAL Team 8) and Special Boat Unit 26, ... numbering perhaps 16 men for several months, train and advise the Peruvians who will eventually do the same for their own forces. Direct U.S. participation in pursuits and raids is forbidden. 'We train the customs, police and coast guard on boat maintenance, board and search techniques and small-arms firing,' said Riverine Det. B commander Lt. Cliff Bruner. ... 'Detachment B is currently training the Peruvians from the lowest level of drown proofing and motor maintenance to procedures for boarding and searching vessels,' according to Sgt. Maj. Daniel Bonilla, Special Operations Command's (South) senior enlisted advisor.[11]

JCET

Special-forces activity in Latin America and the Caribbean also takes place under the Joint Combined Exchange Training (JCET) program. JCET involves sending small special forces teams overseas to work with, or to train with, foreign militaries. The average JCET group is comprised of 10 to 40 troops, though groups can include as many as 100. The JCET program operated in 101 countries worldwide in 1997, and is operating in about 95 countries in 1998.

The law (section 2011 of Title 10, U.S. Code) dictates that training U.S. personnel must be these activities' primary purpose. The JCET program, according to Defense Department spokesman Kenneth Bacon, "is not designed to train the forces of other countries. It's designed to train our special forces in how forces of other countries operate."[12] In a later briefing, Bacon explained:

> It's to give them an opportunity to learn about the geography, topography of other nations, and to build up relationships with the military in other nations in case they're called upon to do hostage rescue operations or evacuations of American citizens or peacekeeping work or help training with forces of other nations.[13]

Some JCET groups operating in Latin America and the Caribbean may have counternarcotics missions, as the following citation from the U.S. State Department's 1998 International Narcotics Control Strategy Report indicates in the case of Venezuela:

> [T]he US armed forces have conducted 16 joint exercises for training (JCET) with the Venezuelan armed forces focused on improving capabilities for planning, coordinating and conducting counternarcotics operations. Riverine forces in particular are better prepared, organized and focused to conduct interdiction operations.[14]

In Colombia, however, Pentagon spokesman Bacon told reporters in May 1998 that the JCET program is separate from Defense Department counternarcotics activities:

> In Colombia, we have had JCET programs going on for several years, but it's actually a relatively small part of our overall military involvement in Colombia. In the current fiscal year, which is fiscal 1998, we plan to have six JCET missions in Colombia involving 32 people – a total of 32 people and six missions. That is dwarfed by our counter-narcotics program in Colombia which will involve 18 separate deployments involving 252 people in Colombia.
>
> Now the counter-narcotics program is under another program. It's separate from the JCET program. In Colombia, we have worked on counter-terrorism training with Colombia forces and we've also worked on hostage rescue training with Colombian forces.[15]

Recent revelations in the media of JCET activity in Colombia and Indonesia – countries where, for human rights reasons, units of the armed forces are prohibited from receiving training through standard security assistance channels – have created controversy, particularly in the U.S. Congress. Observers have voiced concern that JCET can be used as a way to avoid congressionally-imposed restrictions on other sources of training, such as IMET. One key restriction that can potentially be circumvented is the Leahy Amendment, a provision in the Foreign Operations Appropriations Act which prevents foreign military units from receiving assistance if their members face credible allegations of human rights abuse and are not being brought to justice.

Critics of JCET warn that foreign participants in the program are not fully screened for past records of human rights abuse or corruption. Bacon, the Pentagon spokesman, told reporters recently that "we follow the State Department's human rights rules in designing these programs and picking the people who will participate in the programs."[16] Ambassadors and the Special Operations Command approve each JCET mission; the Assistant Secretary of Defense for Special Operations and Low Intensity Conflict is to be added to the approval process in mid-1998. Vetting procedures for potential JCET participants, however, appear to be far less systematic than those being employed by State to enforce the Leahy Amendment.

Law:

The U.S. Special Operations Command (USSOCOM) is governed by section 167 of Title 10, U.S. Code ("Unified combatant command for special operations forces"). Section 167 was added as part of the 1986 "Goldwater-Nichols" legislation which restructured the Department of Defense.

USSOCOM is responsible for developing strategy, doctrine and tactics, directing the expenditure of funds, training assigned forces, and ensuring special forces' combat readiness.

Special operations activities, according to section 167, include:

1. Direct action;
2. Strategic reconnaissance;
3. Unconventional warfare;
4. Foreign internal defense;
5. Civil affairs;
6. Psychological operations;
7. Counterterrorism;
8. Humanitarian assistance;
9. Theater search and rescue; and
10. Such other activities as may be specified by the President or the Secretary of Defense.

Section 2011 of Title 10 governs special operations forces' training with foreign militaries. It allows the commander of USSOCOM to pay expenses associated with:

1. Training, and training with, armed forces and other security forces of a friendly foreign country;

2. Deploying special operations forces for that training; and
3. The friendly foreign country's incremental expenses incurred as a result of the training.

["'Incremental expenses' ... means the reasonable and proper cost of the goods and services that are consumed by a developing country as a direct result of that country's participation in a bilateral or multilateral military exercise with the United States." These may include rations, fuel, training ammunition and transportation. Incremental expenses do not include pay, allowances, and other normal costs.]

The law dictates that the primary purpose of this cooperative training must be to train the U.S. special forces.

Every April 1, the Secretary of Defense must submit a report to Congress discussing special forces' training with foreign forces. The report must specify:

1. All countries in which that training was conducted;
2. The type of training conducted, including whether the training was related to counter-narcotics or counter-terrorism activities, the duration of the training, the number of members of the armed forces involved, and expenses paid in connection with the training;
3. The extent of foreign military forces' participation, including the number and service affiliation of foreign military personnel involved, and the host nation's "physical and financial contribution" to the training effort; and
4. The training's relationship to other overseas training programs conducted by the armed forces, such as:
   - Military exercise programs sponsored by the Joint Chiefs of Staff;
   - Military exercise programs sponsored by a combatant command; and
   - Military training activities sponsored by a military department (including deployments for training, short duration exercises, and other similar unit training events).

Foreign Military Interaction

(Also known as "military-to-military contact")

Description:

The U.S. military relationship with Latin America and the Caribbean goes well beyond security assistance programs, exercises and deployments. The Defense Department carries out a large number of other initiatives whose primary goal is to maintain military-to-military contact with the region. These "foreign military interaction" (or "FMI") initiatives range from formal mechanisms like exchange programs and confidence-building measures to the informal contact that occurs during receptions, meetings and even telephone conversations.

Clearly, all security assistance programs, including arms transfers and military training programs, involve some degree of foreign military interaction. For the efforts described here, however, military-to-military contact is the main objective, not a subsidiary goal.

U.S. defense agencies -- in Latin America and the Caribbean, particularly the U.S. Southern Command (Southcom) – assert that foreign military interaction is necessary for several reasons. Maintaining regular contact, they contend, is essential for confidence-building and exchanges of information relevant to regional security. Knowledge of how other militaries "work" -- procedures, capabilities, command and control -- are regarded as important for future cooperation. The U.S. military seeks the interpersonal relationships that FMI programs build with foreign officers; friendships and acquaintances with top officers, the argument goes, can increase "access" to the region's militaries, making them likely allies in future conflicts, more amenable to U.S. foreign policy concerns, and more inclined to "internalize" U.S. values regarding human rights and civil-military relations in a democracy.

Southcom manages most military-to-military contacts within its area of responsibility (all of Latin America and the Caribbean except Mexico). The command places a high priority on foreign military interaction programs, which it sees as fulfilling a strategy of "cooperative regional peacetime engagement."

Critics caution that FMI programs must undergo greater oversight and scrutiny from civilian leaders, in order to avoid the development of a "parallel foreign policy" that values military objectives over political goals. Some also express concern about the tacit message of U.S. "approval" that these activities might convey when they involve militaries with poor human rights records or democratic credentials.

Types of FMI:

Though many FMI initiatives are too informal or ephemeral to document, several permanent programs exist and merit some description. The following list, which is not comprehensive, documents the military-to-military contact activities that this study has encountered.

Embassy personnel

- **Defense Attaché Offices (DAOs)**

Defense attachés are Defense Department personnel assigned to U.S. embassies; in most cases, they do not perform security-assistance functions. DAO duties include "overt gathering of military information, representing the U.S. Department of Defense in the conduct of military liaison activities, and performing as a component of the U.S. country team." All of these functions, particularly the first two, call for a very close relationship with host-country military personnel.[1]

- **Security Assistance Organizations (SAOs)**

Security Assistance Organizations (SAOs), Defense Department personnel stationed, like DAOs, in U.S. embassies throughout the region, play a key role in military-to-military contact. Their management of security-assistance programs requires SAO members to cultivate relationships with host-country military officers through regular visits, meetings, and other contact.

Exchange programs

Exchanges between U.S. and foreign military personnel are governed by section 544 of the Foreign Assistance Act of 1961 (P.L. 87-195, or the "FAA"), as amended. Section 544 specifies that exchanges must take place on a one-to-one basis, at comparable institutions, and at no cost to the United States.

- **Personnel Exchange Program (PEP)**

The Personnel Exchange Program is defined as "a reciprocal exchange of personnel between a U.S. military service and a counterpart unit in another nation's military service."[2]

- **Subject Matter Expert Exchanges (SMEE)**

    Subject Matter Expert Exchanges are short visits by 3 or 4 U.S. military experts who exchange information with host-nation counterparts on a mutually-agreed topic. Topics may include "personnel, intelligence, operations, logistics, civil affairs, information processing, and others that may be of interest." Usually, both countries' subject-matter experts brief each other on their methods and procedures for dealing with the topic.[3]

- **Schools of Other Nations (SON) Program**

    Officers participating in the Schools of Other Nations program attend a foreign military school and get credit for courses attended.

- **Foreign Area Officer (FAO) Program**

    The Foreign Area Officer program is an "immersion" training program. Participating officers must speak the local language, have a graduate degree, and have lived in the area for one or two years. The FAO attends schools in the country without receiving credit.

Office of the Secretary of Defense

- **Bilateral Working Groups**

    Assistant Secretaries of Defense and their staffs maintain regular contacts with counterparts in foreign civilian defense ministries. Their meetings are usually accompanied by a "military cooperation committee," in which military officers from both countries meet separately.

Joint Chiefs of Staff

- **Joint Staff Talks**

    Members of the U.S. Joint Staff hold annual bilateral consultations with counterparts from Argentina, Brazil and Chile. Participants in these formal meetings share information about structures and activities. The talks, largely regarded as confidence and security-building measures, are normally accompanied by a good deal of informal contact.

- **Joint Mexico-U.S. Defense Commission (JMUSDC)**

    JMUSDC, staffed by representatives of the Joint Staffs of the United States and Mexico, has been largely inactive for years. It may soon be revived, as military-to-military contact with Mexico is now in a period of rapid growth.

U.S. Army

- **Conference of American Armies**

    Founded in 1960, the Conference of American Armies is a biennial meeting of leaders of the hemisphere's armies. The conference has seven specialized sub-conferences, including a Training and Military Education Conference. Technical meetings usually occur between the formal meetings.

- **U.S. Army War College Peacekeeping Round Table**

    A discussion of peacekeeping attended by representatives of the armies of Argentina, Brazil, Chile, Mexico, Uruguay and the United States.

- **Brazil-U.S. Army Staff Talks**

    These discussions are usually held annually.

U.S. Navy

- **Inter-American Naval Conference (IANC)**

    This conference, similar to the Conference of American Armies, meets biennially and has seven specialized supporting conferences.

- **International Seapower Symposium (ISS)**

    The International Seapower Symposium is hosted by the U.S. Navy and attended by 70 states worldwide, including 18 states from the Western Hemisphere.

- **FMI with Argentina:**
    - **Navy Staff Talks**
      These discussions are held regularly between Argentina, Canada and the United States.
    - **Navy Trilateral Wargame**
      A simulation held between Argentina, Canada and the United States.
    - **Standing Naval Committee between Argentina and the U.S. (Atlantic Fleet).**

U.S. Air Force

- **System of Cooperation Among American Air Forces (SICOFAA)**

The SICOFAA hosts an annual Conference of the Chiefs of the American Air Forces (CONJEFAMER), attended by 18 member states from the hemisphere. It has a Permanent Secretariat and nine functional committees.

International Organizations

The bodies discussed in this category are not coordinated by the U.S. government. They are internationally-managed forums for FMI in which U.S. military representatives participate.

- **Inter-American Defense Board (IADB)**

Founded in 1942, the Inter-American Defense Board is a security body within the Organization of American States (OAS). It has four major components: the Council of Delegates, the Staff, the Secretariat, and the Inter-American Defense College.

The Council of Delegates advises the OAS in military matters and serves as "an organ of planning and preparation for the defense and security of the American Continent."[4] The Staff performs planning and advisory functions. The Secretariat performs administrative and support functions.

- **Inter-American Defense College (IADC)**

The Inter-American Defense College offers military officers and civilians with defense responsibilities a one-year post-graduate curriculum. Each student researches and publishes a monograph on a hemispheric defense issue. The IADC hosts symposia and conferences, as well as organizing visits to hemispheric defense institutions throughout the region.[5]

- **Caribbean Island Nations Security Conference (CINSEC)**

CINSEC is an annual meeting attended by representatives from Antigua and Barbuda, the Bahamas, Barbados, Dominica, Dominican Republic, Grenada, Haiti, Jamaica, St. Kitts and Nevis, St. Lucia, St. Vincent and the Grenadines, Trinidad and Tobago, and the United States. Canada attends as an observer.

Other FMI

- **Familiarization Visits**

The U.S. military frequently invites officers or small groups from foreign countries to observe an exercise or operation to become familiar with U.S. methods, procedures and equipment.

- **"Defense Diplomacy"**

The 1996 *Strategic Assessment* published by the National Defense University's Institute for National Strategic Studies coins a term, "defense diplomacy," to describe the wide variety of high-level professional contacts and policy-related outreach activities the U.S. Defense Department conducts with defense establishments worldwide. This category incorporates everything from the biennial meetings of the region's defense ministers (1995 in Williamsburg, VA; 1996 in Bariloche, Argentina) to roundtable discussions between experts.

The *Strategic Assessment* divides "defense diplomacy" into five rough categories:

- **High-level contacts:** official visits overseas, counterpart visits to the United States, defense ministerial meetings, bilateral-security working groups, contact with the Washington diplomatic corps, and personal associations with senior foreign leaders that mature over time.
- **Staff talks:** bilateral Joint Staff talks, multinational service conferences, and both joint and service expert exchange opportunities (relating to subjects such as military law, simulations, and force development).
- **Sharing professional expertise:** OSD briefing (teaching) teams from such staff offices as Program Analysis and Evaluation, the Emergency Planning Directorate, and the Defense Intelligence Agency; the U.S.-U.K. Kermit Roosevelt exchange military lecture series; NDU's collaboration with the Inter-American Defense College; and various DOD outreach programs.
- **Developing an understanding of defense issues and requirements among civilian defense officials:** foreign attendance of courses in service and defense education systems for DOD's civilian professionals; meetings between visiting government and legislative officials and DOD's civilian functional area experts; and short workshops in Washington designed to address this need.
- **Academic/research support of policy:** formal affiliation with sister institutions for military education; counterpart exchange visits by directors of military colleges and universities; roundtable discussions and workshops to share ideas with visiting civilian and military dignitaries, academics, and journalists on topics of their in-

terest; and the distribution of magazines, reports, and other professional literature published by service and defense academic and research institutions--ideally material published in foreign languages.[6]

Accounts that pay for FMI programs

Joint Staff and armed-service funds for operations and maintenance pay for many FMI activities. Some accounts, however, are specifically designed for this purpose.

- **CINC Initiative Fund (CIF)**
- **Traditional CINC Activities (TCA)**
- **Latin American Cooperation**

The Commander-in-Chief (CINC) of Southcom is given a certain amount of money each year to pay for FMI and training activities. The chiefs of the Army, Navy, and Air Force have "Latin American cooperation funds"for similar activities.

The CINC Initiative Fund is governed by section 166a of Title 10, U.S. Code. It authorizes the use of this account for the following activities:

1. Force training (activities whose primary purpose is to train U.S. forces);
2. Contingencies;
3. Selected operations;
4. Command and control;
5. Joint exercises (including activities of participating foreign countries);
6. Humanitarian and civic assistance;
7. Military education and training to military and related civilian personnel of foreign countries (including transportation, translation, and administrative expenses); and
8. Personnel expenses of defense personnel for bilateral or regional cooperation programs.

Other limitations on the fund's use include the following:

- No more than $7 million may be used to buy items whose individual unit cost exceeds $15,000;
- No more than $1 million can pay for expenses of foreign countries participating in joint exercises;
- No more than $2 million can pay for military education and training; and
- Funds may not be provided for an activity that has been denied Congressional authorization.

Section 1050 of Title 10, U.S. Code authorizes Latin American cooperation funds, allowing the secretary of an armed service to "pay the travel, subsistence, and special compensation of officers and students of Latin American countries and other expenses that the Secretary considers necessary for Latin American cooperation."

CIF, TCA and co-op funds generally pay for travel, per diems, lodging, and "representational expenses" (small gifts, meals and social functions) associated with military-to-military contact programs. In Latin America and the Caribbean, these funds also pay for Familiarization Visits and Subject Matter Expert Exchanges.

Non-Lethal Excess Property Transfers

Program description:

The Defense Department "provides selected countries with non-lethal, excess DOD [Defense Department] property to meet specific humanitarian needs."[1] In Latin America and the Caribbean, these are mainly medical and disaster-relief supplies. The law requires that these supplies be transferred to the State Department, which is responsible for distributing them.

In 1997, the Excess Property program provided 28 shipments to 20 countries in Latin America and the Caribbean. The U.S. Southern Command (Southcom) expects to provide another 28 shipments to 22 countries in 1998.[2]

Excess property, humanitarian assistance, and humanitarian and civic assistance

The Excess Property program should be distinguished from the Defense Department's Humanitarian Assistance (HA) program, which is authorized by a separate law (section 2551 of Title 10, U.S. Code). The HA program uses Pentagon funds to provide equipment and other humanitarian services that are not considered "excess."

The HA program has not been very active in Latin America; that is expected to change, however, as some projects are planned for 1998. According to Southcom Commander-in-Chief Gen. Charles Wilhelm, the $2.1 million 1998 HA budget for Latin America and the Caribbean "includes purchasing equipment for medical/disease surveillance systems, assisting malaria eradication efforts, and shipping disaster relief supplies, medical supplies, and fire-fighting equipment throughout the region."[3]

The HA program is itself to be distinguished from "Humanitarian and Civic Assistance (HCA)," the practice of providing construction, medical and other services in connection with a military exercise. Unlike HCA, military personnel participating in the HA program can provide humanitarian services outside the context of an exercise.

Law:

The Excess Property program is authorized by section 2547 of Title 10, U.S. Code, which allows the Secretary of Defense to "make available for humanitarian relief purposes any nonlethal excess supplies of the Department of Defense."

The term "nonlethal excess property" means property, other than real estate:

1. That is excess property, as defined by Defense Department regulations; and
2. That is not a weapon, ammunition, or other equipment or material that is designed to inflict serious bodily harm or death.

Excess property transfers by country, 1997[4]:

Country	Type of Property	Quantity	Value	Transportation costs
Antigua and Barbuda	Medical/Disaster Relief	30,908 lbs	$264,719	$19,522
Antigua and Barbuda	Medical Supplies	16,000 lbs	$346,405	$9,600
Barbados	Medical/Disaster Relief	26,660 lbs	$153,509	$20,226
Barbados	Medical Supplies	23,961 lbs	$101,541	$20,700
Belize	Medical Supplies	88,108 lbs	$692,152	$42,540
Brazil	Ambulance (2)	14,740 lbs	$74,818	$13,168
Costa Rica	Medical Supplies	55,368 lbs	$661,082	$34,204
Dominica	Medical/Disaster Relief	16,445 lbs	$93,954	$9,868
Dominica	Medical Supplies	23,316 lbs	$112,482	$20,725
Dominican Republic	Medical Supplies	27,640 lbs	$152,753	$18,300
Dominican Republic	Medical Supplies	25,582 lbs	$297,170	$16,200
Dominican Republic	Medical/Disaster Relief	59,563 lbs	$472,042	$34,719
Ecuador	Medical Supplies	75,582 lbs	$520,200	$96,778
Ecuador	Medical Supplies	47,238 lbs	$472,668	$63,984
El Salvador	Medical Supplies	78,661 lbs	$593,742	$51,000
Grenada	Medical Supplies	10,997 lbs	$59,502	$10,400
Guatemala	Medical Supplies	70,714 lbs	$467,775	$57,545
Guyana	Medical Supplies	87,782 lbs	$420,346	$59,484
Guyana	Medical Supplies	66,759 lbs	$508,143	$49,570
Haiti	Medical Supplies	70,990 lbs	$917,473	$43,140
Haiti	Medical Supplies	30,337 lbs	$255,569	$17,204
Haiti	Medical Supplies	29,986 lbs	$433,778	$16,500
Honduras	Medical Supplies	110,322 lbs	$353,026	$47,278
Jamaica	Medical/Disaster Relief	122,383 lbs	$1,139,625	$66,352
Jamaica	Disaster Relief	31,672 lbs	$313,192	$16,412
Jamaica	Medical Supplies	32,163 lbs	$225,720	$17,125
Mexico	Medical Supplies	14,447 lbs	$157,666	$10,200

Country	Type of Property	Quantity	Value	Transportation costs
Mexico	Medical Supplies	13,955 lbs	$165,194	$10,100
Nicaragua	Medical Supplies	83,014 lbs	$468,617	$47,278
Nicaragua	Medical Supplies	66,672 lbs	$564,921	$42,400
Peru	Medical Supplies	85,394 lbs	$417,273	$49,848
Peru	Medical Supplies	69,400 lbs	$524,103	$47,048
Suriname	Medical Supplies	69,653 lbs	$567,665	$51,788
Trinidad	Medical Supplies	14,444 lbs	$83,527	$10,420
Total		**1,690,856 lbs**	**$13,052,352**	**$1,141,626**

Excess property transfers by country, 1996[4]:

Country	Type of Property	Quantity	Value	Transportation costs
Belize	Medical Supplies/Equipment	83,058 lbs	$420,458	$62,322
Chile	Medical Supplies/Equipment	50,072 lbs	$305,742	$62,984
Dominican Republic	Medical Supplies/Equipment	16,150 lbs	$29,932	$18,505
Ecuador	Medical Supplies/Equipment	61,089 lbs	$522,980	$56,112
El Salvador	Medical Supplies/Equipment	31,288 lbs	$385,518	$37,956
Guatemala	Medical Supplies/Equipment	95,670 lbs	$493,081	$64,885
Guyana	Medical Supplies/Equipment	47,161 lbs	$583,489	$40,280
Honduras	Medical Supplies/Equipment	60,056 lbs	$556,678	$56,742
Nicaragua	Medical Supplies/Equipment	58,560 lbs	$646,222	$41,640
Paraguay	Medical Supplies/Equipment	32,566 lbs	$503,463	$32,320
Peru	Medical Supplies/Equipment	86,874 lbs	$401,211	$58,206
Suriname	Medical Supplies/Equipment	91,210 lbs	$483,081	$70,092
Total		**713,754 lbs**	**$5,331,855**	**$602,044**

Bases and Other Overseas Military Presences

- U.S. Southern Command

- Security Assistance Organizations

- U.S. Bases in Panama

- Enrique Soto Cano Air Base, Honduras

- Guantánamo Bay Naval Station, Cuba

- Operation Laser Strike

- U.S. Support Group Haiti

- Operation Safe Border, Ecuador-Peru

- Demining in Central America

U.S. Southern Command

A "unified command" is a permanent U.S. military body with components from at least two military services, set up to carry out a specific responsibility. The U.S. Southern Command (or "Southcom") is one of five unified commands whose area of responsibility (frequently referred to as an "AOR") is geographic. Southcom's AOR includes 19 nations -- all of Latin America and the Caribbean excluding Mexico and French Guiana. In 1997, waters surrounding Central and South America, the Caribbean Sea, the Gulf of Mexico and Caribbean island nations were transferred from Atlantic Command to Southern Command responsibility.

Southcom is responsible for implementing U.S. security assistance programs within its AOR. It supports Security Assistance Organizations (SAOs) at U.S. embassies, groups of military personnel who implement U.S. military aid programs most closely (described in the next section). Southcom also carries out exercises, ongoing operations, military-to-military contact programs, special-forces training, and most other U.S. military activities that occur in its area.

According to Southcom publications, the command's specific missions include arms control and non-proliferation, military-to-military contacts, anti-terrorism operations, and counter-insurgency programs, as well as less traditionally "military" roles such as "conducting cooperative counterdrug operations, supporting foreign military [drug] interdiction programs, supporting humanitarian and civic assistance, conducting non-combatant evacuations, conducting search and rescue and disaster relief, and conducting contingency operations."[1]

Southcom operates several bases in Latin America, the Caribbean, Puerto Rico and the United States. The command includes eight component units representing all armed services and several joint efforts:

Component	Headquarters	Personnel (if available, as of May 1997)
U.S. Army South (USARSO)	Fort Clayton, Panama	3,200 military / 2,500 civilians
U.S. Southern Air Force (USSOUTHAF - Forward, 24th Wing, the "forward element" of 12th Air Force, which is based at Davis-Monthan Air Force Base near Tucson, AZ)	Howard AFB, Panama	1,900 military / 2,500 civilians
U.S. Navy Atlantic Fleet Southern Detachment (CINCLANTFLT Detachment South, a detachment of U.S. Commander in Chief, Atlantic Fleet, Norfolk, VA)	Rodman Naval Station, Panama	185 military / 23 civilians

Component	Headquarters	Personnel (if available, as of May 1997)
Marine Forces South (MARFORSOUTH)	Camp Lejeune, NC, "small planning and liaison element" in Panama	20 military in Panama
U.S. Special Operations Command South (SOCSOUTH)	Fort Clayton, Panama	460 military / 15 civilians
Joint Task Force-Bravo (JTF-Bravo)	Enrique Soto Cano Air Base (Honduran-owned), Comayagua, Honduras	499 military
Joint Task Force-Panama (JTF-Panama)	Fort Clayton, Panama	
Security Assistance Organizations (SAOs)	Attached to U.S. embassies in sixteen countries	72 military, 23 civilian, 66 local (1998)

Special Operations Command South is tasked with all special-forces activity in the region, including a large amount of counterdrug training and operational support. In addition to humanitarian, disaster relief and counterdrug operations, Joint Task Force-Bravo assists Central American armed forces in "restructuring their militaries to fit changing security requirements."[2] Joint Task Force-Panama is under the direction of USARSO's commander and is "responsible for the defense of the Panama Canal and protecting U.S. personnel, property, and interests in Panama."[3] The Security Assistance Organizations (SAO) manage U.S. military activities in their respective countries, serve as Southcom's representatives to U.S. ambassadors and embassy country teams, and act as liaisons to foreign militaries throughout the region. There are 20 SAOs in the region, including Mexico.[4]

Southcom is gradually leaving Panama in compliance with the 1977 Panama Canal accords. As of January 1998, the United States still maintains six primary installations or bases in Panama: Fort Clayton, Fort Kobbe, Howard Air Force Base, Rodman Naval Station, Fort Sherman, and the Galeta Island Communications Facility.

After over 80 years in Panama, Southcom's headquarters were transferred in September 1997 from Quarry Heights, Panama to a new high-tech facility in Miami, Florida. Advanced equipment at the site is used for field communication and surveillance throughout Southcom's area of operation. Seven hundred military and civilian personnel are employed at the headquarters facility. When located in Panama, Southern Command headquarters' average annual operating budget was $27 million -- no new budget figures are available for the new headquarters. The Department of Defense allocated $566 million to Southcom as a whole in 1997.[5]

About 5,700 U.S. military personnel and 5,000 civilians are stationed throughout Southcom's AOR. In addition, over 50,000 temporarily assigned personnel -- about 40 percent reservists -- circulate through the region each year to participate in counterdrug operations, exercises, and other deployments.

Counter-drug mission

Counter-drug activities and the maintenance of military-to-military contact are two of the command's highest priorities in the region. Current Southcom Commander-In-Chief Gen. Charles Wilhelm argues that it is essential to offer a proper combination of these two elements:

> Success in our theater requires a balanced approach to conducting regional engagement and counterdrug operations. A strategic link exists in varying degrees between these two missions in each country in our region. We seek to establish the correct balance between these missions in each country to meet that country's specific requirements.[6]

Many of Southcom's current duties owe to the Defense Department's designation as the lead U.S. government agency for international narcotics interdiction. Interdiction and counter-drug assistance are the rationale behind many ongoing operations (particularly "Laser Strike"), traditional security-assistance programs, exercises, military training and other activities funded through special defense-budget authorizations.

U.S. troops do not directly engage foreign drug producers or smugglers, but they help foreign governments do so by providing intelligence and other support. Two Joint Inter-agency Task Forces (JIATFs), equipped with planes, radar, and sophisticated communications equipment, have extensive detection and monitoring missions. The JIATFs pass information about drug shipments to foreign law-enforcement agencies "for appropriate action."[7] They are staffed by personnel from military services, the Drug Enforcement Administration (DEA), the U.S. Customs Service and civilian intelligence agencies.

JIATF-South, located at Howard Air Force Base in Panama, also includes military representatives from Argentina, Brazil, Colombia, Ecuador, Peru and Venezuela. It is also known by its former name, the Joint Air Operations Center. This facility provides intelligence about drug-related activities, training, planning assistance, logistics and communications support to U.S. and Latin American drug-interdiction agencies. JIATF-South focuses on the "source zone," where drugs are produced. JIATF-East, in Key West, Florida, performs similar missions in the "transit zone," where drugs are transshipped to the United States.

Southcom also maintains about 17 radar sites in its AOR to detect possible drug-smuggling flights.[8]

Security Assistance Organizations

Description:

Security Assistance Organizations (SAOs) are military and civilian personnel stationed in foreign countries to manage security assistance and other military programs. SAOs are closest to these programs' operation and have the closest contact with host-country militaries.

SAOs go by different names in different countries. In Latin America and the Caribbean, names include Military Groups (MILGROUPs), Military Assistance Advisory Groups (MAAGs), Military Liaison Offices (MLOs), and Offices of the Defense Representative (ODRs). In general, they are not to be confused with defense attachés, who normally play a more diplomatic role; many embassies have both defense attachés and SAOs.

SAOs' duties are officially referred to as "overseas military program management." Specific responsibilities may include:

- Managing Foreign Military Sales (FMS) cases;
- Managing training programs;
- Monitoring security-assistance programs;
- Evaluating and planning the host country's military capabilities and requirements;
- Promoting international defense cooperation and interoperability between forces;
- Providing administrative support; and
- Carrying out other liaison functions.

Typically, these responsibilities require an SAO to carry out the following tasks listed in The Management of Security Assistance, a Defense Department manual:

- Provide foreign governments with information they need to help them decide whether to buy U.S. defense articles and services. This information might concern the acquisition, use, and training needed to obtain these items;
- Evaluate host countries' military capabilities, in order to process security assistance requests;
- Acquire information concerning foreign governments' potential future defense acquisitions;
- Help U.S. military departments (such as the Army or Navy) arrange security assistance for recipient countries;
- Assist host governments in identifying, administering, and disposing of excess security assistance materiel;
- Report on the use of defense articles and services granted as aid to the host country, as well as personnel trained by the United States;
- Inform other Defense Department offices with security-assistance responsibilities of security assistance activities in host countries;
- Perform secondary functions, such as advisory and training services and negotiation on non-security assistance military matters; and

Security Assistance Organizations

- Perform command and administrative functions.[1]

SAOs also coordinate or participate in activities not traditionally regarded as "security assistance," such as exercises and deployments, humanitarian civic assistance activities, exchanges, conferences and other military-to-military contact programs.

Section 515(e) of the Foreign Assistance Act states that SAOs are to be under the direct supervision of the Ambassador to the country in which they are stationed. However, The Management of Security Assistance probably reflects reality more closely: "The Chief of the SAO is essentially responsible to three authorities: the Ambassador (who heads up the country team), the Commander of the Unified Command [in this case the U.S. Southern Command], and the Director, Defense Security Assistance Agency."[2]

Funding for the portion of SAO salaries and operating costs used to manage security assistance comes from the Foreign Military Financing (FMF) program and from administrative surcharges on Foreign Military Sales (FMS).

Law:

Section 515 of the Foreign Assistance Act of 1961 (P.L. 87-195, or the "FAA"), as amended, governs SAO staffing and responsibilities.

Limitations

Section 515(b) mandates that SAOs keep advisory and training assistance to an absolute minimum. This provision's intent is to specify that SAOs should manage training and advice provided by others, not carry it out themselves.

The number of military members of an SAO cannot exceed six unless specifically authorized by Congress. Colombia, El Salvador and Honduras are the only Western Hemisphere countries allowed to exceed this limit.

Section 515(f) orders the President to instruct SAOs that they "should not encourage, promote, or influence the purchase by any foreign country of United States-made military equipment, unless they are specifically instructed to do so by an appropriate official of the executive branch."

Reporting

SAO staff sizes must be included in the <u>Congressional Presentation</u> documents submitted each February with the administration's budget request.

Notification

If the President wishes to exceed the maximum of six military SAO members, the Senate Foreign Relations Committee and the House International Relations Committee must be notified 30 days in advance.

If the President wishes to exceed the number of military SAO members listed in the yearly State Department <u>Congressional Presentation</u> (even if the number will not exceed six), the Senate Foreign Relations Committee and the House International Relations Committee must be notified 30 days in advance.

SAO funding by country:

Actual assigned strengths for FY 1997 and FY 1998 may be less than the authorized levels shown. Staffing requirements may change as individual country programs develop.

(Thousands of U.S. dollars.)

1996-97:

Country	Organi-zation*	1996 actual[3]			1997 actual[4]		
		FMF	FMS	Total	FMF	FMS	Total
Argentina	USMILGP	$276	$92	$368	$334	$111	$445
Belize	USMLO	$147	$63	$210	$158	$68	$226
Bolivia	USMILGP	$686	$191	$877	$202	$375	$577
Brazil	USMLO	$255	$131	$386	$366	$197	$563
Chile	USMILGP	$164	$71	$235	$196	$84	$280
Colombia	USMILGP	$596	$266	$862	$670	$447	$1,117
Costa Rica	ODR	$229	$26	$255	$204	$23	$227
Dominican Republic	DAO (a) / USMAAG	$168	$86	$254	$244	$61	$305
Eastern Caribbean	USMLO (b)	$276	$60	$336	$260	$87	$347
Ecuador	USMILGP	$239	$93	$332	$245	$105	$350
El Salvador	USMILGP	$523	$207	$730	$195	$585	$780
Guatemala	USMILGP	$202	$92	$294	$186	$33	$219
Haiti	USMLO	$278	$23	$301	$206	$137	$343

Country	Organi- zation*	1996 actual[3]			1997 actual[4]		
		FMF	FMS	Total	FMF	FMS	Total
Honduras	USMILGP	$536	$239	$775	$395	$310	$705
Jamaica	USMLO	$126	$82	$208	$150	$122	$272
Mexico	DAO (a)	$139	$64	$203	$171	$140	$311
Panama	DAO (a)	$37	$99	$136	$29	$43	$72
Paraguay	ODC	$176	$42	$218	$268	$30	$298
Peru	MAAG	$324	$115	$439	$392	$43	$435
Uruguay	ODC	$197	$84	$281	$222	$95	$317
Venezuela	USMILGP	$304	$426	$730	$367	$245	$612
Total, Latin America		$5,878	$2,552	$8,430	$5,478	$3,342	$8,820

1998-99:

Country	Organi- zation*	1998 estimate[4]			1999 request[4]		
		FMF	FMS	Total	FMF	FMS	Total
Argentina	USMILGP	$391	$98	$489	$383	$96	$479
Belize	USMLO	$217	$73	$290	$209	$70	$279
Bolivia	USMILGP	$369	$451	$820	$344	$420	$764
Brazil	USMLO	$434	$186	$620	$419	$180	$599
Chile	USMILGP	$346	$116	$462	$333	$111	$444
Colombia	USMILGP	$813	$435	$1,248	$773	$417	$1,190
Costa Rica	ODR	$230	$26	$256	$218	$24	$242
Domini- can Republic	DAO (a) / USMAAG	$297	$53	$350	$304	$54	$358
Eastern Caribbean	USMLO (b)	$239	$42	$281	$234	$59	$293
Ecuador	USMILGP	$302	$101	$403	$315	$105	$420
El Salvador	USMILGP	$470	$384	$854	$491	$401	$892
Guate- mala	USMILGP	$213	$24	$237	$122	$14	$136
Haiti	USMLO	$116	$63	$179	$125	$67	$192
Honduras	USMILGP	$481	$259	$740	$470	$253	$723
Jamaica	USMLO	$279	$186	$465	$279	$186	$465
Mexico	DAO (a)	$197	$131	$328	$182	$121	$303
Panama	DAO (a)	$65	$22	$87	$59	$25	$84
Paraguay	ODC	$270	$30	$300	$257	$28	$285
Peru	MAAG	$572	$64	$636	$546	$61	$607
Uruguay	ODC	$290	$97	$387	$280	$93	$373
Venezuela	USMILGP	$408	$219	$627	$380	$204	$584
Total, Latin America		$7,043	$3,062	$10,105	$6,769	$2,991	$9,760

Staffing by country:

1996-97:

Country	Organization	1996 actual[5]				1997 actual[6]			
		Military	Civilian	Local	Total	Military	Civilian	Local	Total
Argentina	USMILGP	3	1	2	6	3	1	2	6
Belize	USMLO	2	1	1	4	2	1	0	3
Bolivia	USMILGP	6	5	3	14	5	5	3	13
Brazil	USMLO	3	2	1	6	3	2	1	6
Chile	USMILGP	2	0	1	3	2	0	2	4
Colombia	USMILGP	9	3	10	22	9	3	10	22
Costa Rica	ODR	1	2	3	6	1	0	2	3
Dominican Republic	USMAAG	3	0	2	5	3	0	1	4
Eastern Caribbean	USMLO	4	0	0	4	4	0	0	4
Ecuador	USMILGP	5	1	5	11	5	1	5	11
El Salvador	USMILGP	7	1	11	19	5	1	10	16
Guatemala	USMILGP	3	0	2	5	2	0	1	3
Haiti	USMLO	2	0	1	3	2	0	1	3
Honduras	USMILGP	7	2	9	18	5	2	7	14
Jamaica	USMLO	3	1	0	4	3	1	0	4
Mexico	DAO	3	0	3	6	3	0	3	6
Panama	DAO	1	0	1	2	1	0	1	2
Paraguay	ODC	2	0	3	5	1	0	3	4
Peru	MAAG	2	1	5	8	3	2	5	10
Uruguay	ODC	1	0	4	5	1	0	4	5
Venezuela	USMILGP	6	4	5	15	5	4	5	14
Total, Latin America		**75**	**24**	**72**	**171**	**72**	**23**	**66**	**161**

1998-99

Country	Organization	1998 estimate[6]				1999 request[6]			
		Military	Civilian	Local	Total	Military	Civilian	Local	Total
Argentina	USMILGP	3	1	2	6	3	0	2	5
Belize	USMLO	2	1	0	3	2	1	0	3
Bolivia	USMILGP	4	5	3	12	4	4	3	11
Brazil	USMLO	3	2	1	6	3	2	1	6
Chile	USMILGP	2	0	2	4	2	0	2	4
Colombia	USMILGP	9	3	10	22	8	3	10	21
Costa Rica	ODR	1	0	2	3	1	0	2	3
Dominican Republic	USMAAG	3	0	1	4	3	0	1	4
Eastern Caribbean	USMLO	4	0	0	4				
Ecuador	USMILGP	5	1	5	11	5	1	5	11
El Salvador	USMILGP	5	1	10	16	5	1	8	14
Guatemala	USMILGP	2	0	1	3	2	0	1	3
Haiti	USMLO	2	0	1	3	2	0	1	3
Honduras	USMILGP	5	2	7	14	5	2	7	14

Security Assistance Organizations

Country	Organization	1998 estimate[6]				1999 request[6]			
		Military	Civilian	Local	Total	Military	Civilian	Local	Total
Jamaica	USMLO	3	1	0	4	3	1	0	4
Mexico	DAO	3	0	3	6	3	0	3	6
Panama	DAO	1	0	1	2	1	0	1	2
Paraguay	ODC	1	0	3	4	1	0	3	4
Peru	MAAG	3	2	5	10	3	2	5	10
Uruguay	ODC	1	0	4	5	1	0	4	5
Venezuela	USMILGP	5	4	4	13	5	4	4	13
Total, Latin America		72	23	66	161	72	23	66	161

*Organizations	
DAO (a)	Defense Attaché Office (Augmented)
USMAAG	Military Assistance Advisory Group
USMILGP	Military Group
USMLO	Military Liaison Office
ODR	Office of Defense Representative

U.S. Bases in Panama

The United States has maintained a military presence in Panama since construction of the Panama Canal began in 1903. According to the 1977 Carter-Torrijos Panama Canal accords, the Canal and all U.S. military bases in Panama are to be handed over to the Panamanian government on December 31, 1999. U.S. military bases in Panama have been closing gradually in recent years; six significant sites remain in use.

Howard Air Force Base

In 1917 the U.S. established its first air force contingent in Panama, the Capt. Harold H. Arnold Command, at an area called France Field. This command was responsible for patrolling Panama's Atlantic coastal waters at the end of World War I. Today, the United States' 24th Wing -- the U.S. Southern Command (Southcom) component responsible for air operations over Latin America and the Caribbean -- is stationed at Howard Air Force Base, which was constructed in 1939. Howard Air Force Base accommodates 2,100 air force members, 400 U.S. civilians, 800 Panamanian employees, and 3,000 family members.[1]

The 24th Wing's peacetime mission includes humanitarian and civil support, security assistance, intra-theatre air-lifts, environmental operations, disaster relief, peace operations, defense of the Panama Canal, Panama Canal treaty implementation, arms control and non-proliferation, military-to-military contacts, and counter-drug, terrorism and insurgency operations. The 24th Wing has one flying squadron, the 310th Airlift Squadron, including C-130, C-21, C-27A, and CT-43 cargo aircraft.[2] As of February 1996, the 24th Wing's budget amounted to $85 million.[3]

Three support squadrons are also stationed at Howard. The 640th Air Mobility Support Squadron provides maintenance support and manages C-17, C-141 and C-5 aircraft. Coronet Oak is a unit of Air National Guard and Air Force Reserve C-130 aircraft, manned by reservists who rotate in and out of the region, responsible for airlifting cargo and providing personnel support for Southcom. Coronet Nighthawk is a rotational Air National Guard unit of F-16 and F-15 fighter planes.[4]

Howard is also the home of Joint Inter-Agency Task Force South (JIATF-South, formerly known as the Joint Air Operations Center). This facility was established in 1992 to assist in counter-drug efforts, specifically ground and aerial surveillance of unauthorized aircraft throughout South America (see discussion on page 126).

Like all U.S. installations in Panama, Howard must return to Panamanian control by the end of 1999. However, negotiations continue on a proposal to create a U.S. military-supported multinational counter-drug control center using Howard facilities, especially JIATF-South, after 1999.

Rodman Naval Station

A permanent U.S. Navy presence was first established in Panama in 1917, and expanded in 1943, when construction of U.S. Naval Station Panama Canal (Rodman) was completed on the Pacific side of the Canal.

Today, the 600-acre facility's primary purpose has been to provide fuel, provisions and other support to 12 tenant commands, local Defense Department units, forward-deployed ships, and all ships that call at the Naval Station. It is staffed by over 200 military and civilian personnel. The naval station includes a port facility with three docks, 87 housing units, warehouses, industrial areas, an office building, and other facilities.

Rodman, which is to be handed over to Panama in December 1999, hosts the Southern Detachment of the Atlantic Fleet (CINCLANTFLT Detachment South), the naval component of the U.S. Southern Command (Southcom). CINCLANTFLT takes the lead in Southcom naval exercises.

Rodman also hosts the Navy Small Craft Instruction and Technical Training School (NAVSCIATTS), which trains maritime units from throughout the region, including the National Maritime Service (SMN) of Panama's National Police force.

Fort Clayton

U.S. Army infantry units were first assigned to Panama in 1911, and were permanently established in 1917 to defend the Panama Canal. Today Fort Clayton, a U.S. Army installation located at the Pacific opening of the Panama Canal, hosts the largest number of U.S. military and civilian personnel in Latin America. In 1994, prior to troop drawdowns, Fort Clayton accommodated 20,000 military and civilian personnel including family members. Currently, close to 6,000 U.S. military and civilian personnel reside at the army installation.[5]

U.S. Army South (USARSO), the ground component of the U.S. Southern Command (Southcom), is headquartered at Fort Clayton. USARSO forces include an infantry battalion and aviation, engineer, intelligence, logistics and military police units. USARSO provides "the Army command and control structure for Southcom's area of operation, ... supports regional disaster relief and counterdrug efforts and provides oversight, planning and logistical support for humanitarian and civic assistance projects."[6] USARSO also maintains the Army's Jungle Operations Training Center (JOTC), a facility at Fort Sherman.

Following "Operation Just Cause" in 1989, its last wartime activity, USARSO's mission -- like that of the U.S. Navy and Air force contingent -- has been focused on peacetime activities including security assistance, counterdrug operations, and protecting U.S. personnel, property and the Panama Canal.[8] USARSO headquarters is scheduled to move to Puerto Rico in October 1998.

Fort Clayton's 2,180 acres host the U.S. Army Garrison-Panama, the Military Police Command, and the 106th Signal Brigade. The base also encompasses 1,392 homes, dormitories for 1,754, schools for dependents and several recreational facilities.[9]

Corozal, a sub-installation, is also located at Fort Clayton and hosts the U.S. Army Tropic Test Center, the 470th Military Intelligence Brigade and several residences.[10]

Fort Sherman

Fort Sherman, a 23,100-acre facility on Panama's Atlantic side, includes an airstrip, training facilities, 67 homes and dormitories for 300 people, and recreational areas. Over half of Fort Sherman's land area is covered by tropical forest.[11]

Much of this forest is put to use by the Jungle Operations Training Center (JOTC), a facility run by U.S. Army South (USARSO) that trains U.S. and Latin American personnel in jungle warfare and survival techniques. The JOTC "conducts 11 infantry battalion rotations, 4 engineer company rotations, and 4 Aircrew Survival Courses annually and offers training in jungle survival techniques, land navigation, waterborne operations, and combat tactics." The facility's annual budget is $5.7 million per year. [12]

Soldiers from Central and South America receive jungle and waterborne training at the JOTC. "One of the requirements here," a special-forces instructor stationed at the JOTC told an Army publication, "is that we also teach Latin American soldiers the same things we teach U.S. soldiers -- waterborne operations, air crew survival, cordon and search operations."[13]

Fort Sherman is scheduled to be handed over to Panama on 1999; the last rotation through the JOTC will take place in March 1999.

Galeta Island Communications Facility

Located on the Atlantic side of the Panama Canal, the Galeta Island

Communications Facility uses sophisticated satellite surveillance equipment to gather and share intelligence. Though much of its activities probably have to do with the Defense Department's counter-drug effort, Galeta Island's mission and capabilities are classified.

After a Naval Security Group Activity was deactivated in 1995, Galeta Island passed from U.S. Navy to Army control. The facility is to be turned over to Panama by December 1999.

Fort Kobbe

Fort Kobbe, a 5,196-acre army base on the Pacific side of the Panama Canal, hosts the following units:[14]

- 536th Engineer Combat Battalion (Heavy)
- 1st Battalion, 228th Aviation Regiment
- 5th Battalion, 87th Infantry

Fort Kobbe includes 264 housing units and dormitories for over 1,000, as well as a school and warehouses. Its handover to Panama is scheduled for 1999.[15]

Proposed "Multi-National Counter-Drug Center"

On 23 December 1997, an agreement "in principle" was drafted between the United States and Panama regarding a possible Multinational Anti-Drug Center (CMA, by its Spanish initials) to be established at facilities on several U.S. military bases near the Panama canal.

After it became clear that Panama would not allow a renegotiation of the 1977 treaties to allow U.S. bases to remain in their present state, the United States and Panama held nearly a year of informal talks and often difficult negotiations about the CMA. The idea, originally proposed by Panamanian President Ernesto Pérez Balladares, was to create a civilian-run facility at which civil and military personnel from several countries work to detect and monitor narcotics-trafficking activity. It will also, however, allow the United States to keep troops in Panama after 1999. Critics of the CMA call it a disguised military base.

The agreement, a draft of which appeared in the Mexican daily Excelsior in January 1998, revealed details about the CMA that had been hidden by the negotiations' secrecy.

This early draft has since been disavowed by both sides, and negotiations continue. It nonetheless remains the only source of information on plans for the CMA. The document includes the following points[16]:

The functions of the Center (which the agreement calls the "CLN," or Multi-national Center for the Fight against Narcotrafficking), will be (1) to gather, analyze and exchange intelligence about counternarcotics activities; (2) to detect and monitor the production and trafficking of narcotics and precursor chemicals, as well as money-laundering activities; and (3) to offer training in skills needed for counternarcotics activities.

The Center will incorporate facilities at the following U.S. military installations:

- Howard Air Force Base - at least 93 buildings, including the Joint Air Operations Center, the runway and control tower, recreational areas (including softball fields and a swimming pool), among others;
- Farfán Naval Radio Station - sixteen buildings and a baseball field.
- Fort Kobbe - At least 56 buildings and other complexes, and playing fields.
- Rodman Naval Station - Six buildings and other lots, and the use of three docks.
- The grounds of the old Panama Canal College;
- Galeta Island, currently a super-secret communications facility;
- The Corozal communications complex; and
- Other unspecified training fields and firing ranges.

The Center will be overseen by a council made up of the foreign ministers of the participating countries, and managed by a Permanent Committee made up of representatives selected by the participating countries. These officials, as well as the secretariat managing the center on a day-to-day basis, will enjoy immunity from prosecution in Panamanian courts. In addition, soldiers and other CLN personnel will be exempt from all taxes, tolls, and customs inspections within Panama.

The Center will have three components:

- An Information Directorate, which will coordinate the gathering, analysis and distribution of information about drug trafficking, precursor chemicals, and related activities. Each participating country will be responsible for its own intelligence-gathering activities;
- A Training Institute, which will provide professional education and technical training in law enforcement, administration of justice, investigative techniques, counternarcotics tactics, use and maintenance of equipment, intelligence-gathering, police tactics and techniques, maritime operations, land operations, small-boat repair, and other areas "as required"; and
- A Permanent Committee for Community Affairs, which will oversee housing, security and other quality-of-life issues for personnel participating in the center.

The Panamanian government is chiefly responsible for guaranteeing the Center's security, though it may enter into agreements with member countries to allow them to provide security for certain installations. A separate agreement allows U.S. personnel to guard several sites, including much of what is now Howard Air Force Base. It is the government's responsibility to provide public security in the housing areas and other public services to the Center's personnel.

Each participating country must provide equipment, supplies and personnel to the Center, and must pay a corresponding contribution for its operating costs. Each will remain in control of its equipment, personnel and other resources.

Participating-country (particularly U.S.) forces at the Center may carry out "search and rescue, training, logistical support, and disaster assistance" missions in Panama and the rest of the region, though the Panamanian government may withdraw consent for particular missions.

Panama is charged with negotiating agreements with third countries interested in participating in the Center.

The government of Panama is prohibited from enacting or enforcing any laws that interfere with the Center's activities.

Panama's National Police will be responsible for administering and maintaining training areas and firing ranges. CLN use of these ranges, however, will be given priority over Panamanian authorities' use.

The agreement will be in place for twelve years, after which it can be renewed for five-year periods. No party can abandon the agreement within the initial twelve-year period; after this period, participants may do so after giving one year's notice.

As this book went to press (May 1998), the CMA negotiations had clearly stalled and the Panamanian government appeared to be backing out of the December 1997 agreement.

Enrique Soto Cano Air Base

Honduras

Description:

Joint Task Force Bravo (JTF-Bravo), one of eight components of the U.S. Southern Command (Southcom), was established in August 1984 and stationed at the Enrique Soto Cano semi-permanent air base, a Honduran-owned facility near Comayagua, Honduras.

The joint task force was originally established to support U.S. efforts on behalf of Central American allies in the region's civil wars of the 1980s. With the region at peace, JTF-Bravo's current stated mission is "to enhance cooperative regional security through forward presence and peacetime engagement operations."[1] Specific activities include exercises, humanitarian and civic assistance projects, disaster relief, and support for counterdrug operations. Few troops are permanently assigned to Soto Cano; almost all rotate through for very short periods. While the force numbered in the thousands at its 1980s height, JTF-Bravo now has about 500 troops present at any given time.[2]

In 1995, JTF-Bravo underwent a review by Congress's General Accounting Office (GAO) to determine its post-cold war security relevance. The GAO determined that Soto Cano provided useful and convenient support to some U.S. government activities, such as counternarcotics, but is no longer critical to such activities or current U.S. policy objectives in the region, such as economic growth and democratic reform.[3]

U.S. bases in Panama are scheduled to be turned over to the Panamanian government by the end of 1999. If that occurs as planned, Soto Cano will be the only U.S. airfield on the Latin American mainland. As a result, the Defense Department argues that Soto Cano, which is likely to play a greater anti-drug role, is highly relevant to its future activities.

The Honduran Constitution does not permit a permanent foreign presence in Honduras. A "handshake" agreement between the United States and Honduras allows JTF-Bravo to remain in Honduras on a "semi-permanent" basis. This agreement, an annex to the 1954 military assistance agreement between the United States and Honduras, can be abrogated with little notice.

Budget:

Although the base was downsized and reorganized in 1995, little information is available regarding current costs and levels of equipment used to maintain the base. Prior to the 1995 reorganization, the GAO reported that the total cost of operating and maintaining Soto Cano Air Force Base was over $38 million (see table). This cost was shouldered primarily by the Department of Defense, through operations and maintenance funds.[4]

During the 1995 review, the U.S. General Accounting Office suggested that Defense Department resources for base operations and maintenance (i.e., human, financial, supplies and equipment, and contracts and fees) could be eliminated and costs would either decrease or be redistributed to other agencies.

The GAO's cost estimate for 1994 was the most recent figure this study has been able to uncover so far. A subsequent GAO report released at the end of fiscal year 1995 found that "current data on the cost of the U.S. presence is not available."[5]

Costs to Operate and Maintain U.S. Military Presence at Soto Cano Base, 1994

(Thousands of U.S. dollars)

Cost Elements	1994
Contracts and fees	9,510.9
Army Flying Hours Program	7,900.0
Supplies and Equipment	6,075.6
Per Diem and Transport	6,000.0
Travel and Transport	1,012.2
Civilian Salaries	1,003.2
U.S. Air Force Costs	6,790.0
Total	**38,291.90**

Guantánamo Bay Naval Station
Cuba

The Guantánamo Bay Naval Station is located in an isolated area at the southeastern tip of the island of Cuba. The U.S. Navy has maintained a presence at Guantánamo since 1903, when the area was acquired as a coaling and naval station. The original lease agreement signed between U.S. President Theodore Roosevelt and Cuban President Estrada Palma gave the United States "the right to exercise complete jurisdiction and control within and over the area. In turn, the U.S. recognized the ultimate sovereignty of Cuba over the leased areas."[1] This original agreement was reaffirmed by a treaty signed in 1934 by President Franklin Roosevelt.

The lease on the Guantánamo property is perpetual, with no termination date or fixed number of years. The land can revert to Cuban control only if abandoned or by mutual agreement, neither of which has occurred. Fidel Castro's assumption of power in Cuba in 1959 did not change the status of the Guantánamo Bay base; the naval station may be the only permanent overseas U.S. presence within a country that U.S. foreign policy regards as hostile. For decades the base's perimeter has been guarded by barbed wire, land mines and other measures.

Guantánamo Bay divides the base's land area into a "leeward" and "windward" side, connected by ferry boats and utility boats. The leeward side hosts all flight operations; the larger windward side contains housing units, a naval hospital, recreational facilities and other services. The mission statement makes no mention of U.S.-Cuban relations.

The base's mission, according to its web page, is to provide "logistical support to Caribbean operations, to limited joint forces training and to humanitarian operations."[2]

As of September 30, 1997, according to a regular Defense Department report, there were 1,527 active-duty U.S. military personnel stationed at the base (7 Army, 1,006 Navy, 513 Marine Corps, and 1 Air Force).[3] This number does not include reservists, who may or may not have been present as well.

Operation Laser Strike

Much U.S. drug-interdiction activity in Latin American "source" countries takes place within the framework of Operation Laser Strike. Begun in April 1996, Laser Strike is an ongoing military operation, not an exercise. It seeks to block drugs transiting from source countries to the United States, whether by air, land or water. While overseen by the U.S. Southern Command and carried out mainly by military personnel, other U.S. agencies, such as the Drug Enforcement Administration (DEA) and the Coast Guard, take part in the operation. Laser Strike operates in seven countries: Bolivia, Brazil, Colombia, Ecuador, Panama, Peru and Venezuela.

According to a U.S. Army War College publication, Laser Strike evolved from several series of operations held during the early 1990s. Operations Support Justice, Steady State and Green Clover sought to interdict air traffic in the Andean countries between 1991 and 1996. While these focused on aerial interdiction only, Operation Ghost Zone in Bolivia's Chapare region combined air, land, and riverine activities.[1]

Laser Strike, too, is an aerial, maritime and terrestrial operation. According to a Pentagon spokesman, it is "what we would call in military terms, a multi-phased operation. So there's times when we would concentrate on maritime interdiction and other times we might be concentrating more on ground interdiction or air interdiction. But the idea is to sort of mesh all of these operations as often as possible so that we provide a fairly complete screen."[2]

The U.S. role in Laser Strike is "support and assistance." U.S. personnel provide training and technical support, as well as intelligence to help host countries track, identify, and interdict narcotrafficking. Host-country security forces themselves are encouraged to use these skills and intelligence for what the military calls "endgame" operations -- activities such as intercepting planes, boarding boats or shutting down drug-processing laboratories. "Southcom's efforts during Laser Strike," reports the White House's Office of National Drug Control Policy (ONDCP), "have sparked wide-sweeping river and ground-based counterdrug operations by the Colombian military and has motivated significant cooperation between the governments of Peru, Colombia, and Brazil to improve interdiction effectiveness."[3]

The operation has focused strongly on the "air bridge" through which narcotraffickers fly cocaine base between cultivation areas in Peru and processing sites in Colombia. U.S. personnel monitor the region's skies for suspicious aircraft, which host-country forces then interdict. "Last year alone," reports Southcom chief Gen. Charles Wilhelm, "27 narcotrafficking aircraft were either shot down, strafed, or seized by Peruvian and Colombian endgame forces."[4]

As part of Laser Strike, Venezuela has allowed U.S. aircraft to over-fly its territory to monitor suspicious aircraft. In 1997, according to the State Department's March 1998 *International Narcotics Control Strategy Report (INCSR)*, Venezuelan forces cooperated with U.S. counterparts on sixteen hot pursuits.[5] In Peru and Ecuador, Coast Guard and U.S. Customs teams carried out port security surveys in 1997 "in cooperation with Operation Laser Strike."[6]

U.S. troops participating in the operation are generally on temporary assignments, rotated in and out with some frequency. Many of those -- including 40 percent of flight crews -- are either reservists or National Guard personnel. Their presence is nonetheless significant, as ONDCP chief (or "Drug Czar") Barry McCaffrey explained to a congressional committee in 1996:

> On any particular day there are about 20 U.S. Coast Guard, Customs, and DOD [Department of Defense] aircraft involved in source country counter-drug operations. Approximately 300 additional military personnel are deployed in South America supporting operation Laser Strike. These military personnel operate Ground Based Radar sites in remote Andean locations, fly detection and monitoring aircraft, and provide operational and intelligence support to our allies participating in this regional operation. Our AWACS, P3B's, SIGINT (Signals Intelligence), PHOTINT (Photographic Intelligence), and FLIR (Forward Looking Infrared Radar) aircraft all operate in complete prior coordination with regional governments and military authorities.[7]

Aircraft used to detect possible drug flights, according to a Southcom publication, "include E-3 Sentry AWACS [Airborne Warning and Control System aircraft], C-130 Hercules, P-3 Orions and the unique C-27 (only 10 exist in the Air Force)."[8] The U.S. Air Force's 24th Wing, based at Howard Air Force Base in Panama, handles most of these flights. Eighty percent of flights in and out of Howard today are counter-drug related.

Howard also hosts Joint Inter-Agency Task Force South (JIATF-South), also known as the Joint Air Operations Center, which coordinates the planes carrying out counter-drug monitoring missions. Established in August 1992, JIATF-South "detects, monitors, and tracks suspected drug activity in the source zone with a focus on the Republic of Panama and the landmass of South America."[9] The task force passes the information it gathers about drug shipments to host-country law enforcement agencies. Colombia, Ecuador, Peru and Venezuela maintain liaison officers at JIATF-South, who "assist in passing information between the United States and their countries, and help in acquiring clearances concerning drug enforcement-related flights that cross their borders."[10] JIATF-South is manned by 20 to 25 airmen per 12-hour shift; many of these are on temporary duty.[11]

JIATF-South also coordinates information gathered by ground-based radar stations (GBRs). Three of these are located in Peru (Iquitos, Andoas and Pucallpa) and two in Colombia. Most are located on host-country military bases; within the stations themselves, however, U.S. personnel are in charge of their own security. The radar sites are usually manned by personnel from several branches of the U.S. military, including some National Guard and reserves. One is operated entirely by marines. "A typical detachment," according to a Southcom publication, "consists of 36 to 45 personnel. Perhaps 30 to 40 percent are radar technicians. Since GBRs are essentially self-contained units, everyone from cooks to security guards are among those based at the sites. ... Duty at these remote posts varies from two weeks to six months, depending on service status, rank and specialty."[12]

U.S. Support Group
Haiti

In October 1994, the United States led a multinational effort to remove a military government in Haiti that had deposed elected President Jean-Bertrand Aristide three years earlier. Though the U.S. military quickly scaled down its participation in United Nations-led peacekeeping efforts, the U.S. Southern Command (Southcom) maintains a significant exercise and humanitarian-assistance presence in Haiti.

"U.S. Support Group Haiti," established by presidential order and designed by a U.S. government inter-agency working group, is an open-ended mission, meaning that no end date has been set. As of March 1998 there were about 200 Army personnel deployed in Haiti; according to a Defense Department fact sheet, 239 military personnel (204 Army and 35 Marines) were in Haiti on September 30, 1997.[1]

The support group, according to Southcom Commander-in Chief Gen. Charles Wilhelm, is in Haiti "to provide command, control and logistical support to U.S. forces conducting port calls and exercises."[2] Its only security mission, adds Wilhelm, is the protection of U.S. forces carrying out exercises, training and humanitarian missions.

The military's humanitarian and civic assistance mission is extensive in Haiti. In 1998, U.S. forces will build or renovate six schools, drill five wells and conduct 130 medical site visits. Nine Navy and Coast Guard port calls in Port-au-Prince will include civic assistance projects.[3]

U.S. forces in Haiti are also assisting the country's new Coast Guard, which must confront a great deal of drug smuggling through Haitian waters. The U.S. military will begin building a "maritime operational facility" in Jacmel in mid-summer 1998, which "will enhance the U.S. and Haitian Coast Guard's ability to combat the illegal flow of drugs from South America into Haiti."[4]

Special forces under Southcom form Ministerial Advisory Teams, attached to the U.S. Embassy in Haiti, which "provide advice and assistance at the highest levels of the Haitian government on issues such as prisoner registry, enforcing customs laws and contraband control."[5]

Operation Safe Border

Ecuador – Peru

The Military Observer Mission Ecuador - Peru (MOMEP) is an international peacekeeping force established to oversee the cease-fire agreement that ended a brief 1995 border conflict between Ecuador and Peru. The mission remains in place pending the approval of a treaty settling the two countries' border dispute.

MOMEP, which includes personnel from the United States, Argentina, Brazil and Chile, was "conceived and implemented by U.S. Southern Command," according to a Pentagon publication.[1] The mission is fully funded by Peru and Ecuador. The peacekeepers' presence allowed 5,000 Ecuadorian and Peruvian troops to vacate the zone of conflict.

"Operation Safe Border" is the name given to the U.S. Southern Command (Southcom) military contingent participating in MOMEP. The operation was the first use of U.S. special forces in a muliti-national observer mission in South America.[2]

In December 1997, Southcom transferred most MOMEP support responsibilities to Brazil, Chile and Argentina. Brazil now has "the lead support role for supply and services, base support, maps and photos, ground transportation and general security."[3] By mid-January 1998, Operation Safe Border (the U.S. contingent) was scheduled to be reduced from 62 to 21 people.[4]

Southcom Commander-in-Chief Gen. Charles Wilhelm supports this reduced U.S. role, telling Congress in March 1998, "I believe MOMEP serves as a model for future peacekeeping situations as the U.S. transitions to a guiding vice leading role."[5]

Demining in Central America

Special operations forces within the U.S. Southern Command (Southcom) are assisting the Organization of American States (OAS) and the Inter-American Defense Board (IADB) in efforts to clear the tens of thousands of land mines left behind after Central America's civil wars. The OAS/IADB Assistance Mission for the Removal of Mines in Central America (MOMENCA), based in the Honduran town of Danlí near the Nicaraguan border, is made up of soldiers from the United States, Honduras, Nicaragua, Costa Rica, Colombia, Venezuela and Brazil. U.S. forces provide training, technical advice and logistical support.

Demining operations are ongoing in Honduras, Costa Rica and Nicaragua; on February 5, 1998, Guatemala was approved for demining as well. The IADB and Southcom carried out "a resource determination and site survey in Guatemala" in March 1998, and on-site demining was set to begin shortly afterward.[1]

"As a derivative benefit," notes Southcom Commander-in-Chief Gen. Charles Wilhelm, "the Department of Defense has been actively engaged with the Nicaraguan military for the first time in over a decade."[2]

Assistance by Country

Antigua and Barbuda

Arms Transfers

Subcategory	Program	1996 actual	1997 actual	1998 estimated	1999 requested
Sales and Leases	Foreign Military Sales	$174,000	$262,000	$110	$110,000
	Direct Commercial Sales	$12,363 (Licenses) Less than $500 (Deliveries as of March 1997)	$1,000 (Licenses) $0 (Deliveries as of March 1998)	$1,000 (Expected deliveries)	$1,000 (Expected deliveries)
	Section 1004 Counterdrug		Amount for equipment unknown; total account $18,000	$0	
	Excess Property	$0	Disaster relief and medical supplies $640,246		
	Emergency Drawdowns	$8,500,000 (Shared with Eastern Caribbean)	$1,500,000 (Shared with Eastern Caribbean)		
	Foreign Military Financing	$2,000,000 (Caribbean Regional Fund)	$2,000,000 (Caribbean Regional Fund)	$3,000,000 (Caribbean Regional Fund)	$3,000,000 (Caribbean Regional Fund)

Training and Education

Subcategory	Program	1996 actual	1997 actual	1998 estimate	1999 requested
Funding	International Military Education and Training	$100,000; 11 students	$93,000; 13 students	$115,000; 16 students	$115,000; 16 students
	Expanded IMET	$6,091; 1 student, 0 civilians	$4,958; 1 student, 0 civilians		
	Section 1004 Counterdrug		Amount for training unknown; total account $18,000	$0	

Argentina

Highlights of U.S. security assistance to Argentina

- Argentina is the only country in Latin America and the Caribbean to have gained major non-NATO ally (MNNA) status.
- Argentina was offered more excess defense articles (EDA) than any other country in Latin America and the Caribbean in 1996 and 1997.
- Argentina was second in the region in Direct Commercial Sales (DCS) licenses in 1997.
- Argentina was the region's second-largest recipient of International Military Education and Training (IMET) assistance in 1996, and the third-largest in 1997.
- Argentina was the region's second-largest recipient of Expanded IMET assistance in 1996, and the fourth-largest in 1997.

Arms Transfers

Subcategory	Program	1996 actual	1997 actual	1998 estimated	1999 requested
Sales and Leases	Foreign Military Sales	$17,382,000	$18,981,000	$20,000,000	$20,000,000
	Direct Commercial Sales	$81,579,458 (Licenses)	$198,780,000 (Licenses)		
		$741,000 (Deliveries as of March 1997)	$3,283,000 (Deliveries as of March 1998)	$25,626,000 (Estimated deliveries)	$99,423 (Estimated deliveries)
Grants	Excess Defense Articles Grants	$17,879,800 offered (current value)	$23,352 offered (current value)		
	Section 1004 Counterdrug		Amount for equipment unknown; total account $274,000	Amount for equipment unknown; total account $261,000	

Training and Education

Subcategory	Program	1996 actual	1997 actual	1998 estimated	1999 requested
Funding	International Military Education and Training	$542,000; 186 students	$603,000; 179 students	$600,000; 178 students	$600,000; 178 students
	Expanded IMET	$213,259; 140 students, 78 civilians	$141,724; 55 students, 28 civilians		
	Sales of training and education through FMS	$0	$506,029 (included in FMS above)		
	Section 1004 Counterdrug		Amount for training unknown; total account $274,000	Amount for training unknown; total account $261,000	
Spanish-language institutions	School of the Americas	14 students, 1.5% of total	18 students, 2.0% of total		
	Inter-American Air Forces Academy	7 students, 1.1% of total	19 students, 3.0% of total		
Exercises			- Fuerzas Unidas Cabanas 97, 10/96 - Skills Exchange, 3-4/97 - UNITAS 97, 7-11/97 - Skills Exchange, 7-8/97 - Fuerzas Unidas Southam Peacekeeping 97, 8/97 - Fuerzas Unidas Counterdrug 97, 8/97	- Skills Exchange, 7-8/98 - Cabanas 98, 7-9/98	

Aruba

Arms Transfers

Subcategory	Program	1996 actual	1997 actual	1998 estimated	1999 requested
Sales and Leases	Direct Commercial Sales	$190,871 (Licenses)	$62,000 (Licenses)		
		$2,000 (Deliveries as of March 1997)	$5,000 (Deliveries as of March 1998)	$25,000 (Expected deliveries)	$31,000 (Expected deliveries)

The Bahamas

Highlights of U.S. security assistance to the Bahamas

- In 1996 and 1997, the Bahamas was the number-one recipient of International Narcotics Control (INC) assistance among Caribbean countries.
- In 1997, the Bahamas received more counternarcotics assistance through the Defense Department's "section 1004" account than any other Caribbean country.

Arms Transfers

Subcategory	Program	1996 actual	1997 actual	1998 estimated	1999 requested
Sales and Leases	Foreign Military Sales	$0	$51,000	$2,010,000	$2,010,000
	Direct Commercial Sales	$59,680 (Licenses)	$9,000 (Licenses)		
		$0 (Deliveries as of March 1997)	$6,000 (Deliveries as of March 1998)	$7,000 (Expected deliveries)	$5,000 (Expected deliveries)

Grants	**Section 1004 Counterdrug**		Amount for equipment unknown; total account $507,000	Amount for equipment unknown; total account $150,000	
	Foreign Military Financing	$2,000,000 (Caribbean Regional Fund)	$2,000,000 (Caribbean Regional Fund)	$3,000,000 (Caribbean Regional Fund)	$3,000,000 (Caribbean Regional Fund)
	FMF "in the pipeline" from previous years	$64,000			
	International Narcotics Control	Amount for equipment unknown; total account $700,000	Amount for equipment unknown; total account $800,000	Amount for equipment unknown; total account $500,000	Amount for equipment unknown; total account $1,000,000

Training and Education

Subcategory	Program	1996 actual	1997 actual	1998 estimated	1999 requested
Funding	**International Military Education and Training**	$100,000; 19 students	$107,000; 12 students	$100,000; 11 students	$100,000; 11 students
	Expanded IMET	$11,429; 1 student, 0 civilians	$15,430; 2 students, 0 civilians		
	International Narcotics Control	Amount for training unknown; total account $700,000	Amount for training unknown; total account $800,000	Amount for training unknown; total account $500,000	Amount for training unknown; total account $1,000,000
	Section 1004 Counterdrug			Amount for training unknown; total account $507,000	Amount for training unknown, total account $150,000

Bases and Other Presences

- **Operation Bahamas and Turks and Caicos (OPBAT)**

Barbados

Arms Transfers

Subcategory	Program	1996 actual	1997 actual	1998 estimated	1999 requested
Sales and Leases	Foreign Military Sales	$ 539,000	$139,000	$110,000	$110,000
	Direct Commercial Sales	$45,993 (Licenses)	$96,000 (Licenses)		
		$9,000 (Deliveries as of March 1997)	$8,000 (Deliveries as of March 1998)	$14,000 (Expected deliveries)	$47,000 (Expected deliveries)
Grants	Emergency Drawdowns	$8,500,000 shared with Eastern Caribbean	$1,500,000 shared with Eastern Caribbean		
	Excess Property	$0	Disaster relief and medical supplies $295,976		
	Section 1004 Counterdrug		Amount for equipment unknown; total account $151,000	Amount for equipment unknown; total account $391,000	
	Foreign Military Financing	$2,000,000 (Caribbean Regional Fund)	$2,000,000 (Caribbean Regional Fund)	$3,000,000 (Caribbean Regional Fund)	$3,000,000 (Caribbean Regional Fund)

Training and Education

Subcategory	Program	1996 actual	1997 actual	1998 estimate	1999 requested
Funding	International Military Education and Training	$100,000; 12 students	$103,000; 9 students	$92,000; 8 students	$90,000; 8 students
	Expanded IMET	$3,705; 2 students, 0 civilians	$0		
	Section 1004 Counterdrug		Amount for training unknown; total account $151,000	Amount for training unknown; total account $391,000	

155

Belize

Highlights of U.S. security assistance to Belize

- Belize was the only Central American country to be offered excess defense articles (EDA) in 1997.
- Belize hosted "New Horizons," a six-month humanitarian and civic assistance (HCA) exercise, in 1997.

Arms Transfers

Subcategory	Program	1996 actual	1997 actual	1998 estimated	1999 requested
Sales and Leases	Foreign Military Sales	$314,000	$327,000	$10,000	$10,000
	Direct Commercial Sales	$1,411,548 (Licenses)	$95,000 (Licenses)		
		$14,000 (Deliveries as of March 1997)	$6,000 (Deliveries as of March 1998)	$125,000 (Expected deliveries)	$706,000 (Expected deliveries)
Grants	Excess Property	Medical supplies / equipment $482,780	Medical supplies $734,692		
	Section 1004 Counterdrug		Amount for equipment unknown; total account $224,000	Amount for equipment unknown; total account $219,000	
	Foreign Military Financing "in the pipeline" from previous years	$11,000 pre-1992 MAP funds			

Training and Education

Subcategory	Program	1996 actual	1997 actual	1998 estimated	1999 requested
Funding	International Military Education and Training	$250,000; 81 students	$208,000; 49 students	$250,000; 59 students	$250,000; 59 students
	Expanded IMET	$43,980; 81 students, 1 civilians	$14,634; 2 students, 0 civilians		
	Section 1004 Counterdrug		Amount for training unknown; total account $224,000	Amount for training unknown; total account $219,000	
Spanish-language Institutions	Inter-American Air Forces Academy	0 students	2 students, 2.1% of total		
Exercises			- Fuerzas Aliadas Humanitarian, February 1997; - Fuerzas Aliadas Centam Peacekeeping, May 1997; - New Horizons, January-June 1997	- Fuerzas Aliadas Humanitarian, January-February 1998; - Fuerzas Aliadas Centam Peacekeeping, May 1998	
	Humanitarian and Civic Assistance incidental costs	$263,859.53	$389,141		

Bermuda

Arms Transfers

Subcategory	Program	1996 actual	1997 actual	1998 estimated	1999 requested
Sales and Leases	Direct Commercial Sales	$1,071,319 (Licenses)	$68,000 (Licenses)		
		$10,000 (Deliveries as of March 1997)	$6,000 (Deliveries as of March 1998)	$114,000 (Expected deliveries)	$536,000 (Expected deliveries)

Bolivia

Highlights of U.S. security assistance to Bolivia

- The International Narcotics Control (INC) program spent more in Bolivia than in any other Latin American or Caribbean country in 1996 and 1997 (not including inter-regional aviation funds, which are counted separately). Bolivia's INC funding, however, is expected to fall by almost 75 percent in 1998. The State Department's 1999 Congressional Presentation for Foreign Operations calls for a restoration of 1997 funding levels in 1999.
- Bolivia was the region's fourth-largest recipient of International Military Education and Training (IMET) assistance in 1996 and 1997.
- Bolivia was the region's fourth-largest recipient of Expanded IMET assistance in 1996, and the sixth-largest in 1997.
- Bolivian personnel ranked sixth in the region in attendance at the School of the Americas in 1996, and fifth in 1997.
- Bolivian personnel ranked fifth in the region in attendance at the Inter-American Air Forces Academy in 1996, and third in 1997.

Arms Transfers

Subcategory	Program	1996 actual	1997 actual	1998 estimated	1999 requested
Sales and Leases	Foreign Military Sales	$378,000	$3,000	$1,500,000	$1,500,000
		Intl. Narc. $10,265,000	Intl. Narc. $9,124,000	Intl. Narc. $4,600,000	Intl. Narc. $4,900,000
	Direct Commercial Sales	$2,158,361 (Licenses)	$1,666,000 (Licenses)		
		$249,000 (Deliveries as of March 1997)	$94,000 (Deliveries as of March 1998)	$384,000 (Expected deliveries)	$1,087,000 (Expected deliveries)
	Excess Defense Articles Grants	$4,500 offered (current value)	$0		

Subcategory	Program	1996 actual	1997 actual	1998 estimated	1999 requested
Grants	Section 1004 Counterdrug		Amount for equipment unknown; total account $2,147,000	Amount for equipment unknown; total account $2,052,000	
	Foreign Military Financing "in the pipeline" from previous years	$10,000 pre-1992 MAP funds; $21,000 uncommitted FMF; $236,000 counternarcotics FMF			
	International Narcotics Control	Amount for equipment unknown; total account: $30,000,000	Amount for equipment unknown; total account: $45,500,000	Amount for equipment unknown; total account: $12,000,000	Amount for equipment unknown; total account: $45,000,000

Training and Education

Subcategory	Program	1996 actual	1997 actual	1998 estimated	1999 requested
Funding	International Military Education and Training	$535,000; 133 students	$509,000; 163 students	$550,000; 176 students	$550,000; 176 students
	Expanded IMET	$170,557; 42 students, 0 civilians	$125,700; 44 students		
	International Narcotics Control	Amount for training unknown; total account $15,000,000	Amount for training unknown; total account: $45,500,000	Amount for training unknown; total account: $12,000,000	Amount for training unknown; total account: $45,000,000
	Sales of training and education through FMS	Int'l Narc. $1,744,990 (included in FMS above)	$0		
	Section 1004 Counterdrug		Amount for training unknown; total account $2,147,000	Amount for training unknown; total account $2,052,000	
Spanish-language institutions	School of the Americas	55 students; 5.9% of total	42 students; 4.6% of total		
	Inter-American Air Forces Academy	61 students, 9.7% of total	91 students, 10.3% of total		

Subcategory	Program	1996 actual	1997 actual	1998 estimated	1999 requested
Exercises			- Fuerzas Unidas Cabanas 97, October 1996; - Fuerzas Unidas Southam Peacekeeping 97, August 1997	- Skills Exchange, February-March 1998; - Cabanas 98, July-September 1998	
	Humanitarian and Civic Assistance incidental costs	$21,300.92	$148,849		

Bases and Other Presences

Subcategory	Program	1997 actual	1998 estimated
Counternarcotics detection, monitoring and interdiction	Section 1004/124	$70,000	$51,000

Brazil

Highlights of U.S. security assistance to Brazil

- Brazil was first in the region in Foreign Military Sales (FMS) agreements in 1996, and fourth in 1997.
- Brazil was fifth in the region in Direct Commercial Sales (DCS) licenses in 1996, and third in 1997.
- In 1997, Brazil was fifth in the region in counternarcotics assistance through the Defense Department's "section 1004" account.

Arms Transfers

Subcategory	Program	1996 actual	1997 actual	1998 estimated	1999 requested
Sales and Leases	Foreign Military Sales	$169,283,000	$24,962,000	$28,000,000	$23,500,000
	Direct Commercial Sales	$75,941,338 (Licenses)	$191,334,000 (Licenses)		
		$945,000 (Deliveries as of March 1997)	$4,029,000 (Deliveries as of March 1998)	$22,584,000 (Expected deliveries)	$91,261,000 (Expected deliveries)
	Leased Defense Articles	$14,176,000 replacement value; $0 total rental charge			
Grants	Excess Property	$0	2 ambulances $87,986		
	Section 1004 Counterdrug		Amount for equipment unknown; total account $3,096,000	Amount for equipment unknown; total account $3,632,000	
	International Narcotics Control	Amount for equipment unknown; total account: $290,000	Amount for equipment unknown; Total account: $700,000	Amount for equipment unknown; Total account: $500,000	Amount for equipment unknown; total account: $1,200,000

Training and Education

Subcategory	Program	1996 actual	1997 actual	1998 estimated	1999 requested
Funding	International Military Education and Training	$200,000; 38 students	$222,000; 41 students	$225,000; 42 students	$225,000; 42 students
	Expanded IMET	$555; 1 student, 0 civilians	$0		
	International Narcotics Control	Amount for training unknown; total account $290,000	Amount for training unknown; total account $700,000	Amount for training unknown; total account $500,000	Amount for training unknown; total account $1,200,000
	Sales of training and education through FMS	$1,942,025 (included in FMS above)	$1,019,791 (included in FMS above)		
	Section 1004 Counterdrug		Amount for training unknown; total account $3,096,000	Amount for training unknown; total account $3,632,000	
Spanish-language institutions	School of the Americas	2 students; 0.2% of total	1 student; 0.1% of total		
	Inter-American Air Forces Academy	2 students; 0.32% of total	24 students; 2.7% of total		
Exercises			- Skills Exchange, March-April 1997; - UNITAS 97, July- November 1997; - Skills Exchange, July-August 1997; - Fuerzas Unidas Southam Peacekeeping 97, August 1997; - Fuerzas Unidas Counterdrug 97, August 1997	Skills Exchange, July- August 1998	

British Virgin Islands

Arms Transfers

Subcategory	Program	1996 actual	1997 actual	1998 estimate	1999 estimate
Sales and Leases	Direct Commercial Sales	$346 (Licenses)	$4,000 (Licenses)		
		"Less than $500" (Deliveries as of March 1997)	$4,000 (Deliveries as of March 1998)	"Less than $500" (Expected deliveries)	

Cayman Islands

Arms Transfers

Subcategory	Program	1996 actual	1997 actual	1998 estimate	1999 estimate
Sales and Leases	Direct Commercial Sales	$0 (Licenses)	$7,000 (Licenses)		
			$0 (Deliveries as of March 1998)	$4,000 (Expected deliveries)	$14,000 (Expected deliveries)

Chile

Highlights of U.S. security assistance to Chile

- Chilean personnel ranked first in the region in attendance at the School of the Americas in 1996, and second in 1997.
- Chile was sixth in the region in Direct Commercial Sales (DCS) licenses in 1996, and fifth in 1997.

Arms Transfers

Subcategory	Program	1996 actual	1997 actual	1998 estimated	1999 requested
Sales and Leases	Foreign Military Sales	$2,512,000	$2,322,000	$16,500,000	$26,000,000
	Direct Commercial Sales	$44,527,076 (Licenses)	$32,564,000 (Licenses)		
		$417,000 (Deliveries as of March 1997)	$1,028,000 (Deliveries as of March 1998)	$5,737,000 (Expected deliveries)	$12,271,000 (Expected deliveries)
	Leased Defense Articles	$6,364,000 replacement value; $1,004,000 rental cost	$5,303,000 replacement value; $1,148,000 rental cost		
	Excess Defense Articles Sales	$0	$47,000 offered (current value)		
Grants	Excess property	Medical supplies / equipment $368,726	$0		
	Excess Defense Articles Grants	$486,700 offered (current value)	$0		
	Section 1004 Counterdrug			Amount for equipment unknown; total account $112,000	Amount for equipment unknown; total account $68,000

Training and Education

Subcategory	Program	1996 actual	1997 actual	1998 estimated	1999 requested
Funding	International Military Education and Training	$366,000; 187 students	$395,000; 167 students	$450,000; 190 students	$450,000; 190 students
	Expanded IMET	$77,803; 13 students, 9 civilians	$40,985; 8 students, 6 civilians		
	Sales of training and education through FMS	$36,115 (included in FMS above)	$0		
	Section 1004 Counterdrug			Amount for training unknown; total account $112,000	Amount for training unknown; total account $68,000

Subcategory	Program	1996 actual	1997 actual	1998 estimated	1999 requested
Spanish-language institutions	School of the Americas	150 students; 16% of total	145 students; 16.0% of total		
	Inter-American Air Forces Academy	5 students; 0.8% of total	3 students; 0.3% of total		
Exercises			- Skills Exchange March-April 1997; - UNITAS 97, July-November 1997; - Fuerzas Unidas Chile, July 1997; - Skills Exchange, July-August 1997	- Cabanas 98, July-September 1998	

Colombia

Highlights of U.S. security assistance to Colombia

- Colombia was the region's third-largest recipient of funding through the International Narcotics Control (INC) program in 1996, and the second-largest in 1997. INC funding for Colombia, however, is expected to rise dramatically in 1998. Non-binding report language accompanying the 1998 foreign operations appropriations law (P.L. 105-118) instructs the State Department to use $36 million of the 1998 INC account to buy three UH-60 Blackhawk helicopters for Colombia's National Police. An additional $14 million will be spent to upgrade ten to twelve UH-1H Huey utility helicopters.
- Together with Peru, Colombia will receive counternarcotics military assistance through a special authorization in the defense budget (known as "section 1033") between 1998 and 2002.
- In 1997, Colombia was first in the region in counternarcotics assistance through the Defense Department's "section 1004" account.
- Colombia was second in the region in Foreign Military Sales (FMS) agreements in 1996, and first in 1997.
- Colombian personnel ranked third in the region in attendance at the School of the Americas in 1996 and 1997.
- Colombian personnel ranked second in the region in attendance at the Inter-American Air Forces Academy in 1996 and 1997.
- Colombia was fourth in the region in Direct Commercial Sales (DCS) licenses in 1997.
- Narcotics decertification kept Colombia from receiving International Military Education and Training (IMET) assistance for most of 1996 and all of 1997.

Arms Transfers

Subcategory	Program	1996 actual	1997 actual	1998 estimated	1999 requested
Sales and Leases	Foreign Military Sales	$45,822,000	$74,987,000	$18,000,000	$18,000,000
		Intl. Narc. $19,425,000	Intl. Narc. $0	Intl. Narc. $10,000,000	Intl. Narc. $10,000,000
	Direct Commercial Sales	$27,934.542 (Licenses)	$39,077,000 (Licenses)		
		$5,536,000 (Deliveries as of March 1997)	$6,223,000 (Deliveries as of March 1998)	$5,217,000 (Expected deliveries)	$19,617,000 (Expected deliveries)

Subcategory	Program	1996 actual	1997 actual	1998 estimated	1999 requested
Grants	Emergency Drawdowns	$40,500,000	$14,200,000		
	Section 1033 Counterdrug	$0	$0	$1,000,000	
	Section 1004 Counterdrug		Amount for equipment unknown; total account $7,411,000	Amount for equipment unknown; total account $7,341,000	
	Foreign Military Financing "in the pipeline" from previous years	$70,000 pre-1992 MAP funds; Up to $7,131,000 counternarcotico FMF Note: A special presidential waiver in August 1997 released unspent FMF valued at up to $30,000,000.			
	International Narcotics Control	Amount for equipment unknown; total account $16,000,000	Amount for equipment unknown; total account $33,450,000	Amount for equipment unknown; total account $80,000,000	Amount for equipment unknown; total account $45,000,000
	ONDCP discretionary funds	$0	$500,000	$0	

Training and Education

Subcategory	Program	1996 actual	1997 actual	1998 estimated	1999 requested
Funding	International Military Education and Training	$147,000; 32 students	$0; 0 students	$900,000; 100 students	$800,000 89 students
	Expanded IMET	$50,679; 3 students, 0 civilians	$0		
	International Narcotics Control	Amount for training unknown; total account $16,000,000	Amount for training unknown; total account $33,450,000	Amount for training unknown; total account $80,000,000	Amount for training unknown; total account $45,000,000
	Sales of training and education through FMS	$635,615 (included in FMS above)	$1,376,673 (included in FMS above)		
		Int'l Narc. $129,625 (included in FMS above)	$0		
	Section 1004 Counterdrug		Amount for training unknown; total account $7,411,000	Amount for training unknown; total account $7,341,000	

167

Subcategory	Program	1996 actual	1997 actual	1998 estimated	1999 requested
Spanish-language institutions	School of the Americas	139 students; 14.8% of total	99 students; 10.9% of total		
	Inter-American Air Forces Academy	92 students; 14.6% of total	128 students; 14.5% of total		
Exercises			- UNITAS 97, 7-11/97 - Fuerzas Unidas Counterdrug 97, 8/97	Skills Exchange, 2-3/98	

Bases and Other Presences

Subcategory	Program	1997 actual	1998 estimate
Counternarcotics detection, monitoring and interdiction	Section 1004/124	$25,472,000	$14,687,000
	Section 124	$7,872,000	$9,480,000

Costa Rica

Highlights of U.S. security assistance to Costa Rica

- Costa Rican personnel ranked first among Central American nations in attendance at the Inter-American Air Forces Academy in 1997.

Arms Transfers

Subcategory	Program	1996 actual	1997 actual	1998 estimated	1999 requested
Sales and Leases	Foreign Military Sales	$916,000	$175,000	$4,400,000	$11,010,000
	Direct Commercial Sales	$6,614,808 (Licenses)	$1,653,000 (Licenses)		
		$172,000 (Deliveries as of March 1997)	$215,000 (Deliveries as of March 1998)	$327,000 (Expected deliveries)	$810,000 (Expected deliveries)
	Excess Defense Articles Grants	$137.75 offered (current value)	$0		
Grants	Excess Property	$0	Medical supplies $695,286		
	Section 1004 Counterdrug		Amount for equipment unknown; total account $133,000	Amount for equipment unknown; total account $127,000	
	FMF "in the pipeline" from previous years	$3,000 pre-1992 MAP funds			

169

Training and Education

Subcategory	Program	1996 actual	1997 actual	1998 estimated	1999 requested
Funding	International Military Education and Training	$198,000; 69 students	$200,000; 92 students	$200,000; 92 students	$200,000; 92 students
	Expanded IMET	$43,236; 13 students, 0 civilians	$67,244; 19 students, 0 civilians		
	Section 1004 Counterdrug		Amount for training unknown; total account $133,000	Amount for training unknown; total account $127,000	
Spanish-language institutions	School of the Americas	17 students; 1.8% of total	22 students; 2.4% of total		
	Inter-American Air Forces Academy	21 students; 3.3% of total	32 students; 3.6% of total		
Exercises			Fuerzas Aliadas Humanitarian 97, February 1997		
	Humanitarian Civic Assistance incidental costs	$54,052.29	$57,038		

Bases and Other Presences

- **De-mining (MOMENCA)**

Dominica

Arms Transfers

Subcategory	Program	1996 actual	1997 actual	1998 estimated	1999 requested
Sales and Leases	Foreign Military Sales	$182,000	$0	$110,000	$110,000
	Direct Commercial Sales	$6,400 (Licenses)	$0 (Licenses)		
		$0 (Deliveries as of March 1997)	$0 (Deliveries as of March 1998)	$1,000 (Expected deliveries)	$3,000 (Expected deliveries)
Grants	Excess property	$0	Disaster relief and medical supplies $237,029		
	Emergency Drawdowns	$8,500,000 (Shared with Eastern Caribbean)	$1,500,000 (Shared with Eastern Caribbean)		
	Section 1004 Counterdrug		Amount for equipment unknown; total account $101,000	$0	
	Foreign Military Financing	$2,000,000 (Caribbean Regional Fund)	$2,000,000 (Caribbean Regional Fund)	$3,000,000 (Caribbean Regional Fund)	$3,000,000 (Caribbean Regional Fund)

Training and Education

Subcategory	Program	1996 actual	1997 actual	1998 estimated	1999 requested
Funding	International Military Education and Training	$40,000; 6 students	$32,000; 5 students	$38,000; 6 students	$40,000; 7 students
	Expanded IMET	$6,357; 1 student, 0 civilians	$2,671; 1 student, 0 civilians		
	Section 1004 Counterdrug		Amount for training unknown; total account $101,000	$0	
Exercises	Humanitarian and Civic Assistance incidental costs	$0	$75,000		

Dominican Republic

Highlights of U.S. security assistance to the Dominican Republic

- The Dominican Republic ranked first among Caribbean countries in Direct Commercial Sales (DCS) licenses in 1996 and 1997.
- The Dominican Republic was the Western Hemisphere's fifth-largest recipient of International Military Education and Training (IMET) assistance in 1996, and the second-largest in 1997. The Dominican Republic led all Caribbean nations in this category in both years.
- The Dominican Republic was the Western Hemisphere's seventh-largest recipient of Expanded IMET assistance in 1996, and the fifth in 1997. The Dominican Republic led all Caribbean nations in this category in both years.
- In 1997, the Dominican Republic was second among Caribbean countries in counternarcotics assistance received through the Defense Department's "section 1004" account.
- The Dominican Republic is the only Caribbean country to have sent students to the School of the Americas and the Inter-American Air Forces Academy in 1996 and 1997.

Arms Transfers

Subcategory	Program	1996 actual	1997 actual	1998 estimated	1999 requested
Sales and Leases	Foreign Military Sales	$418,000	$187,000	$2,000,000	$2,000,000
	Direct Commercial Sales	$2,714,978 (Licenses)	$7,319,000 (Licenses)		
		$5,000 (Deliveries as of March 1997)	$254,000 (Deliveries as of March 1998)	$1,003,000 (Expected deliveries)	$1,358,000 (Expected deliveries)

Subcategory	Program	1996 actual	1997 actual	1998 estimated	1999 requested
Grants	Excess property	Medical supplies and equipment $48,437	Medical and disaster relief supplies $990,184		
	Excess Defense Articles Grants	$17,000 offered and delivered (current value)	$223,000 offered and delivered (current value)		
	Section 1004 Counterdrug		Amount for equipment unknown; total account $436,000	Amount for equipment unknown; total account $54,000	
	Foreign Military Financing	$2,000,000 (Caribbean regional fund)	$2,000,000 (Caribbean regional fund)	$3,000,000 (Caribbean regional fund)	$3,000,000 (Caribbean regional fund)
	FMF "in the pipeline" from previous years	$56,000 pre-1992 MAP funds; $90,000 uncommitted FMF			

Training and Education

Subcategory	Program	1996 actual	1997 actual	1998 estimated	1999 requested
Funding	International Military Education and Training	$500,000; 70 students	$622,000; 70 students	$500,000; 56 students	$500,000; 56 students
	Expanded IMET	$118,828; 7 students, 0 civilians	$135,787; 11 students, 0 civilians		
	Sales of training and education through FMS	$0	$78,285		
	Section 1004 Counterdrug		Amount for training unknown; total account $436,000	Amount for training unknown; total account $54,000	
Spanish-language institutions	School of the Americas	39 students; 4.2% of total	26 students; 2.9% of total		
	Inter-American Air Forces Academy	15 students, 2.4% of total	27 students, 3.1% of total		
Exercises	Humanitarian and Civic Assistance incidental costs	$0	$75,000		

Ecuador

Highlights of U.S. security assistance to Ecuador

- Ecuador co-hosts the Ecuador-Peru Military Observer Mission (MOMEP), an international peacekeeping force -- including a U.S. military contingent -- which oversees the cease-fire that ended both countries' brief 1995 border conflict.

Arms Transfers

Subcategory	Program	1996 actual	1997 actual	1998 estimated	1999 requested
Sales and Leases	Foreign Military Sales	$1,508,000	$4,158,000	$8,510,000	$8,000,000
		Intl. Narc. $168,000	Intl. Narc. $1,812,000	Intl. Narc. $3,410,000	Intl. Narc. $1,200,000
	Direct Commercial Sales	$23,694,504 (Licenses)	$7,540,000 (Licenses)		
		$1,506,000 (Deliveries as of March 1997)	$2,720,000 (Deliveries as of March 1998)	$2,040,000 (Expected deliveries)	$6,302,000 (Expected deliveries)
Grants	Excess property	Medical supplies and equipment $579,092	Medical supplies $1,153,630		
	Excess Defense Articles Grants	$14,000 offered and delivered (current value)	$77,000 offered and delivered (current value)		
	Section 1004 Counterdrug		Amount for equipment unknown; total account $3,014,000	Amount for equipment unknown; total account $2,365,000	
	Foreign Military Financing "In the pipeline" from previous years	$24,000 pre-1992 MAP funds; $194,000 uncommitted FMF; $190,000 uncommitted counternarcotics FMF			
	International Narcotics Control	Amount for equipment unknown; total account: $500,000	Amount for equipment unknown; total account: $600,000	Amount for equipment unknown; total account: $500,000	Amount for equipment unknown; total account: $1,500,000

Training and Education

Subcategory	Program	1996 actual	1997 actual	1998 estimated	1999 requested
Funding	International Military Education and Training	$500,000; 135 students	$425,000; 118 students	$500,000; 139 students	$500,000; 139 students
	Expanded IMET	$46,621; 13 students, 1 civilians	$56,477; 15 students, 2 civilians		
	International Narcotics Control	Amount for training unknown; total account $500,000	Amount for training unknown; total account $600,000	Amount for training unknown; total account $500,000	Amount for training unknown; total account $1,500,000
	Sales of training and education through FMS	$0	Int'l Narc. $6,500 (included in FMS above)		
	Section 1004 Counterdrug		Amount for training unknown; total account $3,014,000	Amount for training unknown; total account $2,365,000	
Spanish-language institutions	School of the Americas	28 students; 3.0% of total	9 students; 1.0% of total		
	Inter-American Air Forces Academy	65 students, 10.3% of total	69 students, 7.8% of total		
Exercises			- UNITAS 97, July-November 1997; - Fuerzas Unidas Counterdrug, August 1997	- New Horizons 98, February-April 1998; - Skills Exchange, February-March 1998	
	Humanitarian Civic Assistance incidental costs	$349,504.38	$349,390		

Bases and Other Presences

• **Operation Safe Border (MOMEP)**

El Salvador

Highlights of U.S. security assistance to El Salvador

- El Salvador was the hemisphere's third-largest recipient of International Military Education and Training (IMET) assistance in 1996, and the seventh in 1997. El Salvador was first in this category among Central American countries in both years.
- El Salvador was the hemisphere's third-largest recipient of Expanded IMET assistance in 1996, and the largest recipient overall in 1997. El Salvador was first in this category among Central American countries in both years.
- El Salvador was first among Central American countries in Foreign Military Sales (FMS) agreements in 1997.
- El Salvador was second in Central America in Direct Commercial Sales (DCS) in 1996 and 1997.
- Salvadoran personnel ranked second in Central America in attendance at the School of the Americas in 1996.
- Salvadoran personnel ranked third in the hemisphere and first in Central America in attendance at the Inter-American Air Forces Academy in 1996, and second in Central America in 1997.

Arms Transfers

Subcategory	Program	1996 actual	1997 actual	1998 estimated	1999 requested
Sales and Leases	Foreign Military Sales	$19,173,000	$6,703,000	$2,100,000	$2,100,000
	Direct Commercial Sales	$7,978,534 (Licenses)	$8,244,000 (Licenses)		
		$324,000 (Deliveries as of March 1997)	$52,000 (Deliveries as of March 1998)	$1,631,000 (Expected deliveries)	$4,032,000 (Expected deliveries)
Grants	Excess property	Medical supplies and equipment $423,474	Medical supplies $644,742		
	Section 1004 Counterdrug		Amount for equipment unknown; total account $279,000	Amount for equipment unknown; total account $271,000	
	Foreign Military Financing "in the pipeline" from previous years	$1,655,000 pre-1992 MAP funds; $59,000 uncommitted FMF			

Training and Education

Subcategory	Program	1996 actual	1997 actual	1998 estimated	1999 requested
Funding	International Military Education and Training	$541,000; 207 students	$455,000; 234 students	$500,000; 257 students	$500,000; 257 students
	Expanded IMET	$212,271; 97 students, 4 civilians	$235,110; 222 students, 114 civilians		
	Sales of training and education through FMS	$27,486 (included in FMS above)	$1,630,968 (included in FMS above)		
	Section 1004 Counterdrug		Amount for training unknown; total account $279,000	Amount for training unknown; total account $271,000	
Spanish-language institutions	School of the Americas	55 students; 5.9% of total	14 students; 1.5% of total		
	Inter-American Air Forces Academy	85 students, 13.4% of total	31 students, 3.5% of total		
Exercises			- Fuerzas Aliadas Humanitarian 97, February 1997; - Fuerzas Aliadas Centam Peacekeeping 97, May 1997; - Skills Exchange, May-June 1997; - Fuerzas Aliadas Riverine 97, July 1997	- Skills Exchange, February-March 1998; - New Horizons 98, February-April 1998; - Fuerzas Aliadas Humanitarian 98, January-February 1998; - Fuerzas Aliadas Centam Peacekeeping 98, May 1998	
	Humanitarian and Civic Assistance incidental costs	$551,676.07	$122,220		

French Guiana

Highlights of U.S. security assistance to French Guiana

- French Guiana's large amount of Direct Commercial Sales (DCS) licenses (third in the hemisphere in 1996) owes to the colony's use as a base of operations for the European Space Agency. Satellite and rocketry equipment account for the vast majority of these licenses.

Arms Transfers

Subcategory	Program	1996 actual	1997 actual	1998 estimate	1999 estimate
Sales and Leases	Direct Commercial Sales	$125,439,680 (Licenses)	$5,538,000 (Licenses)		
		$1,732,000 (Deliveries as of March 1997)	$4,710,000 (Deliveries as of March 1998)	$13,098,000 (Expected deliveries)	$62,720,000 (Expected deliveries)

Grenada

Arms Transfers

Subcategory	Program	1996 actual	1997 actual	1998 estimated	1999 requested
Sales and Leases	Foreign Military Sales	$406,000	$353,000	$110,000	$110,000
	Direct Commercial Sales	$0	$68,000 (Licenses)		
		$0	$10,000 (Deliveries as of March 1998)	$7,000 (Expected deliveries)	$0 (Expected deliveries)
Grants	Excess Property	$0	Medical supplies $69,902		
	Emergency Drawdowns	$8,500,000 (Shared with Eastern Caribbean)	$1,500,000 (Shared with Eastern Caribbean)		
	Foreign Military Financing	$2,000,000 (Caribbean regional fund)	$2,000,000 (Caribbean regional fund)	$3,000,000 (Caribbean regional fund)	$3,000,000 (Caribbean regional fund)

Training and Education

Subcategory	Program	1996 actual	1997 actual	1998 estimated	1999 requested
Funding	International Military Education and Training	$40,000; 9 students	$49,000; 7 students	$49,000; 7 students	$50,000; 7 students
	Expanded IMET	$7,008; 1 student, 0 civilians	$0		

Guatemala

Highlights of U.S. security assistance to Guatemala

- Due to concerns about the military's pattern of human rights abuses, Guatemala was prohibited from receiving any assistance through the International Military Training and Education (IMET) program in 1996, and has not received regular IMET since 1995. Foreign Operations appropriations laws have limited Guatemala to expanded IMET in 1997 and 1998.
- Guatemala was the hemisphere's second-largest recipient of Expanded IMET assistance in 1997.
- Guatemala is the only Central American country for which the International Narcotics Control (INC) program maintains a permanent assistance program. In 1996 and 1997 Guatemala was the fifth-largest recipient of INC assistance in the hemisphere.

Arms Transfers

Subcategory	Program	1996 actual	1997 actual	1998 estimated	1999 requested
Sales and Leases	Direct Commercial Sales	$3,011,536 (Licenses)	$2,211,000 (Licenses)		
		$272,000 (Deliveries as of March 1997)	$303,000 (Deliveries as of March 1998)	$512,000 (Expected deliveries)	$1,517,000 (Expected deliveries)

Subcategory	Program	1996 actual	1997 actual	1998 estimated	1999 requested
Grants	Excess property	Medical supplies and equipment $557,966	Medical supplies $525,320		
	Section 1004 Counterdrug		Amount for equipment unknown; total account $806,000	Amount for equipment unknown; total account $774,000	
	Foreign Military Financing "In the pipeline" from previous years	$2,274,000 pre-1992 MAP funds; $303,000 uncommitted FMF			
	International Narcotics Control	Amount for equipment unknown; total account: $2,000,000	Amount for equipment unknown; total account: $2,000,000	Amount for equipment unknown; total account: $3,000,000	Amount for equipment unknown; total account: $4,000,000

Training and Education

Subcategory	Program	1996 actual	1997 actual	1998 estimated	1999 requested
Funding	International Military Education and Training	$0	$205,000; 122 students	$225,000; 134 students	$225,000; 134 students
	Expanded IMET	$0	$157,000; 87 students, 21 civilians		
	International Narcotics Control	Amount for training unknown; total account $2,000,000	Amount for training unknown; total account $2,000,000	Amount for training unknown; total account $3,000,000	Amount for training unknown; total account $4,000,000
	Section 1004 Counterdrug		Amount for training unknown; total account $806,000	Amount for training unknown; total account $774,000	
Spanish-language Institutions	School of the Americas	0 students	1 student, 0.1% of total		
	Inter-American Air Forces Academy	0 students	4 students, 0.5% of total		

Subcategory	Program	1996 actual	1997 actual	1998 estimated	1999 requested
Exercises			- Fuerzas Aliadas Humanitarian 97, February 1997; - Fuerzas Aliadas Centam Peacekeeping 97, May 1997; - Skills Exchange, May- June 1997	- Skills Exchange, February- March 1998; - Fuerzas Aliadas Humanitarian 98, January- February 1998; - Fuerzas Aliadas Centam Peacekeeping 98, May 1998	
	Humanitarian Civic Assistance incidental costs	$49,844.99	$117,851		

Guyana

Highlights of U.S. security assistance to Guyana

- Guyana hosted "New Horizons," a three-month humanitarian and civic assistance (HCA) exercise, in 1997.

Arms Transfers

Subcategory	Program	1996 actual	1997 actual	1998 estimated	1999 requested
Sales and Leases	Foreign Military Sales	$10,000	$70,000	$80,000	$80,000
	Direct Commercial Sales	$185,974 (Licenses)	$108,000 (Licenses)		
		$10,000 (Deliveries as of March 1997)	$22,000 (Deliveries as of March 1998)	$29,000 (Expected deliveries)	$93,000 (Expected deliveries)
Grants	Excess property	Medical supplies and equipment $623,769	Medical supplies $1,037,543		
	Foreign Military Financing "in the pipeline" from previous years	$52,000 uncommitted FMF			

Training and Education

Subcategory	Program	1996 actual	1997 actual	1998 estimated	1999 requested
Funding	International Military Education and Training	$214,000; 31 students	$178,000; 72 students	$175,000; 71 students	$175,000; 71 students
	Expanded IMET	$39,264; 3 students, 0 civilians	$37,000; 50 students, 2 civilians		
Exercises			- Fuerzas Unidas Counterdrug 97, August 1997 - New Horizons 97, July-September 1997		
	Humanitarian Civic Assistance incidental costs	$18,200	$424,541		

Haiti

Highlights of U.S. security assistance to Haiti

- Haiti hosts U.S. Support Group Haiti, a roughly 200-person U.S. military mission whose tasks include logistical support for training, exercises, and humanitarian and civic assistance deployments.
- Haiti was first among Caribbean countries in Foreign Military Sales (FMS) agreements in 1997, and second in 1996.
- Haiti was the Caribbean's third-largest recipient of International Military Education and Training (IMET) assistance in 1996 and 1997.
- Haiti was the Caribbean's second-largest recipient of Expanded IMET assistance in 1996 and 1997.

Arms Transfers

Subcategory	Program	1996 actual	1997 actual	1998 estimated	1999 requested
Sales and Leases	Foreign Military Sales	$2,063,000	$877,000	$1,000,000	$1,000,000
	Direct Commercial Sales	$157,487 (Licenses)	$61,000 (Licenses)		
		$46,000 (Deliveries as of March 1997)	$0 (Deliveries as of March 1998)	$22,000 (Expected deliveries)	$79,000 (Expected deliveries)
Grants	Emergency Drawdowns	Up to $3,000,000	$0		
	Excess Property	$0	Medical supplies $1,683,664		
	Foreign Military Financing	$2,000,000 (Caribbean regional fund)	$2,000,000 (Caribbean regional fund)	$3,000,000 (Caribbean regional fund)	$3,000,000 (Caribbean regional fund)
	FMF "in the pipeline" from previous years	$40,000 pre-1992 MAP funds; $1,000 uncommitted FMF			

Training and Education

Subcategory	Program	1996 actual	1997 actual	1998 estimated	1999 requested
Funding	International Military Education and Training	$250,000; 9 students	$275,000; 125 students	$300,000; 136 students	$300,000; 136 students
	Expanded IMET	$16,058; 1 student, 1 civilian	$67,000; 2 students, 0 civilians		
	Sales of training and education through FMS	$490,502 (included in FMS above)	$0		

Bases and Other Presences

- **U.S. Support Group Haiti**

Honduras

Highlights of U.S. security assistance to Honduras

- Honduras hosts Joint Task Force Bravo, a 500-person component of the U.S. Southern Command based at Enrique Soto Cano Air Base near Comayagua.
- Honduras was first in Central America and fourth in the hemisphere in Foreign Military Sales (FMS) agreements in 1996, and second in Central America and eleventh in the hemisphere in 1997.
- Honduran personnel ranked fourth in the hemisphere in attendance at the School of the Americas in 1996, and sixth in 1997. Honduras led all Central American countries in this category in both years.
- In 1997, Honduras was second in Central America, and ninth in the hemisphere, in counternarcotics assistance received through the Defense Department's "section 1004" account.
- Honduras was the hemisphere's seventh-largest recipient of International Military Education and Training (IMET) assistance in 1996, and the ninth in 1997. Honduras was second in this category among Central American countries in both years.

Arms Transfers

Subcategory	Program	1996 actual	1997 actual	1998 estimate	1999 request
Sales and Leases	Foreign Military Sales	$19,183,000	$910,000	$1,000,000	$950,000
	Direct Commercial Sales	$5,089,128 (Licenses)	$3,696,000 (Licenses)		
		$123,000 (Deliveries as of March 1997)	$70,000 (Deliveries as of March 1998)	$878,000 (Expected deliveries)	$2,545,000 (Expected deliveries)
Grants	Excess Property	Medical supplies and equipment $613,420	Medical supplies $400,304		
	Section 1004 Counterdrug		Amount for equipment unknown; total account $418,000	Amount for equipment unknown; total account $404,000	
	Foreign Military Financing "in the pipeline" from previous years	$227,000 pre-1992 MAP funds; $1,015,000 uncommitted FMF			

Training and Education

Subcategory	Program	1996 actual	1997 actual	1998 estimate	1999 request
Funding	International Military Education and Training	$500,000; 213 students	$425,000; 164 students	$500,000; 193 students	$500,000; 193 students
	Expanded IMET	$140,495; 168 students, 8 civilians	$46,000; 59 students, 3 civilians		
	Sales of training and education through FMS	$253,541	$0		
	Section 1004 Counterdrug		Amount for training unknown; total account $418,000	Amount for training unknown; total account $404,000	
Spanish-language institutions	School of the Americas	123 students; 13.1% of total	33 students; 3.6% of total		
	Inter-American Air Forces Academy	29 students, 4.6% of total	18 students, 2.0% of total		

Subcategory	Program	1996 actual	1997 actual	1998 estimate	1999 request
Exercises			- Fuerzas Aliadas Humanitarian 97, February 1997; - Fuerzas Aliadas Centam Peacekeeping 97, May 1997; - Skills Exchange, May-June 1997; - Fuerzas Aliadas Riverine 97, July 1997	- New Horizons 98, January-June 1998; - Skills Exchange, February-March 1998; - Fuerzas Aliadas Humanitarian 98, January-February 1998; - Fuerzas Aliadas Centam Peacekeeping 98, May 1998	
	Humanitarian Civic Assistance incidental costs	$493,227.85	$84,643		

Bases and Other Presences

Subcategory	Program	1997 actual	1998 estimate
Counternarcotics detection, monitoring and interdiction	Section 1004/124	$400,000	$400,000
Bases	Joint Task Force Bravo		
De-mining	De-mining (MOMENCA)		

Jamaica

Highlights of U.S. security assistance to Jamaica

- Jamaica was first in the Caribbean in Foreign Military Sales (FMS) agreements in 1996.
- Jamaica was the hemisphere's eighth-largest recipient of International Military Education and Training (IMET) assistance in 1996, and the fifth-largest 1997. Jamaica was second among Caribbean countries in this category in both years.

Arms Transfers

Subcategory	Program	1996 actual	1997 actual	1998 estimated	1999 requested
Sales and Leases	Foreign Military Sales	$2,374,000	$50,000	$2,000,000	$2,000,000
	Direct Commercial Sales	$430,818 (Licenses)	$335,000 (Licenses)		
		$5,000 (Deliveries as of March 1997)	$97,000 (Deliveries as of March 1998)	$77,000 (Expected deliveries)	$215,000 (Expected deliveries)
Grants	Excess Property	$0	Disaster relief and medical supplies $1,778,426		
	Excess Defense Articles Grants	$618,700 offered (current value)	$0		
	Section 1004 Counterdrug		Amount for equipment unknown; total account $137,000	Amount for equipment unknown; total account $6,000	
	Foreign Military Financing	$2,000,000 (Caribbean Regional Fund)	$2,000,000 (Caribbean Regional Fund)	$3,000,000 (Caribbean Regional Fund)	$3,000,000 (Caribbean Regional Fund)
	FMF "in the pipeline" from previous years	$5,000 pre-1992 MAP funds; $1,000 uncommitted FMF			
	International Narcotics Control	Amount for equipment unknown; Total account: $700,000	Amount for equipment unknown; Total account: $650,000	Amount for equipment unknown; Total account: $600,000	Amount for equipment unknown; Total account: $800,000

Training and Education

Subcategory	Program	1996 actual	1997 actual	1998 estimated	1999 requested
Funding	International Military Education and Training	$450,000; 73 students	$487,000; 66 students	$500,000; 68 students	$500,000; 68 students
	Expanded IMET	$3,232; 2 students, 0 civilians	$18,000; 2 students, 0 civilians		
	International Narcotics Control	Amount for training unknown; total account $700,000	Amount for training unknown; total account $650,000	Amount for training unknown; total account $600,000	Amount for training unknown; total account $800,000
	Section 1004 Counterdrug		Amount for training unknown; total account $137,000	Amount for training unknown; total account $6,000	

Mexico

Highlights of U.S. security assistance to Mexico

- Mexico received more assistance through the International Military Education and Training (IMET) program than any other country in the region in 1996 and 1997.
- Mexican personnel ranked first in the region in attendance at the School of the Americas in 1997, and second in 1996.
- Mexican personnel ranked first in the region in attendance at the Inter-American Air Forces Academy in 1996 and 1997.
- In 1997, Mexico was second in the region in counternarcotics assistance received through the Defense Department's "section 1004" account.

Arms Transfers

Subcategory	Program	1996 actual	1997 actual	1998 estimated	1999 requested
Sales and Leases	Foreign Military Sales	$4,430,000	$27,663,000	$15,000,000	$15,000,000
	Direct Commercial Sales	$146,617,738 (Licenses)	$22,153,000 (Licenses)		
		$991,000 (Deliveries as of March 1997)	$12,642,000 (Expected deliveries)	$11,665,000 (Expected deliveries)	$47,225,000 (Expected deliveries)
	Excess Defense Articles Sales	$6,863,000 offered (current value)	$0		
Grants	Excess Defense Articles Grants	$2,372,000 offered (current value)	$3,023,000 offered and delivered (current value)		
	Section 1031 Counterdrug	$0	$8,000,000		
	Excess Property	$0	Medical supplies $343,160		
	Emergency Drawdowns	$0	$37,000,000		
	Section 1004 Counterdrug		Amount for equipment unknown, total account: $28,905,000	Amount for equipment unknown, total account: $20,079,000	
	International Narcotics Control	Amount for equipment unknown, total account $2,200,000	Amount for equipment unknown, total account $5,000,000	Amount for equipment unknown, total account $5,000,000	Amount for equipment unknown, total account $8,000,000

Training and Education

Subcategory	Program	1996 actual	1997 actual	1998 estimated	1999 requested
Funding	International Military Education and Training	$1,000,000; 221 students	$1,008,000; 192 students	$1,000,000; 190 students	$1,000,000; 190 students
	Expanded IMET	$96,366; 26 students, 0 civilians	$108,000; 21 students, 0 civilians		
	International Narcotics Control	Amount for training unknown; total account $2,200,000	Amount for training unknown; total account $5,000,000	Amount for training unknown; total account $5,000,000	Amount for training unknown; total account $8,000,000
	Section 1004 Counterdrug		Amount for training $10,800,000; total account: $28,905,000	Amount for training $13,000,000; total account: $20,079,000	
Spanish-language institutions	School of the Americas	149 students, 15.9% of total; one instructor	305 students, 33.6% of total		
	Inter-American Air Forces Academy	141 students, 22.3% of total	260 students, 29.4% of total		

Bases and Other Presences

Subcategory	Program	1997 actual	1998 estimate
Narcotics detection, monitoring and interdiction	Section 1004/124	$3,172,000	$3,126,000

Montserrat

Arms Transfers

Subcategory	Program	1996 actual	1997 actual	1998 estimated	1999 requested
Sales and Leases	Direct Commercial Sales	$3,340 (Licenses) $0 (Deliveries as of March 1997)	$3,000 (Licenses)		

Netherlands Antilles

Arms Transfers

Subcategory	Program	1996 actual	1997 actual	1998 estimated	1999 requested
Sales and Leases	Direct Commercial Sales	$1,353,602 (Licenses) $2,000 (Deliveries as of March 1997)	$136,000 (Licenses) $32,000 (Deliveries as of March 1998)	$28,000 (Expected deliveries)	$72,000 (Expected deliveries)

Nicaragua

Highlights of U.S. security assistance to Nicaragua

- The Army of Nicaragua receives no assistance from the United States.
- Through Special Operations Forces cooperation in OAS-sponsored demining efforts, the U.S. and Nicaraguan militaries have worked together for the first time since the Somoza period.

Arms Transfers

Subcategory	Program	1996 actual	1997 actual	1998 estimated	1999 requested
Sales and Leases	Direct Commercial Sales	$21,685 (Licenses)	$80,000 (Licenses)		
		$10,000 (Deliveries as of March 1997)	$77,000 (Deliveries as of March 1998)	$10,000 (Estimated deliveries)	$11,000 (Estimated deliveries)
Grants	Excess property	Medical supplies and equipment $687,862	Medical supplies $1,123,216		
	Foreign Military Financing "in the pipeline" from previous years	$28,000 total uncommitted FMF			

Training and Education

Subcategory	Program	1996 actual	1997 actual	1998 estimated	1999 requested
Funding	International Military Education and Training	$0	$57,000; 4 students	$200,000; 14 students	$200,000; 14 students
	Expanded IMET	$0	$25,000; 4 students, 0 civilians		

192

Subcategory	Program	1996 actual	1997 actual	1998 estimated	1999 requested
Exercises			- Fuerzas Aliadas Humanitarian 97, February 1997; - Fuerzas Aliadas Centam Peacekeeping 97, May 1997	- Fuerzas Aliadas Humanitarian 98, January-February 1998; - Fuerzas Aliadas Centam Peacekeeping 98, May 1998	
	Humanitarian Civic Assistance Incidental costs	$21,941.64	$24,787		

Bases and Other Presences

- **De-mining (MOMENCA)**

Panama

Highlights of U.S. security assistance to Panama

- Unless an agreement is completed on a proposed Multinational Anti-Drug Center, all U.S. troops stationed in Panama will vacate the country by December 31, 1999.
- In 1997, Panama was first in Central America, and seventh in the hemisphere, in counternarcotics assistance received through the Defense Department's "section 1004" account.
- Panama was tenth in the hemisphere in Direct Commercial Sales (DCS) licenses in 1996, and eighth in 1997. Panama was first among Central American countries in both years.
- Panama hosted "Nuevos Horizontes," a five-month humanitarian and civic assistance exercise, in 1997.

Arms Transfers

Subcategory	Program	1996 actual	1997 actual	1998 estimated	1999 requested
Sales and Leases	Foreign Military Sales	$146,000	$0	$1,510,000	$1,510,000
	Direct Commercial Sales	$9,148,361 (Licenses)	$11,941,000 (Licenses)		
		$89,000 (Deliveries as of March 1997)	$219,000 (Deliveries as of March 1998)	$2,110,000 (Expected deliveries)	$4,574,000 (Expected deliveries)
Grants	FMF "in the pipeline" from previous years	$247,000 pre-1992 MAP funds; $166,000 uncommitted FMF			
	Section 1004 Counterdrug		Amount for equipment unknown; total account $2,799,000	Amount for equipment unknown; total account $2,234,000	

Training and Education

Subcategory	Program	1996 actual	1997 actual	1998 estimated	1999 requested
Funding	International Military Education and Training	$0	$0	$0	$100,000; 7 students
	Section 1004 Counterdrug		Amount for training unknown; total account $2,799,000	Amount for training unknown; total account $2,234,000	

Subcategory	Program	1996 actual	1997 actual	1998 estimated	1999 requested
Spanish-language Institutions	Inter-American Air Forces Academy	24 students, 3.8% of total	13 students, 1.5% of total		
Exercises			- Blue Advance, February 1997; - New Horizons 97, January-May 1997; - Ellipse Echo, March 1997		
	Humanitarian Civic Assistance incidental costs	$748,395.27	$536,361		

Bases and Other Presences

- **Howard Air Force Base**
- **Rodman Naval Station**
- **Fort Clayton**
- **Fort Sherman / Jungle Operations Training Center**
- **Galeta Island**
- **Fort Kobbe**
- **Three firing ranges (Balboa West, New Empire and Piña)**
- **Proposed "Multinational Counter-Drug Center"**

Paraguay

Arms Transfers

Subcategory	Program	1996 actual	1997 actual	1998 estimated	1999 requested
Sales and Leases	Foreign Military Sales	$204,000	$31,000	$0	$0
	Direct Commercial Sales	$102,712 (Licenses)	$42,000 (Licenses)		
		$13,000 (Deliveries as of March 1997)	$0 (Deliveries as of March 1998)	$14,000 (Expected deliveries)	$51,000 (Expected deliveries)
Grants	Excess Property	Medical supplies and equipment $535,783	$0		
	Excess Defense Articles Grants	$4,000 offered and delivered (current value)	$0		
	Section 1004 Counterdrug		Amount for equipment unknown; total account $522,000	Amount for equipment unknown; total account $539,000	
	FMF "in the pipeline" from previous years	$8,000 total uncommitted FMF			

Training and Education

Subcategory	Program	1996 actual	1997 actual	1998 estimated	1999 requested
Funding	International Military Education and Training	$182,000; 10 students	$284,000; 42 students	$200,000; 30 students	$200,000; 30 students
	Expanded IMET	$36,151; 3 students	$46,000; 7 students, 0 civilians		
	Section 1004 Counterdrug		Amount for training unknown; total account $522,000	Amount for training unknown; total account $539,000	

196

Subcategory	Program	1996 actual	1997 actual	1998 estimated	1999 requested
Spanish-language institutions	School of the Americas	4 students; 0.4% of total	11 students; 1.2% of total		
	Inter-American Air Forces Academy	1 student, 0.16% of total	10 students, 1.1% of total		
Exercises			- Fuerzas Unidas Cabanas 97, October 1996; - UNITAS 97, July-November 1997; - Fuerzas Unidas Southam Peacekeeping 97, August 1997	- Cabanas 98, July-September 1998; - Fuerzas Unidas Southam 98, July 1998	
	Humanitarian Civic Assistance incidental costs	$25,043.10	$31,570		

Peru

Highlights of U.S. security assistance to Peru

- Peru was the region's second-largest recipient of assistance from the International Narcotics Control (INC) program in 1996, and the third-largest in 1997.
- In 1997, Peru was third in the region in counternarcotics assistance received through the Defense Department's "section 1004" account.
- Together with Colombia, Peru will receive counternarcotics military assistance through a special authorization in the defense budget (known as "section 1033") between 1998 and 2002.
- In 1997, Peru received an additional $9.8 million in counternarcotics assistance through a special transfer from the White House's Office of National Drug Control Policy (ONDCP).
- Peruvian personnel ranked fifth in the region in attendance at the School of the Americas in 1996, and fourth in 1997.

Arms Transfers

Subcategory	Program	1996 actual	1997 actual	1998 estimated	1999 requested
Sales and Leases	Foreign Military Sales	$125,000	$285,000	$3,710,000	$3,510,000
		$885,000 (Intl. Narc.)	$100,000 (Intl. Narc.)		
	Direct Commercial Sales	$31,293,666 (Licenses)	$5,367,000 (Licenses)		
		$180,000 (Deliveries as of March 1997)	$95,000 (Deliveries as of March 1998)	$2,170,000 (Expected deliveries)	$8,146,000 (Expected deliveries)

Subcategory	Program	1996 actual	1997 actual	1998 estimated	1999 requested
Grants	Excess Defense Articles	$1,249,200 offered (current value)	$0		
	Emergency Drawdowns	$13,750,000	$2,300,000		
	Excess property	Medical supplies and equipment $459,417	Medical supplies $1,038,272		
	Section 1033 counterdrug	$0	$0	$8,000,000	Up to $20,000,000
	Section 1004 Counterdrug		Amount for equipment unknown; total account $27,086,000	Amount for equipment unknown; total account $25,235,000	
	Foreign Military Financing "in the pipeline" from previous years	$335,000 counternarcotics FMF			
	International Narcotics Control	Amount for equipment unknown; total account $18,500,000	Amount for equipment unknown; total account $25,750,000	Amount for equipment unknown; total account $31,000,000	Amount for equipment unknown; total account $50,000,000
	ONDCP discretionary funds		$9,800,000		

Training and Education

Subcategory	Program	1996 actual	1997 actual	1998 estimated	1999 requested
Funding	International Military Education and Training	$400,000; 75 students	$483,000; 133 students	$450,000; 124 students	$450,000; 124 students
	Expanded IMET	$73,732; 78 students, 16 civilians	$125,000; 16 students, 2 civilians		
	International Narcotics Control	Amount for training unknown; total account $18,500,000	Amount for training unknown; total account $25,750,000	Amount for training unknown; total account $31,000,000	Amount for training unknown; total account $50,000,000
	Sales of training and education through FMS	$5,000	$0		
	Section 1004 Counterdrug		Amount for training unknown; total account $27,086,000	Amount for training unknown; total account $25,235,000	
Spanish-language institutions	School of the Americas	91 students; 9.7% of total	98 students; 10.8% of total		
	Inter-American Air Forces Academy	22 students, 3.5% of total	61 students, 6.9% of total		
Exercises			- UNITAS 97, July-November 1997	- Skills Exchange, February-March 1998	
	Humanitarian Civic Assistance incidental costs	$92,045.10	$82,451		

Bases and Other Presences

• **Operation Safe Border (MOMEP)**

St. Kitts and Nevis

Arms Transfers

Subcategory	Program	1996 actual	1997 actual	1998 estimated	1999 requested
Sales and Leases	Foreign Military Sales	$228,000	$187,000	$110,000	$110,000
	Direct Commercial Sales	$5,824 (Licenses)	$5,000 (Licenses)		
		$3,000 (Deliveries as of March 1997)	$2,000 (Deliveries as of March 1998)	$1,000 (Expected deliveries)	$3,000 (Expected deliveries)
Grants	Emergency Drawdowns	$8,500,000 (Shared with Eastern Caribbean)	$1,500,000 (Shared with Eastern Caribbean)		
	Section 1004 Counterdrug		Amount for equipment unknown; total account $2,000	Amount for equipment unknown; total account $64,000	
	Foreign Military Financing	$2,000,000 (Caribbean regional fund)	$2,000,000 (Caribbean regional fund)	$3,000,000 (Caribbean regional fund)	$3,000,000 (Caribbean regional fund)

Training and Education

Subcategory	Program	1996 actual	1997 actual	1998 estimated	1999 requested
Funding	International Military Education and Training	$48,000; 11 students	$56,000; 10 students	$55,000; 9 students	$55,000; 9 students
	Section 1004 Counterdrug			Amount for training unknown; total account $2,000	Amount for training unknown; total account $64,000

St. Lucia

Arms Transfers

Subcategory	Program	1996 actual	1997 actual	1998 estimated	1999 requested
Sales and Leases	Foreign Military Sales	$610,000	$0	$110,000	$110,000
	Direct Commercial Sales	$26,771 (Licenses)	$44,000 (Licenses)		
		$9,000 (Deliveries as of March 1997)	$8,000 (Deliveries as of March 1998)	$7,000 (Expected deliveries)	$13,000 (Expected deliveries)
Grants	Emergency Drawdowns	$8,500,000 (Shared with Eastern Caribbean)	$1,500,000 (Shared with Eastern Caribbean)		
	Foreign Military Financing	$2,000,000 (Caribbean regional fund)	$2,000,000 (Caribbean regional fund)	$3,000,000 (Caribbean regional fund)	$3,000,000 (Caribbean regional fund)
	FMF "in the pipeline" from previous years	$8,000 pre-1992 MAP funds			

Training and Education

Subcategory	Program	1996 actual	1997 actual	1998 estimated	1999 requested
Funding	International Military Education and Training	$46,000; 9 students	$42,500; 5 students	$47,000; 5 students	$50,000; 7 students
	Expanded IMET	$7,075; 1 student, 0 civilians	$7,000; 1 student, 0 civilians		

St. Vincent and the Grenadines

Arms Transfers

Subcategory	Program	1996 actual	1997 actual	1998 estimated	1999 requested
Sales and Leases	Foreign Military Sales	$1,366,000	$66,000	$110,000	$110,000
	Direct Commercial Sales	$5,169 (Licenses) Less than $500 (Deliveries as of March 1997)	$4,000 (Licenses) $1,000 (Deliveries as of March 1998)	$1,000 (Expected deliveries)	$3,000 (Expected deliveries)
Grants	Emergency Drawdowns	$8,500,000 (Shared with Eastern Caribbean)	$1,500,000 (Shared with Eastern Caribbean)		
	Section 1004 Counterdrug		Amount for equipment unknown; total account $49,000	Amount for equipment unknown; total account $51,000	
	Foreign Military Financing	$2,000,000 (Caribbean regional fund)	$2,000,000 (Caribbean regional fund)	$3,000,000 (Caribbean regional fund)	$3,000,000 (Caribbean regional fund)

Training and Education

Subcategory	Program	1996 actual	1997 actual	1998 estimated	1999 requested
Funding	International Military Education and Training	$46,000; 10 students	$44,000; 6 students	$54,000; 8 students	$50,000; 7 students
	Expanded IMET	$7,316; 1 student, 0 civilians	$0		
	Section 1004 counterdrug		Amount for training unknown; total account $49,000	Amount for training unknown; total account $51,000	

Suriname

Arms Transfers

Subcategory	Program	1996 actual	1997 actual	1998 estimated	1999 requested
Sales and Leases	Foreign Military Sales	$0	$0	$182,000	$110,000
	Direct Commercial Sales	$135,761 (Licenses)	$139,000 (Licenses)		
		$11,000 (Deliveries as of March 1997)	$5,000 (Deliveries as of March 1998)	$27,000 (Expected deliveries)	$68,000 (Expected deliveries)
Grants	Excess Property	Medical supplies and equipment $553,173	Medical supplies $619,453		

Training and Education

Subcategory	Program	1996 actual	1997 actual	1998 estimated	1999 requested
Funding	International Military Education and Training	$79,000; 138 students	$149,000; 100 students	$100,000; 67 students	$100,000; 67 students
	Expanded IMET	$27,514; 88 students, 28 civilians	$38,000; 33 students, 4 civilians		

Trinidad and Tobago

Arms Transfers

Subcategory	Program	1996 actual	1997 actual	1998 estimated	1999 requested
Sales and Leases	Foreign Military Sales	$165,000	$185,000	$110,000	$110,000
	Direct Commercial Sales	$332,302 (Licenses)	$809,000 (Licenses)		
		$25,000 (Deliveries as of March 1997)	$55,000 (Deliveries as of March 1998)	$97,000 (Expected deliveries)	$166,000 (Expected deliveries)
Grants	Excess Property	$0	Medical supplies $93,947		
	Section 1004 Counterdrug		Amount for equipment unknown; total account $188,000	Amount for equipment unknown; total account $504,000	
	Foreign Military Financing	$2,000,000 (Caribbean regional fund)	$2,000,000 (Caribbean regional fund)	$3,000,000 (Caribbean regional fund)	$3,000,000 (Caribbean regional fund)
	FMF "in the pipeline" from previous years	$16,000 total uncommitted FMF			

Training and Education

Subcategory	Program	1996 actual	1997 estimate	1998 estimated	1999 requested
Funding	International Military Education and Training	$57,000; 8 students	$95,000; 12 students	$125,000; 16 students	$125,000; 16 students
	Expanded IMET	$0	$232,000; 1 student, 0 civilians		
	Section 1004 Counterdrug		Amount for training unknown; total account $188,000	Amount for training unknown; total account $504,000	
Exercises	Humanitarian and Civic Assistance incidental costs	$0	$80,178		

Turks and Caicos Islands

Arms Transfers

Subcategory	Program	1996 actual	1997 actual	1998 estimate	1999 estimate
Sales and Leases	Direct Commercial Sales	$0	$1,000 (Licenses) / $0 (Deliveries as of March 1998)	$0 (Expected deliveries)	$0 (Expected deliveries)

Bases and Other Presences

- **Operation Bahamas and Turks and Caicos (OPBAT)**

Uruguay

Arms Transfers

Subcategory	Program	1996 actual	1997 actual	1998 estimated	1999 requested
Sales and Leases	Foreign Military Sales	$1,926,000	$1,078,000	$2,240,000	$2,260,000
	Direct Commercial Sales	$5,101,998 (Licenses) / $121,000 (Deliveries as of March 1997)	$14,723,000 (Licenses) / $111,000 (Deliveries as of March 1998)	$1,995,000 (Expected deliveries)	$2,615,000 (Expected deliveries)
Grants	Excess Defense Articles Grants	$2,794 offered (current value)	$0		
	Section 1004 Counterdrug		Amount for equipment unknown; total account $21,000	Amount for equipment unknown; total account $19,000	
	Foreign Military Financing "in the pipeline" from previous years	$123,000 pre-1992 MAP funds			

Training and Education

Subcategory	Program	1996 actual	1997 actual	1998 estimated	1999 requested
Funding	International Military Education and Training	$330,000; 85 students	$332,000; 65 students	$300,000; 59 students	$300,000; 59 students
	Expanded IMET	$141,043; 7 students, 0 civilians	$71,000; 10 students, 0 civilians		
	Section 1004 Counterdrug		Amount for training unknown, total account $21,000	Amount for training unknown; total account $19,000	
Spanish-language institutions	School of the Americas	3 students; 0.3% of total	8 students; 0.9% of total		
	Inter-American Air Forces Academy	17 students, 2.7% of total	40 students, 4.5% of total		
Exercises			- Fuerzas Unidas Cabanas 97, October 1996; - UNITAS 97, July-November 1997; - Fuerzas Unidas Southam Peacekeeping 97, August 1997	- Skills Exchange, July-August 1998; - Cabanas 98, July-September 1998	

Venezuela

Highlights of U.S. security assistance to Venezuela

- Venezuela was first in the region in Direct Commercial Sales (DCS) licenses in 1996 and 1997.
- Venezuela was third in the region in Foreign Military Sales (FMS) agreements in 1996, and second in 1997.
- In 1997, Venezuela was fourth in the region in counternarcotics assistance funded through the Defense Department's "section 1004" account.
- Venezuela was the region's largest recipient of Expanded IMET assistance in 1996, and the third-largest in 1997.

Arms Transfers

Subcategory	Program	1996 actual	1997 actual	1998 estimated	1999 requested
Sales and Leases	Foreign Military Sales	$21,332,000	$59,421,000	$15,000,000	$15,000,000
	Direct Commercial Sales	$711,891,676 (Licenses)	$342,929,000 (Licenses)		
		$1,103,000 (Deliveries as of March 1997)	$2,101,000 (Deliveries as of March 1998)	$71,945,000 (Expected deliveries)	$188,237,000 (Expected deliveries)
	Leased Defense Articles	$501,000 replacement value; $29,000 total rental value	$3,351,000 replacement value; $88,000 total rental value		
	Excess Defense Articles Sales	$1,058,000 offered (current value)	$0		
Grants	Emergency Drawdowns	$12,250,000	$1,000,000		
	Excess Defense Articles Grants	$208,000 offered and delivered (current value)	$0		
	Section 1004 Counterdrug		Amount for equipment unknown; total account $9,005,000	Amount for equipment unknown; total account $10,250,000	
	International Narcotics Control	Amount for equipment unknown; total account $500,000	Amount for equipment unknown; total account $600,000	Amount for equipment unknown; total account $600,000	Amount for equipment unknown; total account $700,000

Training and Education

Subcategory	Program	1996 actual	1997 actual	1998 estimated	1999 requested
Funding	International Military Education and Training	$430,000; 114 students	$388,000; 100 students	$400,000; 103 students	$400,000; 103 students
	Expanded IMET	$152,361; 60 students, 9 civilians	$143,000; 13 students, 0 civilians		
	International Narcotics Control	Amount for training unknown; total account $500,000	Amount for training unknown; total account $600,000	Amount for training unknown; total account $600,000	Amount for training unknown; total account $700,000
	Sales of training and education through FMS	$167,591	$252,748		
	Section 1004 counterdrug		Amount for training unknown; total account $9,005,000	Amount for training unknown; total account $10,250,000	
Spanish-language institutions	School of the Americas	47 students; 5.0% of total	22 students; 2.4% of total		
	Inter-American Air Forces Academy	43 students, 6.8% of total	19 students, 5.5% of total		
Exercises			- UNITAS 97, July-November 1997; - Fuerzas Unidas Counterdrug 97, August 1997		

Appendix A: Prohibitions on Security Assistance

Prohibitions on assistance in the FAA and AECA:

Most U.S. security assistance carries legal prohibitions that can prevent the U.S. government from providing military and police aid to particular countries. The most rigorously conditioned security assistance programs are those governed by the **Foreign Assistance Act** of 1961 (P.L. 87-195), as amended (hereafter referred to as the "**FAA**") and the **Arms Export Control Act** (P.L. 90-269), as amended (hereafter called the "**AECA**"). These programs, which make up what is traditionally known as "security assistance," include:

> "Security assistance," by its official definition, means defense articles, training or services provided under the FAA and AECA.

- Sales of defense articles, training and services under the Foreign Military Sales (FMS) and Direct Commercial Sales (DCS) programs *(Section 524 FAA; Sections 21-40A, AECA)*;
- Funding of FMS purchases through the Foreign Military Financing (FMF) program *(Section 23 AECA)*;
- Drawdowns of defense articles, training and services *(Section 506 FAA)*;
- Grants and sales of Excess Defense Articles (EDA) *(Section 516 FAA)*;
- Leases of defense articles *(Sections 61-64 AECA)*;
- Funding of training through the International Military Education and Training (IMET) program *(Sections 541-546 FAA)*;
- Counternarcotics assistance through the State Department's International Narcotics Control (INC) program *(Sections 481-490 FAA)*; and
- Economic aid grants under the Economic Support Fund (ESF), which is often placed within the "security assistance" category *(Sections 531-534 FAA)*.

Overall Eligibility:

Not surprisingly, the law forbids the provision of security assistance that would do harm to U.S. interests. In order even to be considered for security assistance under the FAA and AECA, a country must pass a few basic tests.

1. The President must determine that assistance to the country "will strengthen the security of the United States and promote world peace" *(Section 503 FAA, Section 3(a) AECA)*;
2. The President must also find that the country does not have "sufficient wealth to enable it ... to maintain and equip its own military forces at adequate strength without undue burden to its economy" *(Section 503 FAA)*;
3. A country cannot receive more than $3 million in defense articles in one year

unless the President determines that:

a) The country "conforms to the purposes and principles of the United Nations Charter";

b) The country will use the assistance for its own defensive strength;

c) The country "is taking all reasonable measures" to develop its own defense capacities; and

d) The country's ability to defend itself is important to U.S. security *(Section 505(b) AECA)*;

4. The country must agree to keep the assistance from being used by anyone who is not an officer, employee, or agent of that country. It must agree not to transfer the assistance to a third country or to use the assistance for purposes other than those for which it was provided *(Section 505(a) FAA)*;

5. The country must agree to guard the assistance it receives, guaranteeing "substantially the same degree" of security that the U.S. government provides its own articles and services *(Section 505(a) FAA);*

6. The country must agree that it will continuously allow the U.S. government to observe and review the country's use of the assistance, making necessary information available to U.S. officials;

7. Unless the U.S. government says otherwise, the country must agree to return assistance that is no longer needed for the purposes for which it was provided *(Section 505(a) FAA);*

8. The country's official policies or governmental practices must not prevent U.S. personnel from participating in the provision of assistance on the basis of race, religion, national origin or sex; and

9. If the U.S. government has determined that the country seriously violated the requirements listed above, sales and leases cannot go forward until the U.S. government certifies that:

- Stopping the sale or lease would harm U.S. security; or

- The violation has stopped, and the country has given "satisfactory" assurances that it will not happen again *(Section 503 FAA, Section 3(c) AECA).*

Narcotics Certification:

Since 1986, countries deemed eligible for security assistance can still be barred from receiving several forms of aid if they are "decertified" for failing to cooperate with counternarcotics efforts.

Congressional notification of major drug-producing and drug-transit countries

Countries that the law classifies as "major illicit drug producing" and "major drug-transit" states are subject to certification decisions each year, as mandated by section 490 of the FAA. Countries with these classifications can avoid sanction if the U.S. government decides they have fully cooperated with U.S. counternarcotics efforts or have taken steps on their own against drug trafficking.

The law defines "cooperation" as:

1. Meeting the goals and objectives of the United Nations Convention Against Illicit Traffic in Narcotic Drugs and Psychotropic Substances;
2. Accomplishing the goals laid out in bilateral or multilateral counternarcotics agreements involving the United States, usually the result of diplomatic exchanges in late spring or early summer of the year before the certification decision; and
3. Taking legal and law enforcement measures against government corruption -- especially that involving senior state officials -- which aids narcotics production and trafficking.

Presidential determination of certification

A country that does not meet these conditions is "decertified." The President announces certification and decertification decisions on or before March 1 of each year. Sanctions against decertified countries include the following:

Before November 1 of each year the President must notify Congress which countries are considered "major illicit drug producing countries" and "major drug transit countries." A "major drug producing country" is one that cultivates or harvests each year:

- 1,000 hectares or more of illicit opium poppy;
- 1,000 hectares or more of illicit coca; or
- 5,000 hectares or more of illicit cannabis (marijuana).

A "major drug transit country" is one:

- That is a significant direct source of drugs affecting the United States; or
- Through which these drugs are transported.

Thirty-one countries worldwide currently meet one or both of these criteria.

1. Most forms of U.S. assistance for that country are cut off, and previously-granted assistance can be frozen. Humanitarian aid and counterdrug assistance managed by the State Department's International Narcotics Control (INC) program are not cut off. Security assistance through the following programs may be suspended, though aid regarded as necessary for counternarcotics is generally delivered:

- Direct Commercial Sales (DCS);
- Emergency drawdowns of defense articles;
- Excess Defense Articles (EDA);
- Foreign Military Financing (FMF);
- Foreign Military Sales (FMS);
- International Military Education and Training (IMET);
- Leased Defense Articles; and
- Economic-aid grants under the Economic Support Fund (ESF).

The law is not very specific about which aid programs must be cut off. This caused trouble after Colombia was decertified in 1996. The State Department and other Executive Branch agencies, citing "interagency legal concerns as well as differences within the State Department," took about eight months to decide what aid could and could not be provided to Colombia.

2. The U.S. representatives at multilateral development banks (World Bank, Inter-American Development Bank, and others) must automatically vote against all loans or grants to that country.

3. The President also has the option of exercising "discretionary" trade sanctions, such as the removal of trade preferences and suspension of quotas.

National interest waiver

These punishments may be waived, however, if the U.S. government determines that the national interest depends on delivery of the assistance. A "national interest waiver" must be accompanied by:

1. A written description of the vital national interests that would be placed at risk by decertification; and
2. A statement weighing the risk to national interests against that posed by the country's failure to combat narcotics trafficking.

Congressional power to overturn certification decisions

Within thirty days, Congress may approve a joint resolution to overturn the President's certification decision.

These sanctions remain in effect until a country is recertified. Decisions to recertify a country must be accompanied by a description of improvements made since the original decertification decision. These improvements may include either a change of government in the country in question, or a fundamental change in conditions since the original decertification decision was made.

Human Rights:

Section 502B of the FAA, enacted in 1974 and strengthened in 1976, seeks to block security assistance to governments that engage "in a consistent pattern of gross violations of internationally recognized human rights." After first requesting a State Department report on the human rights situation in a given country, Congress may terminate security assistance to that country by approving a joint resolution.

Programs affected by section 502B include:

- Direct Commercial Sales (DCS);
- Emergency drawdowns of defense articles;
- Excess Defense Articles (EDA);
- Foreign Military Financing (FMF);
- Foreign Military Sales (FMS);
- International Military Education and Training (IMET);
- Leased Defense Articles;
- Economic-aid grants under the Economic Support Fund (ESF); and

The law defines "gross violations of internationally recognized human rights" as "torture or cruel, inhuman, or degrading treatment or punishment, prolonged detention without charges and trial, causing the disappearance of persons by the abduction and clandestine detention of those persons, and other flagrant denial of the right to life, liberty or the security of person."

- Peacekeeping and antiterrorism assistance.

Exceptions

If the President certifies in writing to the Speaker of the House and the Senate Foreign Relations and Banking, Housing, and Urban Affairs Committees that "extraordinary circumstances" exist, section 502B permits the following types of assistance to be delivered despite a congressional ban:

1. Security assistance to police, domestic intelligence, or similar law-enforcement forces;
2. Licenses for the export of crime control and detection equipment; and
3. International Military Education and Training (IMET).

Process for reversal

A country whose aid was suspended under section 502B can have the suspension reversed if the President finds that its human rights situation has improved significantly. When doing so, the President must report the following to Congress:

1. The country involved;
2. The amount and kinds of assistance to be provided; and
3. The justification for providing the assistance, including a description of the significant improvements in the country's human rights record.

Police training:

Section 660 of the FAA prohibits the use of security-assistance funds to train, advise or offer financial support to foreign police forces, prisons, internal intelligence programs other law enforcement forces. Programs which cannot pay for police training include the following:

- International Military Education and Training (IMET);
- Foreign Military Financing (FMF);
- Emergency drawdowns;
- Economic-aid grants under the Economic Support Fund (ESF); and
- Peacekeeping and antiterrorism assistance.

Note that some of the above programs may provide equipment to police forces; the prohibition only applies to training.

Exceptions

Several exceptions to section 660 exist. The following types of police training are permitted:

1. Training in maritime law enforcement and other maritime skills;

2. Training of police forces participating in the regional security system (RSS) of the Eastern Caribbean;
3. Training related to the monitoring and enforcement of sanctions;
4. Training provided to help rebuild civilian police authority in post-conflict societies;
5. "Professional public safety training," which includes training in human rights, the rule of law, anti-corruption, and "the promotion of civilian police roles that promote democracy";
6. Training in countries which have longstanding democratic traditions, do not have standing armed forces, and do not engage in consistent patterns of gross human-rights violations; and
7. The Justice Department's International Criminal Investigative Training Assistance Program (ICITAP), authorized by section 534(b)(3) of the FAA. ICITAP carries out the following:
   - Training in investigative and forensic functions;
   - Assistance in the development of law-enforcement instruction and curricula;
   - Programs to improve administrative and management capabilities; and
   - Multilaterally-managed programs to improve prisons.

Foreign police may also be trained by programs authorized by laws other than the Foreign Assistance Act. Defense Department counternarcotics training for foreign police forces, for instance, is authorized by section 1004 of the 1991 National Defense Authorization Act.

Other Prohibitions in the FAA and AECA:

The FAA and AECA contain several other measures that can prevent a Latin American or Caribbean country from receiving security assistance.

1. The present government of Cuba cannot receive any assistance. Before assistance can go to a future Cuban government, Cuba must compensate U.S. citizens who were at least one-half owners of expropriated property -- unless the U.S. government finds that it is in the U.S. interest to provide assistance *(Section 620 (a)(1-2), FAA)*;
2. No assistance can go to countries which do not pay money owed to U.S. citizens for goods and services, in cases where (1) the country does not deny or contest that the debt exists and (2) all legal means have been exhausted *(Section 620(c), FAA)*;
3. Countries are ineligible for assistance if, after 1962:
   - They nationalized, expropriated, or seized property owned by U.S. citizens or corporations without payment; or
   - They broke agreements or contracts with U.S. citizens or corporations without compensation *(Section 620(e), FAA)*;
4. Communist countries cannot receive assistance unless the President finds that:
   a) The assistance is vital to U.S. security;
   b) The country "is not controlled by the international Communist conspiracy"; and
   c) The assistance will promote the country's independence from international Communism *(Section 620(f), (h), FAA)*;

5. Countries which have severed diplomatic relations with the United States are ineligible for security assistance until relations resume *(Section 620(t), FAA);*

6. Countries are excluded from receiving assistance if they support international terrorism, assist the governments of countries that support terrorism, or provide military equipment to the governments of countries that support terrorism. These prohibitions can be overturned by Presidential national-interest waivers *(Section 620A, 620G and 620H, FAA)*;

7. Countries that restrict the delivery of U.S. humanitarian assistance cannot receive aid unless the President submits a national-interest waiver *(Section 620I, FAA)*; and

8. Arms sales and licenses are not to be granted to governments that engage "in a consistent pattern of acts of intimidation or harassment directed against individuals of the United States" *(Section 6 AECA)*.

The following are not prohibitions, but issues that must be "considered" or "taken into account" when making security-assistance decisions:

1. A country's seizure or penalization of U.S. fishing vessels in international waters *(Section 620(o) FAA)*;

2. The country's defense budget as a proportion of total budget and foreign-exchange revenue *(Section 620(s) FAA)*; and

3. The status of the country's dues and arrears with the United Nations *(Section 620(u) FAA)*.

1998 Foreign Operations Appropriations Act:

Congress assigns funds for the security-assistance programs in the FAA through a yearly appropriations bill. The "Foreign Operations, Export Financing, and Related Programs of [Year] Act," as the bill is always named, contains its own eligibility requirements. These are in effect only during the fiscal year for which aid is appropriated.

Eligibility requirements in the 1998 appropriations bill (P.L. 105-118, enacted 11/26/97) which might affect Latin American or Caribbean countries include the following.

IMET and FMF for Guatemala:

Due to continuing human rights concerns, Guatemala is expressly prohibited from receiving funding through the Foreign Military Financing (FMF) program. Guatemala also may not receive training funds through the International Military Education and Training (IMET) program, unless these funds pay for expanded IMET courses.

Section 508 (Military Coups):

No assistance can be given to countries which have had their elected head of government ousted by a military coup or decree. Aid may resume once the President reports to the appropriations committees that a democratically-elected government has taken office.

Section 512 (Limitation on Assistance to Countries in Default):

Any country which is in default for more than a year on loans made under the FAA is barred from receiving assistance. However, this prohibition does not apply in 1998 to Nicaragua or Liberia, or to counternarcotics assistance to Colombia, Bolivia and Peru. (This prohibition is also known as the "Brooke Amendment," after its original sponsor, former Senator Edwin Brooke (R-MA). It is very similar to section 620(q) of the FAA.)

Section 562 (Limitation on Assistance for Haiti)

Haiti cannot receive assistance unless the President reports that the Haitian government is:

1. Conducting investigations of extrajudicial and political killings;
2. Cooperating with the United States in these investigations;
3. Substantially completing the privatization of at least three major public enterprises; and
4. Acting to remove human rights violators from the Haitian National Police, national palace and residential guard, ministerial guard, or other related public security entities.

Humanitarian, electoral, counternarcotics, and law enforcement assistance are exempt from this restriction, and the President can waive the rest every six months by submitting a certification to Congress that the waiver is in the U.S. national interest.

Section 570 (Limitation on Assistance to Security Forces):

Frequently referred to as the "Leahy Amendment" after its sponsor, Sen. Patrick Leahy (D-VT), this provision was first included in the 1997 Foreign Operations Appropriations Act (P.L. 104-208). While in 1997 it only applied to the State Department's International Narcotics Control program, it was broadened to include all security-assistance programs in the FAA during FY 1998.

The Leahy Amendment prohibits a unit of a foreign security force from receiving U.S. assistance if:

1. Credible evidence exists that the unit's members have committed gross violations of human rights; and
2. Effective measures are not being taken to bring the responsible members of the unit to justice.

Assistance not restricted by the FAA and AECA:

The executive branch has means at its disposal to avoid the above-mentioned prohibitions. The FAA gives the President a broad power to waive its provisions. Furthermore, programs authorized by Defense Department funding bills are legally separate from the FAA and AECA -- the prohibitions in the FAA and AECA do not apply.

"614 Waiver"

Section 614 ("Special Authorities") of the FAA allows the President to override any of the prohibitions discussed In the preceding sections. The President may furnish security assistance without regard to FAA and AECA restrictions after notifying the Speaker of the House and the Chairman of the Senate Foreign Relations Committee "that to do so is important to the security interests of the United States."

The 614 waiver carries a few weak limitations. Deliveries resulting from its use cannot exceed $750 million in sales and $250 million in grants in a single fiscal year. No single country may receive more than $50 million in grants unless it is a victim of active aggression, in which case it may not receive more than $500 million in sales and grants.

Counternarcotics Activities of the Department of Defense

With the 1989 inclusion of section 124 in Title 10 of the U.S. Code, the Department of Defense became the lead U.S. agency responsible for detecting and monitoring illegal drugs entering the United States by air or sea. Over the past few years, the annual National Defense Authorization legislation has contained provisions allowing the U.S. military to provide counternarcotics assistance to foreign security forces. The prohibitions found in the FAA and AECA do not apply to these provisions.

Section 1004

"Section 1004," which contains no limitations that would prohibit a country (or a unit of a country's security forces) from receiving assistance, is the most far-reaching of these provisions. This authorization, found in section 1004 ("Additional Support for Counter-Drug Activities") of the 1991 National Defense Authorization Act (P.L. 101-510), as amended, allows the Secretary of Defense to provide support for an array of counternarcotics programs with foreign governments, including:

1. Maintenance, repair and upgrading of equipment;
2. Transport of U.S. and foreign personnel and supplies;

3. Establishment and operation of bases of operation and training;
4. Training of foreign law enforcement personnel;
5. Detection and monitoring;
6. Construction to block drug smuggling across U.S. borders;
7. Communication networks;
8. Linguistic and intelligence services; and
9. Aerial and ground reconnaissance.

Activities authorized by section 1004 take place in nearly every Latin American and Caribbean country.

Authorizations for Specific Countries

Security forces of the following Latin American countries benefited from specific authorizations for counternarcotics assistance in the National Defense Authorization Act.

1. **Mexico**: section 1031 of the 1997 Department of Defense Authorization Act (P.L. 104-201), extended by section 1032 of the 1998-99 Department of Defense Authorization Act (P.L. 105-85).
2. **Colombia and Peru**: section 1033 of the 1998 Department of Defense Authorization Act (P.L. 105-85)

Other Department of Defense Activities

The Defense Department carries out other activities in Latin America and the Caribbean which resemble FAA and AECA security-assistance programs but are not subject to the same eligibility requirements. These include:

1. **Special Operations Forces (SOF) training**: U.S. Special Operations Forces conduct training activities throughout the region using their own resources, particularly through the Joint Combined Exchange Training (JCET) program. The choice of countries in which they operate is not circumscribed by legislation.
2. **Center for Hemispheric Defense Studies**: The CHDS, a newly-established facility at the National Defense University, offers education in defense management and civil-military relations to civilian and military officials with defense responsibilities. As part of the National Defense University, the CDHS is not affected by FAA and AECA restrictions.
3. **Exercises and deployments.** The U.S. Southern Command deploys about 56,000 troops a year to Latin America and the Caribbean, while carrying out 20-25 major exercises. While training is not technically given through these activities, no limitations exist to prohibit countries or units from participating.
4. **Military-to-military contact programs.** Latin American and Caribbean militaries, regardless of their eligibility for security assistance, participate in regular "foreign military interaction" activities, including exchanges, conferences, defense attaché activities, and less formal contact.

5. **Defense Export Loan Guarantee program**. The DELG program, which insures private lenders who finance sales of defense articles, is authorized by section 2540 of Title X, U.S. Code. Western Hemisphere countries cannot currently participate in the DELG program. The law does, however, permit the participation of countries that were major non-NATO allies as of March 31, 1995. In mid-1997, Argentina became the first country in the hemisphere to be granted major non-NATO ally status; a small change in the law would permit Argentina and future hemispheric non-NATO allies to participate in the DELG program.

Appendix B: Calendar of Required Reports

Regular submissions of written information are the most important tool Congress uses to oversee the security assistance programs it funds. Many laws governing security assistance require the executive branch to issue periodic reports explaining the objectives and activities of its programs. These requirements guarantee that Congress receives updates about many activities on a regular basis.

With a few minor exceptions, these reports are considered to be public information. Their availability has made these legally-mandated reports an indispensable source of primary information for this study.

> Section 634B of the Foreign Assistance Act allows the President, "on an extraordinary basis," to classify some information in reports. To do so, the President must submit a separate report justifying the decision.

For ease of presentation, this study divides all legally-mandated written information into two categories: **"reports"** and **"notifications." Reports** are documents that must be submitted by a fixed calendar date. They usually describe the overall activities or strategy of a particular program, providing an overview, for instance, of expenditures during a past fiscal year. Most are submitted annually or quarterly, which means overseers know when to expect them (several, however, frequently end up being delivered well past their deadlines).

Notifications, by contrast, are submitted in response to an action -- such as an arms sale, a waiver or an information request -- that does not take place on a regular basis. Since they occur "on the fly," the submission of these documents cannot be placed on a calendar. A list of major notification requirements is presented in Appendix C.

The rest of this appendix presents, in chronological order, all significant reports submitted over the course of a year.

Reports due as soon as possible

These reports have no deadline; instead, Congress has chosen to freeze some or all of the relevant program's funds until it receives the information requested. All of these reports were mandated in legislation, enacted in 1997, which authorized or made appropriations for foreign assistance or defense.

Report name:	**_Certification and report concerning the School of the Americas (SOA)_**
Deadline:	As soon as possible. Grant financing for students at the School of the Americas through the IMET and INL programs is frozen until information is received.
Relevant law:	Foreign Operations, Export Financing, and Related Programs Appropriations Act, 1998 (P.L. 105-118)
Fre-quency:	One time only
Who must be notified:	House and Senate Appropriations Committees
Descrip-tion:	_Certification:_ The Secretary of Defense must certify: 1. That instruction and training provided at the U.S. Army School of the Americas is fully consistent – especially where human rights are concerned – with training and doctrine provided to U.S. military students at military institutions whose primary purpose is to train U.S. personnel; and 2. That the Secretary of State, in consultation with the Secretary of Defense, "has developed and issued specific guidelines governing the selection and screening of candidates for instruction at the School of the Americas." This certification was received in a January 21, 1998 letter to the appropriations committees from Secretary of Defense William S. Cohen. _Report:_ The Secretary of Defense must also submit "a report detailing the training activities of the School of the Americas and a general assessment of its graduates' performance during 1996." This report has been issued and can be read at the SOA website <http://www.benning.army.mil/usarsa/certif/content.htm>.

Report name:	**_Financial plan for the State Department's International Narcotics Control (INC) program_**
Deadline:	As soon as possible. 10 percent of INC funds were withheld until the report was received.
Relevant law:	Foreign Operations, Export Financing, and Related Programs Appropriations Act, 1998 (P.L. 105-118)
Fre-quency:	One time only
Who must be noti-fied:	House and Senate Appropriations Committees
Descrip-tion:	The Secretary of State must submit a financial plan for funds appropriated to the State Department's Bureau of International Narcotics and Law Enforcement Affairs for International Narcotics Control activities.

Report name:	**_Riverine counter-drug plan for Colombia and Peru_**
Deadline:	As soon as possible. Funding of section 1033 activities is frozen until 60 days after information is received.
Relevant law:	Section 1033, National Defense Authorization Act for Fiscal Year 1998 (P.L. 105-85)
Fre-quency:	One time only
Who must be noti-fied:	House National Security Committee, House International Relations Committee, Senate Armed Services Committee, Senate Foreign Relations Committee

Description:	The Secretary of Defense, in consultation with the Secretary of State, must submit a riverine counter-drug plan for Colombia and Peru. The plan must include the following:
	1. A detailed security assessment, including a discussion of the threat posed by illicit drug traffickers in the foreign country;
	2. An evaluation of previous and ongoing riverine counter-drug operations by the recipient government;
	3. An assessment of the monitoring of past and current assistance provided by the U.S. under this section to ensure the appropriate use of such assistance;
	4. A description of the centralized management of the coordination among Federal agencies involved in the development and implementation of the plan;
	5. A description of the resources to be contributed by the Defense and State Departments for each fiscal year covered by the plan, and the manner in which such resources will be utilized under the plan;
	6. In the plan submitted during the first fiscal year, a schedule for establishing a riverine counter-drug program that can be sustained by the Peruvian and Colombian governments within five years. In plans for subsequent fiscal years, a description of the progress made in establishing and carrying out the program;
	7. A reporting system to measure the effectiveness of the riverine counter-drug program; and
	8. A detailed discussion of how the riverine counter-drug program supports the United States' national drug control strategy.
	Any revisions to this plan must be submitted in subsequent fiscal years.

Report name:	*Certification required for additional support for counter-drug activities of Peru and Colombia*
Deadline:	As soon as possible. Funding of section 1033 activities is frozen until 60 days after certification is received.
Relevant law:	Section 1033, National Defense Authorization Act for Fiscal Year 1998 (P.L. 105-85)
Frequency:	One time only
Who must be notified:	House National Security Committee, House International Relations Committee, Senate Armed Services Committee, Senate Foreign Relations Committee
Description:	The Secretary of Defense must submit a written certification that:
	1. Provision of riverine counterdrug support to Peru and Colombia will not adversely affect the military preparedness of the U.S. Armed Forces;
	2. The equipment provided will be used only by government officials and employees whom the recipient government submits to background investigations and approves for the performance of counter-drug activities;
	3. The recipient government has certified that none of the equipment will be transferred to any other person or entity not authorized by the United States, and that the equipment will be used only for the purposes intended by the U.S government;
	4. The recipient government has agreed to maintain a thorough inventory of the equipment provided, and to allow U.S. government personnel access to any of this equipment or to any records having to do with it; and
	5. The recipient government has agreed to guarantee the equipment's security to a degree deemed satisfactory by the U.S. government, and to permit continuous U.S. government review of the equipment's use.

Reports due in January

Report name:	Report on international narcotics and law enforcement activities
Deadline:	January 25, 1998, 60 days after enactment of the foreign assistance appropriations bill.
Relevant law:	Foreign Operations, Export Financing, and Related Programs Appropriations Act, 1998 (P.L. 105-118)
Fre-quency:	One time only
Who must be noti-fied:	House and Senate Appropriations Committees
Descrip-tion:	In consultation with the Director of the Office of National Drug Control Policy, the Secretary of State must submit a report containing: 1. A list of all countries in which the United States carries out international counter-narcotics activities; 2. The number, mission and agency affiliation of U.S. personnel assigned to each country; and 3. All costs and expenses obligated for each program, project or activity by each U.S. agency in each country.

Report name:	Report on country human rights practices
Deadline:	January 31
Relevant law:	Sections 116 and 502B of the Foreign Assistance Act of 1961 (P.L. 87-195, or the "FAA"), as amended (also known as sections 2151n and 2304 of Title 22, U.S. Code).
Fre-quency:	Annual
Who must be noti-fied:	Speaker of the House, Senate Foreign Relations Committee
Descrip-tion:	The Secretary of State must transmit a report including: 1. The status of internationally-recognized human rights in all foreign countries which belong to the United Nations or receive U.S. economic or security assistance; 2. Coercive population-control measures; 3. The votes of each member of the UN Human Rights Commission at its annual session; 4. The extent to which each country has extended protection to refugees; and 5. Steps taken to alter economic-aid programs in the country due to human-rights considerations. This report -- popularly known as the State Department's annual "Human Rights Country Reports" -- is available online at the State Department website <http://www.state.gov/www/global/human_rights/1997_hrp_report/97hrp_report_toc.html>.

Reports due in February

Report name:	Annual report
Deadline:	February 1

Appendix B - Calendar of Required Reports

Relevant law:	Section 634 of the Foreign Assistance Act of 1961 (P.L. 87-195, or the "FAA"), as amended (also known as section 2394 of Title 22, U.S. Code).
Fre-quency:	Annual
Who must be noti-fied:	Congress

Descrip-tion:	A report must be submitted providing the following information:
	1. The dollar value of all foreign assistance and guaranties, by category and by country, provided by the United States to foreign countries and international organizations:
	  a) From 1946 to the fiscal year immediately preceding the current year;
	  b) As presented to Congress in the past fiscal year;
	  c) As actually obligated in the past fiscal year;
	  d) As planned for the current fiscal year; and
	  e) As proposed for the following fiscal year;
	2. For countries belonging to the Organization for Economic Cooperation and Development (Mexico is the only Latin American or Caribbean country in the OECD) and Organization of Petroleum Exporting Countries (Venezuela is the only Latin American or Caribbean country in OPEC): all security assistance and international narcotic control assistance programs broken down by country, expressed as a dollar value, as a per capita figure, and as a percentage of (a) the country's GDP and (b) the country's budget; and
	3. The aggregate dollar value and quantity of grant military assistance, military education and training, and any other defense articles and services furnished under the FAA.
	
	Most of this information is presented in the State Department's yearly Congressional Presentation for Foreign Operations.

Report name:	*Annual estimate and justification for sales program*
Deadline:	February 1, together with the annual report discussed above.
Relevant law:	Section 25 of the Arms Export Control Act of 1968 (P.L. 90-269, or the "AECA"), as amended (also known as section 2765 of Title 22, U.S. Code).
Fre-quency:	Annual
Who must be noti-fied:	House and Senate Appropriations Committees, House International Relations Committee, Senate Foreign Relations Committee

Descrip-tion:	A report, popularly referred to as the "Javits report," which includes:
	1. An Arms Sales Proposal listing all probable Foreign Military Sales (FMS) or Direct Commercial Sales (DCS) exports for the current calendar year that exceed:
	  • $7 million for major weapons or weapons-related defense equipment; or
	  • $25 million for other weapons or weapons-related defense equipment;
	2. An indication of which sales or licenses are most likely to be approved during the current year;
	3. An estimate of the total amount of FMS sales and DCS licenses expected to be made to each foreign country;
	4. The national security considerations involved in expected sales or licenses to each country. This must include "an analysis of the relationship between anticipated sales to each country and arms control efforts concerning such country" and "an analysis of the impact of such anticipated sales on the stability of the region that includes such country";
	5. An estimate of the total international arms traffic to and from each country

buying defense articles from the United States. This must include "best estimates" of major recipient countries' purchases from all major international
arms suppliers during the preceding fiscal year;

6. An estimate of the aggregate dollar value and quantity of defense articles and
    services, military education and training, grant military assistance, and credits
    and guarantees the United States will furnish each country in the next fiscal
    year;
7. An analysis and description of services U.S. government officers and employ-
    ees have performed during the past year which are reimbursed by proceeds
    from Foreign Military Sales;
8. A list of countries for which the President considers that arms purchases "will
    strengthen the security of the United States and promote world peace";
9. The status of outstanding loans, guaranties and credits made under the FAA
    and AECA; and
10. A description of assistance furnished for de-mining activities.

The Senate Foreign Relations Committee and House International Relations committee may request additional information about the above at any time, in which
case the President has thirty days to respond.

Report name:	Excess defense articles
Deadline:	February 1, together with the annual report discussed above
Relevant law:	Section 516 of the Foreign Assistance Act of 1961 (P.L. 87-195, or the "FAA"), as amended (also known as section 2321j of Title 22, U.S. Code).
Fre-quency:	Annual
Who must be noti-fied:	Congress
Descrip-tion:	Countries eligible to receive Excess Defense Articles (EDA) must be listed. This list must be accompanied by: 1. An explanation of the general purposes of providing EDA; and 2. A table with aggregate totals of EDA grants and sales by country in the previ-ous year, separating total offers, total deliveries, and the articles' original cost and current value. This information is presented in the State Department's yearly Congressional Pres-entation for Foreign Operations.

Report name:	Security Assistance Organizations (SAOs)
Deadline:	February 1, together with the annual report discussed above.
Relevant law:	Section 515 of the Foreign Assistance Act of 1961 (P.L. 87-195, or the "FAA"), as amended (also known as section 2321i of Title 22, U.S. Code).
Fre-quency:	Annual
Who must be noti-fied:	Congress
Descrip-tion:	This report must state the number of members of the Armed Forces assigned to each foreign country in a fiscal year to manage security assistance. This information is presented in the State Department's yearly Congressional Pres-entation for Foreign Operations.

Report name:	National Drug Control Strategy
Deadline:	February 1
Relevant law:	Section 1504 of Title 21, U.S. Code.
Frequency:	Annual
Who must be notified:	Congress
Description:	The President, together with the Director of the White House's Office for National Drug Control Policy (ONDCP, popularly known as the "Drug Czar"), must submit a report detailing the government's goals and objectives for all drug-control activities, both international and domestic. This report is available online at the ONDCP website <http://www.whitehousedrugpolicy.gov/policy/98ndcs/contents.html>.

Report name:	End-use monitoring of defense articles and services
Deadline:	February 1
Relevant law:	Section 40A of the Arms Export Control Act of 1968 (P.L. 90-269, or the "AECA"), as amended (also known as section 2785 of Title 22, U.S. Code).
Frequency:	Annual
Who must be notified:	Congress
Description:	The President must transmit a report describing actions taken "to provide reasonable assurance" that countries which have received defense articles and services from the United States are: 1. Complying with U.S. government requirements concerning their use, transfers and security; and 2. Using these articles and services for the purposes for which they were provided. The report must also detail the costs and number of personnel involved in the end-use monitoring program.

Report name:	Annual military assistance report
Deadline:	February 1
Relevant law:	Section 655 of the Foreign Assistance Act of 1961 (P.L. 87-195, or the "FAA"), as amended (also known as section 2415 of Title 22, U.S. Code).
Frequency:	Annual
Who must be notified:	Congress
Description:	The President must submit a report for the previous fiscal year detailing the dollar value and quantity of defense articles (including excess defense articles), defense services and military training transferred to each foreign country and international organization. The report must specify whether the defense articles were furnished under the Foreign Military Sales (FMS) program or licensed for export under the Direct Commercial Sales (DCS) program. The report must also document foreign military items imported into the United States, by country and by type.

Report name:	Exchanges of training and related support
Deadline:	February 1
Relevant law:	Section 30A of the Arms Export Control Act of 1968 (P.L. 90-269, or the "AECA"), as amended (also known as section 2770a of Title 22, U.S. Code).
Frequency:	Annual
Who must be notified:	Congress
Description:	The President must submit a report on exchanges of military training and related support for military and civilian defense personnel. This report must estimate: 1. The full costs of training and related support provided by the United States to each country or International organization, and 2. The value of training and related support provided by each country or international organization to the United States.

Report name:	Budget proposal for Southern Command
Deadline:	The first Monday in February, in the annual budget of the Department of Defense submitted to Congress.
Relevant law:	Section 166 of Title 10, U.S. Code.
Frequency:	Annual
Who must be notified:	Congress
Description:	The Secretary of Defense must submit separate budget proposals for each of the armed forces' combatant commands. The combatant command with responsibility for all of Latin America and the Caribbean (except Mexico) is the U.S. Southern Command (or "Southcom"), based in Miami, FL. The Southcom budget proposal must contain information about the following activities: 1. Joint exercises; 2. Force training, including amounts for special operations forces' training with foreign forces; 3. Contingencies; and 4. Selected operations.

Report name:	Humanitarian assistance
Deadline:	The first Monday in February, at the time of the defense budget submission for the next fiscal year.
Relevant law:	Section 2551 of Title 10, U.S. Code.
Frequency:	Annual
Who must be notified:	House National Security Committee, House International Relations Committee, Senate Armed Services Committee, Senate Foreign Relations Committee
Description:	The Secretary of Defense must submit a report on the Defense Department's provision of humanitarian assistance during the previous fiscal year. The report must include: 1. The total amount of funds obligated "for the purpose of providing transportation of humanitarian relief and for other humanitarian purposes worldwide";

	2. The number of scheduled and completed transportation missions for purposes of providing humanitarian assistance; and
	3. A description of transfers of excess non-lethal supplies for humanitarian relief purposes. The description should include the date of each transfer, the entity to whom each is made, and the quantity of items transferred.

Report name:	*Report on overseas deployments*
Deadline:	February 16, 1998
Relevant law:	Section 332, National Defense Authorization Act for Fiscal Year 1998 (P.L. 105-85)
Fre-quency:	One time only
Who must be noti-fied:	Congress
Descrip-tion:	A report on the overseas deployments of members of the armed forces (except the Coast Guard) as of June 30, 1996 and June 30, 1997. The report shall include the following information, both in the aggregate and broken down by individual service: 1. The number of military personnel deployed overseas on permanent duty assignments, broken down by country or ocean; 2. The number of military personnel deployed overseas on temporary duty assignments, specifying how many are training with units from a single service, how many are taking part in joint exercises with other branches of the U.S. military, and how many are taking part in exercises with other countries; and 3. The number of military personnel taking part in "contingency operations" such as peacekeeping, humanitarian assistance or other activities.

Report name:	*Arms sales to Latin America report*
Deadline:	February 24, 1998
Relevant law:	House Appropriations Committee Report 105-176 on Foreign Operations, Export Financing, and Related Programs Appropriations Act, 1998 (P.L. 105-118), July 14, 1997.
Fre-quency:	One time only
Who must be noti-fied:	House and Senate Appropriations Committees
Descrip-tion:	The Secretary of State must provide "a report detailing the security needs in Latin America and the impact of lifting the existing U.S. ban on high technology weapons sales to the region."

Reports due in March

Report name:	*International Narcotics Control Strategy Report*
Deadline:	March 1
Relevant law:	Section 489 of the Foreign Assistance Act of 1961 (P.L. 87-195, or the "FAA"), as amended (also known as section 2291h of Title 22, U.S. Code).
Fre-quency:	Annual

Who must be noti-fied:	Speaker of the House, Senate Foreign Relations Committee
Descrip-tion:	The International Narcotics Control Strategy Report (INCSR) forms the factual basis for the President's yearly certification decisions. For each country that has received counter-drug assistance during the last 2 fiscal years, the President must determine the extent to which that country has:

1. Met the goals and objectives of the United Nations Convention Against Illicit Traffic in Narcotic Drugs and Psychotropic Substances;
2. Accomplished goals laid out in bilateral or multilateral counternarcotics agreements involving the United States, usually the result of diplomatic exchanges in late spring or early summer of the year before the certification decision; and
3. Taken legal and law enforcement measures against government corruption, especially that involving senior state officials, which aids narcotics production and trafficking.

The INCSR must also include a description of the State Department's international narcotics control policies, agreements and programs. It must provide updates on negotiations dealing with extradition treaties, mutual legal assistance treaties, precursor chemical controls, money laundering, and maritime law enforcement agreements. The report must also include information about bilateral and multilateral strategies to combat narcotics-related money laundering, including descriptions of other agencies' efforts.

The report must identify countries that are major illicit drug-producing countries or drug-transit countries (these terms are discussed below), major sources of precursor chemicals, or major money-laundering countries. For each of these countries, the report must provide:

1. A description of the country's counter-drug plans and programs, and "a discussion of the adequacy of the legal and law enforcement measures taken and the accomplishments achieved in accord with those plans";
2. A determination whether the country encourages or facilitates the production or distribution of drugs, or whether senior government officials participate in the drug trade;
3. A detailed status report on the drugs that are being cultivated, produced, processed, or transported in the country;
4. The country's procedures for controlling and regulating precursor chemicals;
5. The presence in the country's banking system of proceeds from sales of illegal drugs;
6. The presence or absence of an agreement to exchange records of narcotics investigations and proceedings;
7. Ratification of the UN Convention, other regional agreements, and bilateral agreements for information exchange with the United States; and
8. Findings on the country's adoption of laws and regulations considered essential to prevent narcotics-related money-laundering.

The INCSR must highlight instances of a country's refusal to cooperate with foreign governments, and actions taken by the United States and international organizations to address them.

The report must also document any available evidence indicating that a foreign country has misused aircraft or other equipment provided by the U.S. for counter-narcotics purposes. U.S. actions to prevent further misuse must be explained (this topic is mandated by section 484(c) of the FAA).

The INCSR incorporates the international narcotics assistance report required by section 489(b) of the FAA. This report supplies the following information about assistance provided, and proposed to be provided, to support international anti-drug efforts:

1. The amount and nature of the assistance;
2. Counter-drug assistance provided by the Drug Enforcement Administration (DEA), Customs Service and Coast Guard; and
3. Transfers of property seized or forfeited in the United States in connection with narcotics-related activity.

The report must also discuss the health and environmental impact of herbicides used for aerial drug eradication (this topic is mandated by section 481(d) of the FAA).

The INCSR is available online at the State Department's website <http://www.state.gov/www/global/narcotics_law/1997_narc_report/index.html>.

Report name:	**Narcotics control certification decisions**
Deadline:	March 1
Relevant law:	Section 490 of the Foreign Assistance Act of 1961 (P.L. 87-195, or the "FAA"), as amended (also known as section 2291j of Title 22, U.S. Code).
Frequency:	Annual
Who must be notified:	Congress
Description:	In a report submitted to Congress the previous November, the President selected countries regarded as "major illicit drug producing countries" or "major drug-transit countries." By March 1, the President must certify whether these countries have cooperated fully with the United States, or taken adequate steps on their own, to comply with the goals of the United Nations Convention Against Illicit Traffic in Narcotic Drugs and Psychotropic Substances.

Countries that do not pass this test are "decertified." A decertified country cannot receive most U.S. assistance, and loans and grants from multilateral development banks are subject to an automatic "no" vote by the U.S. representatives to those banks.

Decertified countries can avoid these sanctions, however, if the President issues a "national interest waiver" stating that the vital national interests of the United States require that the country receives aid. The waiver must include the following:

1. A complete description of the vital national interests that would be placed at risk by application of the sanctions; and
2. A statement weighing the risk to national interests against the risks posed by the country's failure to cooperate in counternarcotics efforts. |

Report name:	**Humanitarian and civic assistance provided in conjunction with military operations**
Deadline:	March 1
Relevant law:	Section 401 of Title 10, U.S. Code.
Frequency:	Annual

Who must be notified:	House National Security Committee, House International Relations Committee, Senate Armed Services Committee, Senate Foreign Relations Committee
Description:	The Secretary of Defense must submit a report including: 1. A list of countries in which humanitarian and civic assistance activities were carried out during the preceding fiscal year; 2. The type and description of such activities carried out in each country during the preceding fiscal year; and 3. The amount spent carrying out each activity in each country during the preceding fiscal year. The term "Humanitarian and civic assistance" includes: 1. Medical, dental and veterinary care provided in rural areas of a country; 2. Construction of rudimentary surface transportation systems; 3. Well drilling and construction of basic sanitation facilities; and 4. Detection and clearance of landmines, including education and technical assistance for the clearing of landmines.

Report name:	*Participation of developing countries in combined exercises: payment of incremental expenses*
Deadline:	March 1
Relevant law:	Section 2010 of Title 10, U.S. Code.
Frequency:	Annual
Who must be notified:	Congress
Description:	The Secretary of Defense must submit a report containing the following information about the past fiscal year: 1. A list of the developing countries which the United States reimbursed for incremental expenses incurred while participating in a military exercise. 2. The amount each country was reimbursed. *["'Incremental expenses' means the reasonable and proper cost of the goods and services that are consumed by a developing country as a direct result of that country's participation in a bilateral or multilateral military exercise with the United States." These may include rations, fuel, training ammunition and transportation. Incremental expenses do not include pay, allowances, and other normal costs.]*

Reports due in April

Report name:	*Special operations forces: training with friendly foreign forces*
Deadline:	April 1
Relevant law:	Section 2011 of Title 10, U.S. Code.
Frequency:	Annual
Who must be notified:	Congress

Descrip-
tion:
	The Secretary of Defense must submit a report discussing training with foreign forces carried out by special operations forces. The report must specify:
	1. All countries in which that training was conducted;
	2. The type of training conducted, including whether the training was related to counter-narcotics or counter-terrorism activities, the duration of the training, the number of members of the armed forces involved, and expenses paid in connection with the training;
	3. The extent of foreign military forces' participation, including the number and service affiliation of foreign military personnel involved, and the host nation's "physical and financial contribution" to the training effort; and
	4. The training's relationship to other overseas training programs conducted by the armed forces, such as:
	  a) Military exercise programs sponsored by the Joint Chiefs of Staff;
	  b) Military exercise programs sponsored by a combatant command; and
	  c) Military training activities sponsored by a military department (including deployments for training, short duration exercises, and other similar unit training events).

Reports due in November

Report name:	Determining major drug-transit and major illicit drug-producing countries
Deadline:	November 1
Relevant law:	Section 490 of the Foreign Assistance Act of 1961 (P.L. 87-195, or the "FAA"), as amended (also known as section 2291j of Title 22, U.S. Code).
Fre-quency:	Annual
Who must be noti-fied:	House and Senate Appropriations Committees, House International Relations Committee, Senate Foreign Relations Committee
Descrip-tion:	Before November 1 of each year the President must notify Congress which countries are considered to be "major illicit drug producing countries" and "major drug transit countries." A "major drug producing country" is one that cultivates or harvests each year: 1. 1,000 hectares or more of illicit opium poppy; 2. 1,000 hectares or more of illicit coca; or 3. 5,000 hectares or more of illicit cannabis. A "major drug transit country" is one: 1. That is a significant direct source of drugs affecting the United States; or 2. Through which these drugs are transported. The countries chosen are considered in the yearly narcotics control certification processes. Certification decisions are made every March 1, at the same time the President submits the yearly International Narcotics Control Strategy Report (see above).

Report name:	International Military Education and Training programs for Latin America
Deadline:	November 26, 1998, twelve months after enactment of the Foreign Operations, Export Financing, and Related Programs Appropriations Act, 1998 (P.L. 105-118)
Relevant law:	Section 584(c), Foreign Operations, Export Financing, and Related Programs Appropriations Act, 1998 (P.L. 105-118)

Fre-quency:	One time only
Who must be noti-fied:	House and Senate Appropriations Committees, House International Relations Committee, Senate Foreign Relations Committee
Descrip-tion:	The Secretary of Defense, in consultation with the Secretary of State, must report in writing on the military training of Latin American students funded by the International Military Education and Training (IMET) program. The report must focus specifically on improvements "in the areas of human rights and civilian control of the military. The Secretary shall include in the report plans for implementing additional expanded IMET programs for Latin America during the next three fiscal years."

Quarterly reports

Report name:	*Report on commercial and governmental military exports*
Deadline:	Within 60 days after the end of each quarter.
Relevant law:	Section 36(a) of the Arms Export Control Act of 1968 (P.L. 90-269, or the "AECA"), as amended (also known as section 2776 of Title 22, U.S. Code).
Who must be noti-fied:	Speaker of the House and chairman of the Senate Foreign Relations Committee

Descrip-tion:	The President must submit an unclassified report containing:
	 1. A listing, by category and by country, of all letters of offer to sell major defense equipment exceeding $1 million that have not yet been accepted or canceled *["Major defense equipment" means any item on the United States Munitions List with a research and development cost of at least $50 million or a total production cost of at least $200 million.]*;
	 2. A listing of all letters of offer that have been accepted during the current fiscal year, together with the total value of all defense articles and services sold to each country that year;
	 3. The cumulative dollar amounts, by country, of sales credit and guaranty agreements for defense articles and services;
	 4. A numbered listing, by country, of licenses and approvals for private exports of defense articles exceeding $1 million, together with the total of licenses for the current year. The listing must detail:
	    a) The items to be exported under the license;
	    b) The quantity and price of each item to be furnished; and
	    c) The name and address of the ultimate user of each item;
	 5. Projections of the dollar amounts of expected Foreign Military Sales (FMS) for the following quarter and the remainder of the fiscal year;
	 6. An estimate of the number of U.S. military personnel, U.S. government civilian personnel and U.S. civilian contractors who were in each foreign country at the end of the quarter, and at any time during the quarter, to implement arms-sales or security-assistance tasks authorized by the FAA and AECA;
	 7. A listing of foreign military construction sales; and
	 8. A listing of consents granted to allow countries to perform third-party transfers of defense articles or services that were originally provided by the United States.

Report name:	*Report on security assistance surveys*
Deadline:	Within 60 days after the end of each quarter, as part of the report on commercial and governmental military exports discussed above.

Appendix B - Calendar of Required Reports

Relevant law:	Section 26 of the Arms Export Control Act of 1968 (P.L. 90-269, or the "AECA"), as amended (also known as section 2766 of Title 22, U.S. Code).
Who must be noti-fied:	Speaker of the House and chairman of the Senate Foreign Relations Committee
Descrip-tion:	A list of all security assistance surveys authorized during the preceding calendar quarter, specifying the country involved, the purpose of the survey, and the number of U.S. personnel carrying out the survey. A "security assistance survey" is "any survey or study conducted in a foreign country by United States Government personnel for the purpose of assessing the needs of that country for security assistance," including "defense requirement surveys, site surveys, general surveys or studies, and engineering assessment surveys." Copies of the surveys themselves are available upon request of the chairman of the Senate Foreign Relations or House International Relations Committee.

Report name:	*Report on leases for international narcotics assistance purposes*
Deadline:	Within 30 days after the end of each quarter.
Relevant law:	Section 488 of the Foreign Assistance Act of 1961 (P.L. 87-195, or the "FAA"), as amended (also known as section 2291g of Title 22, U.S. Code).
Who must be noti-fied:	House International Relations Committee, Senate Foreign Relations Committee
Descrip-tion:	The cost and duration of all leases, a description of the properties leased, and the purpose of the leases.

Source: Applicable laws. All items in quotation marks are direct citations of the law.

Appendix C: Notification Requirements

Most laws governing security-assistance programs contain provisions requiring that Congress be notified of how the programs are being carried out. While reports must be submitted on an annual or quarterly basis, the notification requirements described here are triggered by a particular action, such as a decision to provide assistance, a request for a waiver, or a request for information. Some notification requirements contain provisions allowing Congress to freeze or prohibit transfers of assistance.

The most significant notification requirements affecting U.S. security assistance to Latin America and the Caribbean are listed below. This list is by no means inclusive; it merely encompasses what the authors of this study consider to be the most "essential" notification requirements.

Report name:	Furnishing information on request
Triggering event:	Upon request
Due date:	Within 35 days of the request.
Relevant law:	Section 633A of the Foreign Assistance Act of 1961 (P.L. 87-195, or the "FAA"), as amended (also known as section 2393a of Title 22, U.S. Code).
Who notified:	Whoever made the request (General Accounting Office (GAO), House and Senate Appropriations Committees, House International Relations Committee, Senate Foreign Relations Committee)
Description:	Through a written request to the head of the relevant agency, the GAO or any committee of Congress charged with considering legislation, appropriations or expenditures under the FAA may ask for "any document, paper, communication, audit, review, finding, recommendation, report or other material in its [the agency's] custody or control" related to a program authorized by the FAA. If the agency does not respond within 35 days, funding for that program may be frozen, unless the President certifies that he has forbidden the provision of this information. The President's certification must give a reason for the refusal.

Report name:	Notification of Foreign Military Sales (FMS)
Triggering event:	A letter of offer to sell the following through the Foreign Military Sales (FMS) program: 1. Defense articles or services valued at $50 million or more; 2. Design and construction services valued at $200 million or more; or 3. Major defense equipment valued at $14 million or more. ["Major defense equipment" means any item on the United States Munitions List with a research and development cost of at least $50 million or a total production cost of at least $200 million.]
Due date:	For all Latin American and Caribbean countries, the letter of offer cannot be issued until 30 days after the President submits the certification discussed below. During these 30 days, the Congress may prohibit the sale by enacting a joint resolution.

Appendix C – Notification Requirements

Relevant law:	Section 36(b) of the Arms Export Control Act of 1968 (P.L. 90-269, or the "AECA"), as amended (also known as section 2776 of Title 22, U.S. Code).
Who notified:	Speaker of the House, Chairman of the Senate Foreign Relations Committee
Description:	The President must submit a numbered certification providing the following information: 1. The foreign country or international organization to which the offer is being made; 2. The dollar amount of the offer and the number of defense articles offered; 3. A description of the defense article or service being offered; 4. The U.S. agency (or branch of the armed forces) making the offer; and 5. If construction and design services are being offered, a description of the facilities to be constructed. The certification must also mention any contributions, gifts, commissions or fees paid to help secure the offer. In addition, it must contain a section (which may be classified) identifying sensitive technology contained in the articles to be offered. The President's certification must be published in the *Federal Register*. The President can waive the thirty-day delay and void Congress's power to prohibit the sale by including in this certification a statement that "an emergency exists which requires the proposed sale in the national security interest of the United States." This statement must include a detailed description of these emergency circumstances and a discussion of the national security interests involved. If the Speaker of the House, House International Relations Committee or Senate Foreign Relations Committee requests it, the President must "promptly" submit a statement with the following information: 1. A detailed description of the articles or services being offered, including -- in the case of a defense article -- a brief description of its capabilities; 2. An estimate of the number of U.S. government personnel and contractors who will be needed in the country to carry out the proposed sale; 3. The name of each contractor expected to provide the article or service, and a description of any offset agreements associated with the proposed sale; 4. An evaluation prepared by the director of the Arms Control and Disarmament Agency (ACDA), in consultation with the Secretaries of State and Defense. This evaluation must analyze whether the proposed sale would contribute to an arms race, support international terrorism, increase the possibility of an outbreak or escalation of conflict, prejudice arms control negotiations, or adversely affect U.S. arms control policy; 5. The reasons why the prospective buyer needs the defense articles or services to be offered, and a description of how the country or international organization intends to use them; 6. An analysis by the President of the impact of the proposed sale on U.S. military stocks and preparedness; 7. The reasons why the proposed sale is in the U.S. national interest; 8. An analysis by the President of the impact of the proposed sale on the prospective buyer's military capabilities; 9. An analysis by the President of how the proposed sale would affect the relative military strengths of countries in the prospective buyer's region, and whether other countries in the region have comparable defense articles and services; 10. An estimate of whether the prospective buyer has the trained personnel and maintenance facilities necessary to utilize the defense articles or services effectively; 11. An analysis of the extent to which comparable defense articles and services are available from other countries; 12. An analysis of the impact of the proposed sale on U.S. relations with other countries in the prospective buyer's region;

	13. A description of any agreement whereby the United States will purchase articles from the prospective buyer in connection with the proposed sale. This description must include an analysis of this purchase's impact on domestic economic concerns; 14. The projected delivery dates of the articles or services proposed to be sold; 15. A detailed description of the weapons and munitions that may be required as support for the proposed sale; and 16. An analysis of the relationship of the proposed sale to projected procurements of the same item.

Report name:	Notification of Direct Commercial Sales (DCS) licenses
Triggering event:	Intention to issue an export license under the Direct Commercial Sales (DCS) program for: • Defense articles or services valued at $50 million or more; or • Major defense equipment valued at $14 million or more. ["Major defense equipment" means any item on the United States Munitions List with a research and development cost of at least $50 million or a total production cost of at least $200 million.]
Due date:	For all Latin American and Caribbean countries, the license cannot be issued until 30 days after the President submits the certification discussed below. During these 30 days, the Congress may prohibit the sale by enacting a joint resolution.
Relevant law:	Section 36(c) of the Arms Export Control Act of 1968 (P.L. 90-269, or the "AECA"), as amended (also known as section 2776 of Title 22, U.S. Code).
Who notified:	Speaker of the House, Chairman of the Senate Foreign Relations Committee
Description:	The President must submit an unclassified, numbered certification providing the following information: 1. The foreign country or international organization to which the export will be made; 2. The dollar amount of the items to be exported; and 3. A description of the items to be exported. The President's certification must be published in the *Federal Register*. The President can waive the thirty-day delay and void Congress's power to prohibit the export by including in this certification a statement that "an emergency exists which requires the proposed export in the national security interest of the United States." This statement must include a detailed description of these emergency circumstances and a discussion of the national security interests involved. If the Speaker of the House, House International Relations Committee or Senate Foreign Relations Committee requests it, the President must "promptly" submit a statement with the following information: 1. A description of the capabilities of the items to be exported; 2. An estimate of the number of U.S. government personnel who will be needed in the country in connection with the items to be exported; and 3. An analysis, prepared in consultation with the Secretary of Defense, of the export's arms-control impact.

Report name:	Notification of certain leases of defense equipment
Triggering event:	Intention to enter into, or to renew, a lease or loan of a defense article for over one year.

239

Due date:	For all Latin American and Caribbean countries, the lease cannot take place until 30 days after the President submits the certification discussed under the "Description" heading below. During these 30 days, Congress may prohibit the sale by enacting a joint resolution, if: 1. The value of major defense equipment (replacement cost not including depreciation) is $14,000,000 or more; or 2. The value of the defense articles to be leased is $50,000,000 or more. ["Major defense equipment" means any item on the United States Munitions List with a research and development cost of at least $50 million or a total production cost of at least $200 million.]
Relevant law:	Sections 62 and 63 of the Arms Export Control Act of 1968 (P.L. 90-269, or the "AECA"), as amended (also known as sections 2796a and 2796b of Title 22, U.S. Code).
Who notified:	Speaker of the House, chairman of the Senate Foreign Relations Committee, chairman of the Senate Armed Services Committee
Description:	The President must submit a written certification specifying: 1. The country or international organization to which the defense article is to be leased or loaned; 2. The type, quantity and value (in terms of replacement cost) of the defense article to be leased or loaned; 3. The terms and duration of the lease or loan; and 4. A justification for the lease or loan, including an explanation of why the defense article is being leased or loaned rather than sold. The President can waive the thirty-day delay and void Congress's power to prohibit large leases by including in this certification a statement that "an emergency exists which requires the lease or loan be entered into immediately in the national security interest of the United States." This statement must include a detailed description of these emergency circumstances and a discussion of the national security interests involved.

Report name:	Change in allocation of foreign assistance
Triggering event:	Enactment of a law appropriating funds to carry out any provision of the FAA or AECA. Continuing resolutions are excepted.
Due date:	30 days after the law's enactment.
Relevant law:	Section 653 of the Foreign Assistance Act of 1961 (P.L. 87-195, or the "FAA"), as amended (also known as section 2413 of Title 22, U.S. Code).
Who notified:	Congress
Description:	The President shall list each foreign country or international organization to which the U.S. government plans to provide funds under the appropriation law. For each country or international organization, the President shall state how much the U.S. government plans to provide.

Report name:	Report on country human rights practices
Triggering event:	Request from the House or Senate (by resolution), the House International Relations Committee, or the Senate Foreign Relations Committee
Due date:	30 days after request.
Relevant law:	Section 502B(c) of the Foreign Assistance Act of 1961 (P.L. 87-195, or the "FAA"), as amended (also known as section 2304 of Title 22, U.S. Code).
Who notified:	House International Relations Committee, Senate Foreign Relations Committee

Descrip- tion:	The Secretary of State must transmit a statement, prepared with the Assistant Secretary of State for Democracy, Human Rights and Labor, providing the following information about a specific country: 1. All available information about the observance of and respect for human rights and fundamental freedoms in that country. This must include a detailed description of that government's human-rights practices; 2. The steps the United States has taken to promote human rights and to discourage abuses in that country; 3. The steps the United States has taken to call attention, publicly or privately, to practices that violate human rights, and steps taken to disassociate the United States and its security assistance from these practices; and 4. The Secretary of State's opinion whether, despite these practices, "extraordinary circumstances" warrant the continuation of security assistance. This must be accompanied by a description of these circumstances and the extent to which assistance must be continued. This notification is distinct from the annual reports on country human-rights practices required by section 502B of the FAA.

Report name:	Waiver of human rights prohibition
Triggering event:	Presidential finding that a country's human rights situation has improved sufficiently to warrant a resumption of aid.
Due date:	Immediately
Relevant law:	Section 502B(g) of the Foreign Assistance Act of 1961 (P.L. 87-195, or the "FAA"), as amended (also known as section 2304 of Title 22, U.S. Code).
Who notified:	Congress
Description:	The President must "specify the country involved, the amount and kinds of assistance to be provided, and the justification for providing the assistance, including a description of the significant improvements which have occurred in the country's human rights record."

Report name:	Prior notification of drawdowns
Triggering event:	Drawdown of defense (or other agencies') articles and services for counternarcotics or migration and refugee assistance.
Due date:	Drawdown cannot take place until 15 days after notification.
Relevant law:	Section 506 of the Foreign Assistance Act of 1961 (P.L. 87-195, or the "FAA"), as amended (also known as section 2318 of Title 22, U.S. Code).
Who notified:	House and Senate Appropriations Committees, House International Relations Committee, Senate Foreign Relations Committee
Description:	When a drawdown is performed for international narcotics control assistance or migration and refugee assistance, the President must submit a notification specifying the nature and purpose of the drawdown and the country or countries involved.

Report name:	Report of completed drawdowns
Triggering event:	Upon completion of a drawdown (after all arms, equipment, services, training or education have been delivered).
Due date:	Immediately
Relevant law:	Section 576, Foreign Operations, Export Financing, and Related Programs Appropriations Act, 1998 (P.L. 105-118)
Who notified:	Congress

Description:	A report "detailing all defense articles, defense services, and military education and training" delivered to the country via the drawdown.

Report name:	Transfer of certain excess defense articles
Triggering event:	The transfer of Excess Defense Articles (EDA) that are "significant military equipment" (articles normally subject to export controls) or whose current value exceeds $7,000,000.
Due date:	Transfer cannot take place until 30 days after notification is received.
Relevant law:	Section 516 of the Foreign Assistance Act of 1961 (P.L. 87-195, or the "FAA"), as amended (also known as section 2321j of Title 22, U.S. Code).
Who notified:	House and Senate Appropriations Committees, House International Relations Committee, Senate Foreign Relations Committee
Description:	The President's notification of the EDA transfer must include: 1. A statement outlining the purposes for which the article is being provided to the country, including whether the article has been provided to the country before; 2. An assessment of the impact of the article's transfer on U.S. military readiness; 3. An assessment of the transfer's impact on the national technology and industrial base; and 4. A statement describing the article's current value, and its value when it was originally acquired.

Report name:	Invocation of the President's special waiver authority
Triggering event:	Use of a waiver (known as the "614 waiver") which allows the President to override prohibitions on assistance contained in the Foreign Assistance Act or Arms Export Control Act.
Due date:	Immediately
Relevant law:	Section 614 of the Foreign Assistance Act of 1961 (P.L. 87-195, or the "FAA"), as amended (also known as section 2364 of Title 22, U.S. Code).
Who notified:	House and Senate Appropriations Committees, House International Relations Committee, Senate Foreign Relations Committee
Description:	The President must consult with, and provide a written policy justification to, the congressional committees. Up to $50 million may be transferred under this provision without specifying its destination, upon determination that "it is inadvisable to specify the nature of the use of such funds." Before doing so, however, the President must inform the chairmen and ranking minority members of the committees.

Report name:	Introduction of additional military personnel to manage security assistance in-country
Triggering event:	The introduction of additional military personnel to a foreign country to manage security assistance programs
Due date:	30 days
Relevant law:	Section 515 of the Foreign Assistance Act of 1961 (P.L. 87-195, or the "FAA"), as amended (also known as section 2321i of Title 22, U.S. Code).
Who notified:	House International Relations Committee, Senate Foreign Relations Committee

Descrip-tion:	Members of the Armed Forces (known as Security Assistance Officers, or SAOs) are routinely assigned to a foreign country to manage security assistance programs. If the President wishes to change the number of SAOs in a country so that (a) there are more than six or (b) it exceeds the number justified in the congressional presentation materials for that fiscal year, the congressional committees must be notified at least 30 days before the new personnel are introduced.

Report name:	Designation of major non-NATO allies
Triggering event:	Designation of a country as a major non-NATO ally.
Due date:	Designation cannot take place until 30 days after notification.
Relevant law:	Section 517 of the Foreign Assistance Act of 1961 (P.L. 87-195, or the "FAA"), as amended (also known as section 2321k of Title 22, U.S. Code).
Who notified:	Congress
Descrip-tion:	The President must notify Congress in writing before designating a country as a major non-NATO ally (MNNA), or before terminating a country's MNNA status.

Report name:	Purchases of weapons or ammunition through the International Narcotics Control (INC) program
Triggering event:	Upon transfer of weapons or ammunition through the INC program
Due date:	Transfers cannot take place until 15 days after notification.
Relevant law:	Section 482 of the Foreign Assistance Act of 1961 (P.L. 87-195, or the "FAA"), as amended (also known as section 2291a of Title 22, U.S. Code).
Who notified:	House and Senate Appropriations Committees, House International Relations Committee, Senate Foreign Relations Committee
Descrip-tion:	Section 482(b) allows the State Department's INL program to supply weapons or ammunition only if they are to be used: 1. For the defensive arming of aircraft that are used for counternarcotics purposes; or 2. For defensive purposes by State Department employees or contract personnel engaged in counternarcotics activities. Arms cannot be transferred for either of these reasons until fifteen days after the President notifies the congressional committees.

Report name:	Supply of aircraft through the International Narcotics Control (INC) program
Triggering event:	Grants of aircraft through the INC program.
Due date:	Transfers cannot take place until 15 days after notification.
Relevant law:	Section 484 of the Foreign Assistance Act of 1961 (P.L. 87-195, or the "FAA"), as amended (also known as section 2291c of Title 22, U.S. Code).
Who notified:	House and Senate Appropriations Committees, House International Relations Committee, Senate Foreign Relations Committee
Descrip-tion:	Section 484(a) specifies that aircraft provided to foreign countries through the INL program must be either leased or loaned. The President may grant aircraft through INL, however, by determining that a lease or loan would be "contrary to the national interest of the United States." The aircraft cannot be transferred until fifteen days after the President notifies the congressional committees.

Report name:	Construction of facilities through the International Narcotics and Law Enforcement Affairs (INL) program
Triggering event:	Obligation of INL funds for "construction of facilities for use by foreign military, paramilitary, or law enforcement forces."
Due date:	Funds cannot be obligated until 15 days after notification.
Relevant law:	Section 488 of the Foreign Assistance Act of 1961 (P.L. 87-195, or the "FAA"), as amended (also known as section 2291g of Title 22, U.S. Code).
Who notified:	House and Senate Appropriations Committees, House International Relations Committee, Senate Foreign Relations Committee
Description:	Funds cannot be obligated for the construction until fifteen days after the President notifies the congressional committees.

Source: Applicable laws. All items in quotation marks are direct citations of the law.

Endnotes

Programs governed by the Foreign Assistance Act and the Arms Export Control Act

Foreign Military Sales:

[1] United States, Department of Defense, Defense Institute of Security Assistance Management, "Appendix 6: A Comparison of Direct Commercial Sales and Foreign Military Sales for the Acquisition of U.S. Defense Articles and Services," The Management of Security Assistance, 17th ed. (Wright-Patterson AFB, OH: May 1997).

[2] United States, Department of State, Office of Resources, Plans and Policy, Congressional Presentation for Foreign Operations, Fiscal Year 1998 (Washington: March 1997): 652-3.

[3] United States, Department of Defense, Defense Security Assistance Agency, "Foreign Military Sales of Training: American Republics Region, For the Period FY 1996-1997 to Date As of 17 September 1997," memo in response to congressional inquiry, Washington, October 1997.

[4] United States, Department of State, Office of Resources, Plans and Policy, Congressional Presentation for Foreign Operations, Fiscal Year 1999 (Washington: March 1998): 1136-7.

Direct Commercial Sales:

[1] Federation of American Scientists Arms Sales Monitoring Project, "U.S. Approved $25B in Arms Sales in FY 1996," Arms Sales Monitor 33, (February 24, 1997): 6 <http://www.fas.org/asmp/asm33.html>.

[2] United States, Department of State, Department of Defense, Foreign Military Assistance Act Report To Congress, Fiscal Year 1996 (Washington: September 1997).

[3] United States, Department of State, Office of Resources, Plans and Policy, Congressional Presentation for Foreign Operations, Fiscal Year 1998 (Washington: March 1997): 695-6.

[4] Congressional Record, March 4, 1998: E295-6 <http://thomas.loc.gov/cgi-bin/query/z?r105:E04MR8-342:>.

[5] United States, Department of State, Office of Resources, Plans and Policy, Congressional Presentation for Foreign Operations, Fiscal Year 1999 (Washington: March 1998): 1163-4.

Foreign Military Financing:

[1] United States, General Accounting Office, Drug Control: U.S. Counternarcotics Efforts in Colombia Face Continuing Challenges, document number GAO/NSIAD-98-60, Washington, February 1998: 29 <http://frwebgate.access.gpo.gov/cgi-bin/useftp.cgi?IPaddress=waisback.access.gpo.gov&filename=ns98060.txt&directory=/diskb/wais/data/gao>,
Adobe Acrobat (.pdf) format <http://frwebgate.access.gpo.gov/cgi-bin/useftp.cgi?IPaddress=waisback.access.gpo.gov&filename=ns98060.pdf&directory=/diskb/wais/data/gao>.

[2] General Accounting Office 47.

[3] United States, Department of State, Office of Resources, Plans and Policy, Congressional Presentation for Foreign Operations, Fiscal Year 1999 (Washington: March 1998): 470-1, 999.

[4] United States, Department of Defense, Legislative Affairs, "Foreign Financing (FMF) Program: Prior Year Uncommitted FMF," memo in response to congressional inquiry, Washington, September 15, 1997.

International Military Education and Training:

[1] United States, General Accounting Office, Drug Control: U.S. Counternarcotics Efforts in Colombia Face Continuing Challenges, document number GAO/NSIAD-98-60, Washington, February 1998: 29 <http://frwebgate.access.gpo.gov/cgi-bin/useftp.cgi?IPaddress=waisback.access.gpo.gov&filename=ns98060.txt&directory=/diskb/wais/data/gao>,
Adobe Acrobat (.pdf) format <http://frwebgate.access.gpo.gov/cgi-bin/useftp.cgi?IPaddress=waisback.access.gpo.gov&filename=ns98060.pdf&directory=/diskb/wais/data/gao>.

[2] United States, Department of State, Office of Resources, Plans and Policy, Congressional Presentation for Foreign Operations, Fiscal Year 1998 (Washington: March 1997): 125-6.

[3] United States, Department of State, Office of Resources, Plans and Policy, Congressional Presentation for Foreign Operations, Fiscal Year 1999 (Washington: March 1998): 1013.

Expanded IMET:

[1] United States, Defense Security Assistance Agency, Expanded IMET Handbook, (Washington: February 14, 1997).

[2] United States, Defense Security Assistance Agency, "International Military Education and Training Program: Expanded-IMET Students Trained," memo in response to congressional inquiry, Washington, October 1997: 2-3.

[3] United States, Defense Security Assistance Agency, Standardized Training Listing as of 17 September 1997 (Washington: DSAA, September 1997).

International Narcotics Control:

[1] United States, Department of State, Bureau of International Narcotics and Law Enforcement Affairs, Fiscal Year 1999 Budget Congressional Presentation (Washington: Department of State: March 1998): 2-3.

[2] United States, General Accounting Office, Drug Control: U.S. Counternarcotics Efforts in Colombia Face Continuing Challenges, document number GAO/NSIAD-98-60, Washington, February 1998: 16-7 <http://frwebgate.access.gpo.gov/cgi-bin/useftp.cgi?IPaddress=waisback.access.gpo.gov&filename=ns98060.txt&directory=/diskb/wais/data/gao>,
Adobe Acrobat (.pdf) format <http://frwebgate.access.gpo.gov/cgi-bin/useftp.cgi?IPaddress=waisback.access.gpo.gov&filename=ns98060.pdf&directory=/diskb/wais/data/gao>.

[3] General Accounting Office, U.S. Counternarcotics Efforts in Colombia 20.

[4] Department of State, Fiscal Year 1999 Budget Congressional Presentation 19.

[5] Department of State, Fiscal Year 1999 Budget Congressional Presentation 20.

[6] Department of State, Fiscal Year 1999 Budget Congressional Presentation 20.

[7] United States, Bureau for International Narcotics and Law Enforcement Affairs, Department of State, International Narcotics Control Strategy Report, Washington, March 1998, March 2, 1998 <http://www.state.gov/www/global/narcotics_law/1997_narc_report/index.html>.

United States, Bureau for International Narcotics and Law Enforcement Affairs, Department of State, International Narcotics Control Strategy Report, Washington, March 1997, October 1997 <http://www.state.gov/www/global/narcotics_law/1996_narc_report/index.html>.

[8] Department of State, International Narcotics Control Strategy Report, March 1998.

[9] Department of State, Fiscal Year 1999 Budget Congressional Presentation 21.

Department of State, International Narcotics Control Strategy Report, March 1997.

United States, General Accounting Office, Drug Control: Long-Standing Problems Hinder U.S. International Efforts, document number GAO-NSIAD-97-75 (Washington, GAO, February 1997): 15 <http://frwebgate.access.gpo.gov/cgi-bin/useftp.cgi?IPaddress=waisback.access.gpo.gov&filename=ns97075.txt&directory=/diskb/wai

s/data/gao>,
Adobe Acrobat (.pdf) format <http://frwebgate.access.gpo.gov/cgi-bin/useftp.cgi?IPaddress=waisback.access.gpo.gov&filename=ns97075.pdf&directory=/diskb/wais/data/gao>.

[10] Department of State, Fiscal Year 1999 Budget Congressional Presentation 20.

[11] Department of State, International Narcotics Control Strategy Report, March 1998.

[12] Department of State, Fiscal Year 1999 Budget Congressional Presentation 21.

United States, Department of State, Bureau for International Narcotics and Law Enforcement Affairs, End-Use Monitoring Report, 1995 (Washington: Department of State, February 1997): 70-4.

[13] United States, Senate, Appropriations Committee, Foreign Operations Subcommittee, Committee Report 105-35 (Washington: U.S. Senate, June 24, 1997.) <ftp://ftp.loc.gov/pub/thomas/cp105/sr035.txt> Adobe Acrobat (.pdf) format <http://frwebgate.access.gpo.gov/cgi-bin/getdoc.cgi?dbname=105_cong_reports&docid=f:sr035.105.pdf>.

[14] United States, Department of State, Bureau of International Narcotics and Law Enforcement Affairs, Fiscal Year 1998 Budget Congressional Presentation (Washington: Department of State: March 1997): 13-16.

[15] Department of State, International Narcotics Control Strategy Report, March 1998.

[16] U.S. Senate, Committee Report 105-35.

[17] Department of State, Fiscal Year 1999 Budget Congressional Presentation 21.

[18] Department of State, Fiscal Year 1999 Budget Congressional Presentation 21.

[19] Department of State, Fiscal Year 1999 Budget Congressional Presentation 21.

[20] Department of State, International Narcotics Control Strategy Report, March 1998.

[21] Department of State, International Narcotics Control Strategy Report, March 1998.

[22] Department of State, International Narcotics Control Strategy Report, March 1998.

[23] Department of State, Fiscal Year 1999 Budget Congressional Presentation 30.

[24] Department of State, Fiscal Year 1999 Budget Congressional Presentation 30.

[25] General Accounting Office, U.S. Counternarcotics Efforts in Colombia 35.

[26] Beers.

[27] R. Rand Beers, Acting Assistant Secretary of State, International Narcotics and Law Enforcement Affairs, Statement before the House International Relations Committee, Washington, DC. March 31, 1998 <http://www.state.gov/www/policy_remarks/1998/980331_beers_hirc.html>.

[28] Department of State, Fiscal Year 1999 Budget Congressional Presentation 95.

[29] General Accounting Office, U.S. Counternarcotics Efforts in Colombia 8-9, 33-4.

[30] Department of State, International Narcotics Control Strategy Report, March 1998.

[31] General Accounting Office, U.S. Counternarcotics Efforts in Colombia 8-9, 33-4.

[32] General Accounting Office, U.S. Counternarcotics Efforts in Colombia 8-9, 33-4.

[33] General Accounting Office, U.S. Counternarcotics Efforts in Colombia 4, 7.

[34] General Accounting Office, U.S. Counternarcotics Efforts in Colombia 44.

[35] United States, General Accounting Office, "Drug Control: Status of U.S. International Narcotics Activities," Statement of Benjamin F. Nelson, Director, International Relations and Trade Issues, National Security and International Affairs Division, document number GAO/T-NSIAD-98-116, Washington, March 12, 1998: 3 <http://frwebgate.access.gpo.gov/cgi-bin/useftp.cgi?IPaddress=waisback.access.gpo.gov&filename=ns98116t.txt&directory=/diskb/wais/data/gao>,
Adobe Acrobat (.pdf) format <http://frwebgate.access.gpo.gov/cgi-bin/useftp.cgi?IPaddress=waisback.access.gpo.gov&filename=ns98116t.pdf&directory=/diskb/wais/data/gao>.

Department of State, Fiscal Year 1999 Budget Congressional Presentation 48.

[36] Department of State, <u>Fiscal Year 1999 Budget Congressional Presentation</u> 48.

[37] Department of State, <u>International Narcotics Control Strategy Report</u>, March 1998.

[38] General Accounting Office, "Status of Counternarcotics Efforts in Mexico" 9.

General Accounting Office, " Status of U.S. International Narcotics Activities" 8.

United States, Executive Office of the President, Office of National Drug Control Policy, <u>Report to Congress: Volume I</u>, Washington, September 15, 1997: 16 <http://www.whitehousedrugpolicy.gov/enforce/rpttocong/rpttoc.html>, Adobe Acrobat (.pdf) format <http://www.whitehousedrugpolicy.gov/enforce/rpttocong/report.pdf>.

[39] Department of State, <u>Fiscal Year 1999 Budget Congressional Presentation</u> 49-50.

[40] Department of State, <u>Fiscal Year 1999 Budget Congressional Presentation</u> 49.

Department of State, <u>International Narcotics Control Strategy Report</u>, March 1998.

[41] Department of State, <u>Fiscal Year 1999 Budget Congressional Presentation</u> 49-50.

[42] Department of State, <u>Fiscal Year 1999 Budget Congressional Presentation</u> 50.

[43] Department of State, <u>Fiscal Year 1997 Budget Congressional Presentation</u> 37.

[44] United States, Department of State, Office of Resources, Plans and Policy, <u>Congressional Presentation for Foreign Operations, Fiscal Year 1999</u> (Washington: March 1998): 1103.

[45] Department of State, <u>Fiscal Year 1999 Budget Congressional Presentation</u> 57.

[46] Department of State, <u>Fiscal Year 1997 Budget Congressional Presentation</u> 42.

[47] Department of State, <u>Fiscal Year 1999 Budget Congressional Presentation</u> 58.

[48] Department of State, <u>Congressional Presentation for Foreign Operations, Fiscal Year 1999</u> 3.

Department of State, <u>Fiscal Year 1999 Budget Congressional Presentation</u> 95.

[49] Department of State, <u>Fiscal Year 1999 Budget Congressional Presentation</u> 58.

[50] General Accounting Office, <u>Long-Standing Problems</u> 15.

[51] Department of State, <u>Fiscal Year 1999 Budget Congressional Presentation</u> 57-8.

[52] Department of State, <u>Fiscal Year 1999 Budget Congressional Presentation</u> 95.

[53] General Accounting Office, <u>U.S. Counternarcotics Efforts in Colombia</u> 35.

[54] United States, Executive Office of the President, Office of National Drug Control Policy, <u>The National Drug Control Strategy</u>, Washington, February 1998: 57-8 <http://www.whitehousedrugpolicy.gov/policy/ndcs.html>.

[55] United States, Department of State, Office of Resources, Plans and Policy, <u>Congressional Presentation for Foreign Operations, Fiscal Year 1998</u> (Washington: Department of State, March 1997): 48.

[56] Department of State, <u>Congressional Presentation for Foreign Operations, Fiscal Year 1999</u> 11.

[57] Department of State, <u>Congressional Presentation for Foreign Operations, Fiscal Year 1999</u> 355.

[58] Department of State, <u>Congressional Presentation for Foreign Operations, Fiscal Year 1998</u> 49.

[59] Department of State, <u>Congressional Presentation for Foreign Operations, Fiscal Year 1999</u> 12.

ONDCP Discretionary Funding:

[1] United States, Executive Office of the President, Office of National Drug Control Policy, "Drug Czar McCaffrey Announces New $9.8 million To Fight Drug Traffickers in Peru," press release, June 26, 1997, March 1998 <http://www.whitehousedrugpolicy.gov/news/press/062697.html>.

[2] United States, Executive Office of the President, Office of National Drug Control Policy, memo in response to congressional inquiry, February 1998.

[3] United States, Executive Office of the President, Office of National Drug Control Policy, memo in response to congressional inquiry, February 1998.

[4] United States, Executive Office of the President, Office of National Drug Control Policy, memo in response to congressional inquiry, February 1998.

Excess Defense Articles:

[1] United States, Department of State, Office of Resources, Plans and Policy, Congressional Presentation for Foreign Operations, Fiscal Year 1998 (Washington: March 1997): 668.

Excess Defense Articles Electronic Bulletin Board, United States Department of Defense, Washington, September 1997 <telnet://134.152.212.131>.

United States, Department of State, Department of Defense, Foreign Military Assistance Act Report To Congress, Fiscal Year 1996 (Washington: September 1997).

[2] United States, Department of State, Office of Resources, Plans and Policy, Congressional Presentation for Foreign Operations, Fiscal Year 1999 (Washington: March 1998): 1146.

[3] Congressional Presentation, Fiscal Year 1998 667.

Excess Defense Articles Electronic Bulletin Board.

Foreign Military Assistance Act Report To Congress.

[4] Congressional Presentation, Fiscal Year 1999 1145.

Emergency Drawdowns:

[1] United States, General Accounting Office, Drug Control: U.S. Counternarcotics Efforts in Colombia Face Continuing Challenges, document number GAO/NSIAD-98-60, Washington, February 1998 <http://frwebgate.access.gpo.gov/cgi-bin/useftp.cgi?IPaddress=waisback.access.gpo.gov&filename=ns98060.txt&directory=/diskb/wais/data/gao>
Adobe Acrobat (.pdf) format <http://frwebgate.access.gpo.gov/cgi-bin/useftp.cgi?IPaddress=waisback.access.gpo.gov&filename=ns98060.pdf&directory=/diskb/wais/data/gao>.

[2] General Accounting Office, U.S. Counternarcotics Efforts in Colombia.

[3] General Accounting Office, U.S. Counternarcotics Efforts in Colombia.

[4] General Accounting Office, U.S. Counternarcotics Efforts in Colombia.

[5] United States, General Accounting Office, "Drug Control: Status of Counternarcotics Efforts in Mexico," Statement of Benjamin F. Nelson, Director, International Relations and Trade Issues, National Security and International Affairs Division, before the Subcommittee on National Security, International Affairs, and Criminal Justice, Committee on Government Reform and Oversight, House of Representatives; and the Caucus on International Narcotics Control, U.S. Senate, document number GAO/T-NSIAD-98-129, Washington, March 18, 1998: 9 <http://frwebgate.access.gpo.gov/cgi-bin/useftp.cgi?IPaddress=waisback.access.gpo.gov&filename=ns98129t.txt&directory=/diskb/wais/data/gao>.

[6] United States, Executive Office of the President, Office of National Drug Control Policy, Report to Congress: Volume I, Washington, September 15, 1997: 20 <http://www.whitehousedrugpolicy.gov/enforce/rpttocong/rpttoc.html>,
Adobe Acrobat (.pdf) format
<http://www.whitehousedrugpolicy.gov/enforce/rpttocong/report.pdf>.

[7] United States, General Accounting Office, "Drug Control: Status of U.S. International Narcotics Activities," Statement of Benjamin F. Nelson, Director, International Relations and Trade Issues, National Security and International Affairs Division, document number GAO/T-NSIAD-98-116, Washington, March 12, 1998: 8 <http://frwebgate.access.gpo.gov/cgi-bin/useftp.cgi?IPaddress=waisback.access.gpo.gov&filename=ns98116t.txt&directory=/diskb/wais/data/gao>,

Adobe Acrobat (.pdf) format <http://frwebgate.access.gpo.gov/cgi-bin/useftp.cgi?IPaddress=waisback.access.gpo.gov&filename=ns98116t.pdf&directory=/diskb/wais/data/gao>.

[8] General Accounting Office, "Status of Counternarcotics Efforts in Mexico" 2.

[9] General Accounting Office, "Status of Counternarcotics Efforts in Mexico" 12-13.

[10] General Accounting Office, "Status of U.S. International Narcotics Activities" 10-11.

[11] General Accounting Office, "Status of U.S. International Narcotics Activities" 11.

[12] United States, General Accounting Office, "Drug Control: Observations on Counternarcotics Activities in Mexico," Statement of Jess T. Ford, Associate Director, International Relations and Trade Issues, National Security and International Affairs Division, document number GAO/T-NSIAD-96-239, September 12, 1996: 5-6 <http://frwebgate.access.gpo.gov/cgi-bin/useftp.cgi?IPaddress=wais.access.gpo.gov&filename=ns96239t.txt&directory=/diskb/wais/data/gao>,
Adobe Acrobat (.pdf) format <frwebgate.access.gpo.gov/cgi-bin/useftp.cgi?IPaddress=wais.access.gpo.gov&filename=ns96239t.pdf&directory=/diskb/wais/data/gao>.

[13] United States, Department of State, "Summary Sheet," fax document, September 16, 1997.

Federal Register, October 10, 1997: 53221.

[14] United States, Department of State, "Memorandum of Justification for use of Section 506(a)(2) special authority to draw down articles, services, and military education and training," December 1996.

United States, Department of State, Bureau of Legislative Affairs, "506 (a)(2) Drawdown Package," September 13, 1996.

Federal Register, December 11, 1996: 65149.

[15] Department of State, "Summary Sheet."

[16] United States, Department of State, "Memorandum of Justification for use of Section 506(a)(2) special authority to draw down articles, services, and military education and training," September 1996.

Federal Register, November 4, 1996: 56865.

[17] Federal Register, September 25, 1996: 50417.

[18] Federal Register, June 23, 1995: 35463.

Leased Defense Articles:

[1] United States, Department of State, Office of Resources, Plans and Policy, Congressional Presentation for Foreign Operations, Fiscal Year 1998 (Washington: March 1997): 669-70.

[2] United States, Department of State, Office of Resources, Plans and Policy, Congressional Presentation for Foreign Operations, Fiscal Year 1999 (Washington: March 1998): 1148.

International Criminal Investigative Training Assistance Program:

1 United States, Department of Justice, Annual Report of Organizational Development and Training Activities, 1996, (Washington: Department of Justice, 1997).

2 United States, Bureau for International Narcotics and Law Enforcement Affairs, Department of State, International Narcotics Control Strategy Report, Washington, March 1998, March 2, 1998 <http://www.state.gov/www/global/narcotics_law/1997_narc_report/index.html>.

Defense Department Programs

Section 124/1004:

[1] United States, Executive Office of the President, Office of National Drug Control

Policy (ONDCP), Report to Congress: Volume I, Washington, September 15, 1997: 16 <http://www.whitehousedrugpolicy.gov/enforce/rpttocong/rpttoc.html>, Adobe Acrobat (.pdf) format <http://www.whitehousedrugpolicy.gov/enforce/rpttocong/report.pdf>.

[2] United States, Executive Office of the President, Office of National Drug Control Policy (ONDCP), The National Drug Control Strategy: Budget Summary, Washington, February 1998: 34 <http://www.whitehousedrugpolicy.gov/pdf/sum_pt1.pdf>.

[3] United States, General Accounting Office, "Drug Control: Status of Counternarcotics Efforts in Mexico," Statement of Benjamin F. Nelson, Director, International Relations and Trade Issues, National Security and International Affairs Division, before the Subcommittee on National Security, International Affairs, and Criminal Justice, Committee on Government Reform and Oversight, House of Representatives; and the Caucus on International Narcotics Control, U.S. Senate, document number GAO/T-NSIAD-98-129, Washington, March 18, 1998: 9 <http://http://frwebgate.access.gpo.gov/cgi-bin/useftp.cgi?IPaddress=waisback.access.gpo.gov&filename=ns98129t.txt&directory=/diskb/wais/data/gao>.

Robert J. Newberry, acting deputy assistant secretary for Drug Enforcement Policy and Support, United States Department of Defense, letter to Rep. James P. McGovern (D-MA), December 12, 1997.

[4] United States, Bureau for International Narcotics and Law Enforcement Affairs (INL), Department of State, International Narcotics Control Strategy Report, Washington, March 1998, March 2, 1998, <http://www.state.gov/www/global/narcotics_law/1997_narc_report/index.html>.

[5] ONDCP, Report to Congress: Volume I 20-1.

[6] ONDCP, Report to Congress: Volume I 20-1.

[7] ONDCP, Report to Congress: Volume I 21.

[8] Newberry.

ONDCP, Report to Congress: Volume I 21.

[9] ONDCP, The National Drug Control Strategy: Budget Summary 34-5.

[10] United States, Defense Department, Kenneth H. Bacon, Assistant Secretary of Defense, Public Affairs, News Briefing, Tuesday, May 26, 1998, 1:40 p.m. <http://www.defenselink.mil/news/May1998/t05261998_t0526asd.html>.

[11] INL, International Narcotics Control Strategy Report.

[12] Bacon.

[13] H. Allen Holmes, coordinator for drug enforcement policy and support, United States Department of Defense, letter in response to congressional inquiry, Jan. 23, 1998.

This letter includes the following footnotes:
(1) Caribbean: FY97 reflects actual OPTEMPO; FY98 is estimated.
(2) Colombia: FY97 reflects commercialization of Ground Mobile Radars.

Section 1031:

[1] United States, Executive Office of the President, Office of National Drug Control Policy (ONDCP), Report to Congress: Volume I, Washington, September 15, 1997: 16 <http://www.whitehousedrugpolicy.gov/enforce/rpttocong/rpttoc.html>, Adobe Acrobat (.pdf) format <http://www.whitehousedrugpolicy.gov/enforce/rpttocong/report.pdf>.

Section 1033:

[1] United States, Executive Office of the President, Office of National Drug Control Policy, The National Drug Control Strategy, Washington, February 1998: 57-8 <http://www.whitehousedrugpolicy.gov/policy/ndcs.html>.

[2] United States Southern Command, Statement of General Charles E. Wilhelm, USMC, Commander in Chief, before the Committee on Government Reform and Oversight, Subcommittee on National Security, International Affairs, and Criminal Justice, House of Representatives, March 12, 1998: 8-9.

[3] Wilhelm 18.

[4] H. Allen Holmes, coordinator for drug enforcement policy and support, United States Department of Defense, letter in response to congressional inquiry, Jan. 23, 1998.

School of the Americas:

[1] Spanish Helicopter School Battalion, April 1998, <http://www.snowhill.com/~fig/soa.html>.

[2] United States, General Accounting Office, School of the Americas: U.S. Military Training for Latin American Countries, document no. NSIAD-96-178 (Washington: GAO, August 22, 1996) <http://frwebgate.access.gpo.gov/cgi-bin/useftp.cgi?IPaddress=wais.access.gpo.gov&filename=ns96178.txt&directory=/diskb/wais/data/gao> Adobe Acrobat (.pdf) format <http://frwebgate.access.gpo.gov/cgi-bin/useftp.cgi?IPaddress=wais.access.gpo.gov&filename=ns96178.pdf&directory=/diskb/wais/data/gao>.

[3] United States, Department of Defense, response to inquiry from Rep. Sidney R. Yates, March 13, 1997.

[4] U.S. Army School of the Americas, June 1997 <http://www.benning.army.mil/usarsa/main.htm>.

United States, Department of the Army, Certifications and Report on the U.S. Army School of the Americas, Washington: January 1998 <http://www.benning.army.mil/usarsa/certif/content.htm>.

[5] United States Army School of the Americas, Yearly List of Students Trained at SOA, 1997.

Inter-American Air Forces Academy:

[1] United States, Inter-American Air Forces Academy, Office of the Registrar, e-mail communication with the authors, March 24, 1998.

[2] Inter-American Air Forces Academy, March 1998, <http://www.lak.aetc.af.mil/iaafa/test.htm>.

Center for Hemispheric Defense Studies:

[1] United States, Department of Defense, Center for Hemispheric Defense Studies, "Center for Hemispheric Defense Studies: Understanding and Mutual Trust," pamphlet, 1998.

[2] United States, Department of Defense, Center for Hemispheric Defense Studies, documents from inaugural conference for the CHDS (Washington, September 1997).

[3] "Center for Hemispheric Defense Studies: Understanding and Mutual Trust."

[4] "March 1998 Demographics"; "May 1998 Demographics," Fact sheet from CHDS, 1998.

[5] Documents from inaugural conference for the CHDS.

Foreign Student Program at U.S. Service Academies:

[1] United States, Department of Defense, "Foreign student program at the U.S. service academies," (Washington: 1997).

[2] Department of Defense.

[3] Department of Defense.

[4] Department of Defense.

Exercises:

[1] United States, Department of Defense, Defense Institute of Security Assistance Management, The Management of Security Assistance, 17th ed. (Wright-Patterson AFB, OH: May 1997): 732.

[2] United States, Department of Defense, National Defense University, "Chapter nine:

Defense Engagement in Peacetime," Strategic Assessment 1996: Elements of U.S. Power, 1996, April 1998 <http://www.ndu.edu/ndu/inss/sa96/sa96ch09.html>.

[3] United States Southern Command, Operations Directorate (J3) Exercise Overview, (U.S. Southern Command: May 21, 1997).

[4] Southern Command, Exercise Overview.

[5] United States Southern Command, Statement of General Charles E. Wilhelm, USMC, Commander in Chief, before the Committee on Government Reform and Oversight, Subcommittee on National Security, International Affairs, and Criminal Justice, House of Representatives, March 12, 1998: 9.

[6] Wilhelm 10.

[7] Southern Command, Exercise Overview.

Tentative Exercise Calendar:

[1] United States Southern Command, Operations Directorate (J3) Exercise Overview, (U.S. Southern Command: May 21, 1997).

Humanitarian and Civic Assistance:

[1] United States, Department of Defense, Office of the Assistant Secretary of Defense for Special Operations and Low-Intensity Conflict, Humanitarian and Civic Assistance Program of the Department of Defense, Fiscal Year 1996, (Washington: Department of Defense, March 1, 1997).

[2] United States, Department of Defense, Office of the Assistant Secretary of Defense for Public Affairs, Public Affairs Guidance on Fuertes Caminos in Guatemala, (Washington: Department of Defense, December 1994).

[3] United States, Department of Defense, Office of the Assistant Secretary of Defense for Special Operations and Low-Intensity Conflict, Humanitarian and Civic Assistance Program of the Department of Defense, Fiscal Year 1997, (Washington: Department of Defense, March 1, 1998).

[4] Office of the Assistant Secretary of Defense for Special Operations and Low-Intensity Conflict, Humanitarian and Civic Assistance Program of the Department of Defense, Fiscal Year 1996.

[5] United States Southern Command, Operations Directorate (J3) Exercise Overview, (U.S. Southern Command: May 21, 1997).

Deployments for Training:

[1] Richard K. Kolb, "Tracking the Traffic. U.S. Southcom Counters Cocaine at the Source," Dialogo: The military forum of the Americas, (U.S. Southern Command: July-September 1997) <http://www.allenwayne.com/dialogo/julsep97/frames/article.htm>.

[2] United States Southern Command, Operations Directorate (J3) Exercise Overview, (U.S. Southern Command: May 21, 1997).

[3] United States Southern Command.

[4] United States, Department of Defense, Defense Institute of Security Assistance Management, The Management of Security Assistance, 17th ed. (Wright-Patterson AFB, OH: May 1997): 736.

[5] Defense Institute of Security Assistance Management 736.

[6] Defense Institute of Security Assistance Management 734.

[7] Kenneth H. Bacon, Assistant Secretary of Defense for Public Affairs, U.S. Department of Defense, "Department of Defense News Briefing," The Pentagon, Washington, March 26, 1998, 1:45 PM EST, April 1998 <http://www.defenselink.mil/news/Mar1998/t03261998_t0326asd.html>.

[8] United States, General Accounting Office, Drug Control: Interdiction Efforts in Central America Have Had Little Impact on the Flow of Drugs, document number GAO/NSIAD-94-

233, Washington, August 1994 <http://frwebgate.access.gpo.gov/cgi-bin/useftp.cgi?IPaddress=wais.access.gpo.gov&filename=ns94233.txt&directory=/diskb/wais/data/gao>.

United States, Department of Defense, National Defense University, "Chapter 12: Unconventional Military Instruments," Strategic Assessment 1996: Elements of U.S. Power, 1996, April 1998 <http://www.ndu.edu/ndu/inss/sa96/sa96ch12.html>.

[9] National Defense University.

[10] United States, Mission to the Organization of American States, "Note From the Permanent Mission of the United States of America Forwarding an Inventory of Confidence- and Security-Building Measures," I Regional Conference on Confidence- and Security-Building Measures in the Region, Santiago, Chile, November 8-10, 1995, Document no. OEA/Ser.K/XXIX.2: 10.

Special Operations Forces:

[1] William S. Cohen, Secretary of Defense, United States, Annual Report To the President and Congress, 1998, April 1998 <http://www.dtic.mil/execsec/adr98/index.html>.

[2] Cohen.

[3] Gen. Peter J. Schoomaker, commander, U.S. Special Operations Command, "Special Operations Forces: The Way Ahead," Defense Issues 13:10 (Washington: American Forces Information Service, 1997), April 1998 <http://www.defenselink.mil//di98/di1310.html>.

- **Army** units include:
  - Army Special Forces (known as the "Green Berets"): five active and two Army National Guard groups;
  - Rangers: three active battalions based In the United States;
  - Special Operations Aviation (SOA): one regiment in the United States and one company in Panama;
  - Psychological operations (PSYOP) forces: three groups, one active and two U.S. Army Reserve;
  - Civil affairs (CA) units: three U.S. Army Reserve CA commands, nine Army Reserve CA brigades, 24 Army Reserve CA battalions, and one active-duty CA battalion. 97 percent of civil affairs forces are reservists;
  - Signal, logistical and headquarters units within the U.S. Army Special Operations Command.
- **Navy** units include Sea-Air-Land forces (SEALs), special boat units and SEAL delivery units.
  - Two Naval Special Warfare Groups (NSWGs) are composed of three SEAL teams and a SEAL Delivery Vehicle team;
  - Two Special Boat Squadrons (SBS) have a Special Boat Unit and coastal patrol ships;
  - Naval Special Warfare Units are located outside the United States, either based at a regional command (such as Southcom) or accompanying a naval fleet or task force.
- **Air Force** SOF are organized into one Special Operations Wing, two Special Operations Groups (one each in the Pacific and European Commands), one Special Tactics Group, and a Special Operations Wing in both the Air Force Reserve and Air National Guard. Each of these units has "special operations squadrons" within it, which include special tactics squadrons, a foreign internal defense squadron, and a combat weather squadron.

[4] Cohen.

[5] Gen. Henry H. Shelton, commander in chief, U.S. Special Operations Command, "Special Operations Forces: Key Role in Preventive Defense," Defense Issues 12:12 (Washington: American Forces Information Service, 1997), April 1998 <http://www.defenselink.mil/pubs/di97/di1212.html>.

[6] Shelton.

Schoomaker.

[7] Schoomaker.

[8] Cohen.

[9] Richard K. Kolb, "Tracking the Traffic. U.S. Southcom Counters Cocaine at the Source," Dialogo: The military forum of the Americas. (U.S. Southern Command: July-September 1997) <http://www.allenwayne.com/dialogo/julsep97/frames/article.htm>.

[10] H. Allen Holmes, assistant secretary of defense for special operations and low-intensity conflict, "Military Operations in the Post-Cold War Era," Remarks at the Intelligence in Partnership Conference, Joint Military Intelligence College, Andrews Air Force Base, Md., June 26, 1997, Defense Issues 12:34 (Washington: American Forces Information Service, 1997) April 1998 <http://www.defenselink.mil/pubs/di97/di1234.html>.

United States, Executive Office of the President, Office of National Drug Control Policy, Report to Congress: Volume I, Washington, September 15, 1997: 18 <http://www.whitehousedrugpolicy.gov/enforce/rpttocong/rpttoc.html>, Adobe Acrobat (.pdf) format <http://www.whitehousedrugpolicy.gov/enforce/rpttocong/report.pdf>.

[11] Kolb.

[12] United States, Defense Department, Kenneth H. Bacon, Assistant Secretary of Defense, Public Affairs, News Briefing, Tuesday, March 26, 1998, 1:45 p.m. <http://www.defenselink.mil/news/Mar1998/t03261998_t0326asd.html>.

[13] United States, Defense Department, Kenneth H. Bacon, Assistant Secretary of Defense, Public Affairs, News Briefing, Tuesday, May 26, 1998, 1:40 p.m. <http://www.defenselink.mil/news/May1998/t05261998_t0526asd.html>.

[14] United States, Bureau for International Narcotics and Law Enforcement Affairs (INL), Department of State, International Narcotics Control Strategy Report, Washington, March 1998, March 2, 1998, <http://www.state.gov/www/global/narcotics_law/1997_narc_report/index.html>.

[15] Bacon, May 26, 1998.

[16] Bacon, May 26, 1998.

Foreign Military Interaction:

[1] United States, Department of Defense, Defense Institute of Security Assistance Management, The Management of Security Assistance, 17th ed. (Wright-Patterson AFB, OH: May 1997): 722.

[2] United States, Mission to the Organization of American States, "Note From the Permanent Mission of the United States of America Forwarding an Inventory of Confidence- and Security-Building Measures," I Regional Conference on Confidence- and Security-Building Measures in the Region, Santiago, Chile, November 8-10, 1995, Document no. OEA/Ser.K/XXIX.2: 10.

[3] Mission to the Organization of American States 10.

[4] Inter-American Defense Board, Organization of American States, April 1998 <http://www.jid.org/>.

[5] Inter-American Defense Board.

[6] United States, Department of Defense, National Defense University, "Chapter nine: Defense Engagement in Peacetime," Strategic Assessment 1996: Elements of U.S. Power, 1996, April 1998 <http://www.ndu.edu/ndu/inss/sa96/sa96ch09.html>.

Non-Lethal Excess Property Transfers:

[1] United States Southern Command, Statement of General Charles E. Wilhelm, USMC, Commander in Chief, before the Committee on Government Reform and Oversight, Subcommittee on National Security, International Affairs, and Criminal Justice, House of Representatives, March 12, 1998: 13-4.

[2] Wilhelm 13-4.

[3] Wilhelm 13-4.

[4] United States, Department of Defense, Office of the Secretary of Defense, Humanitarian Assistance, faxed response to inquiry, November 3, 1997.

U.S. Southern Command:

[1] Col. M. L. Olson, USMC, Vice Director, J-5, United States Southern Command, J5 Strategy, Policy and Plans Directorate, document acquired May 1997.

[2] Profile of the U.S. Southern Command, October 1997, United States Southern Command Headquarters, April 1998 <http://www.ussouthcom.com/southcom/graphics/profile.htm>.

[3] Profile of the U.S. Southern Command.

[4] Profile of the U.S. Southern Command.

[5] United States Southern Command, Statement of General Charles E. Wilhelm, USMC, Commander in Chief, before the Committee on Government Reform and Oversight, Subcommittee on National Security, International Affairs, and Criminal Justice, House of Representatives, March 12, 1998: 32.

[6] Wilhelm 4-5.

[7] United States, Department of State, Enhanced Multilateral Drug Control Cooperation: A Counternarcotics Alliance for the Hemisphere, Washington, September 1997: 8. <http://www.whitehousedrugpolicy.gov/enforce/rpttocong/rpttoc.html>, Adobe Acrobat (.pdf) format <http://www.whitehousedrugpolicy.gov/enforce/rpttocong/report.pdf>.

[8] United States, General Accounting Office, Drug Control: Update on U.S. Interdiction Efforts in the Caribbean and Eastern Pacific,document number GAO/NSIAD-98-30, Washington, October, 1997: 22. <http://frwebgate.access.gpo.gov/cgi-bin/useftp.cgi?IPaddress=waisback.access.gpo.gov&filename=ns98030.txt&directory=/diskb/wais/data/gao>, Adobe Acrobat (.pdf) format <http://frwebgate.access.gpo.gov/cgi-bin/useftp.cgi?IPaddress=waisback.access.gpo.gov&filename=ns98030.pdf&directory=/diskb/wais/data/gao>.

Security Assistance Organizations:

[1] United States, Department of Defense, Defense Institute of Security Assistance Management, The Management of Security Assistance, 17th ed. (Wright-Patterson AFB, OH: May 1997): 111-28.

[2] Defense Institute of Security Assistance Management 111-28.

[3] United States, Department of State, Office of Resources, Plans and Policy, Congressional Presentation for Foreign Operations, Fiscal Year 1998 (Washington: March 1997): 660-1.

[4] United States, Department of State, Office of Resources, Plans and Policy, Congressional Presentation for Foreign Operations, Fiscal Year 1999 (Washington: March 1998): 1136-7.

[5] Department of State, Congressional Presentation for Foreign Operations, Fiscal Year 1998 663.

[6] Department of State, Congressional Presentation for Foreign Operations, Fiscal Year 1999 1140.

U.S. Bases in Panama:

[1] United States Southern Command Headquarters, Fact Sheet: U.S. Military in Panama Now, (Panama: January 31, 1997).

[2] Howard Air Force Base, April 1998 <http://www.howard.af.mil/>.

Southern Command, Fact Sheet: U.S. Military in Panama Now.

United States Southern Command, Profile of the U.S. Southern Command, October 1997, United States Southern Command Headquarters, April 1998 <http://www.ussouthcom.com/southcom/graphics/profile.htm>.

[3] Southern Command Headquarters, Fact Sheet: U.S. Military in Panama Now.

[4] Howard Air Force Base.

Southern Command, Fact Sheet: U.S. Military in Panama Now.

Southern Command, Profile of the U.S. Southern Command.

[5] United States Southern Command Headquarters, Fact Sheet: U.S. Military in Panama Now, (Panama: January 31, 1997).

[6] Profile of the U.S. Southern Command, October 1997, United States Southern Command Headquarters, April 1998 <http://www.ussouthcom.com/southcom/graphics/profile.htm>.

[7] Profile of the U.S. Southern Command.

[8] Description of the Military Bases in the Interoceanic Region, Panama, Inter-Oceanic Region Authority (ARI), April 1998 <http://www.ari-panama.com/ari-ing9.htm>.

[9] Description of the Military Bases in the Interoceanic Region.

[10] United States Southern Command Headquarters, Fact Sheet: U.S. Military in Panama Now, (Panama: January 31, 1997).

[11] Description of the Military Bases in the Interoceanic Region, Panama, Inter-Oceanic Region Authority (ARI), April 1998 <http://www.ari-panama.com/ari-ing9.htm>.

[12] Jungle Operations Training Battalion, U.S. Army South, April 1998 <http://www.army.mil/usarso/jotb.htm>.

[13] Staff Sgt. Brian Thomas, "Special Forces soldiers teach waterborne basics in Panama," Army news release, May 6, 1998, May 10, 1998 <http://www.dtic.mil/armylink/news/May1998/a19980506waterops.html>.

[14] United States Southern Command Headquarters, Fact Sheet: U.S. Military in Panama Now, (Panama: January 31, 1997).

[15] Description of the Military Bases in the Interoceanic Region, Panama, Inter-Oceanic Region Authority (ARI), April 1998 <http://www.ari-panama.com/ari-ing9.htm>.

[16] "Panamá Concede "Excesivas Responsabilidades" a Washington en el CMLN: México," Excelsior, January 27, 1998, February 1998 <http://www.excelsior.com.mx/9801/980127/exe03.html>.

Enrique Soto Cano Air Base, Honduras:

[1] United States Southern Command, Profile of the U.S. Southern Command, October 1997, United States Southern Command Headquarters, April 1998 <http://www.ussouthcom.com/southcom/graphics/profile.htm>.

[2] Profile of the U.S. Southern Command.

[3] United States, General Accounting Office, Honduras: Continuing U.S. Military Presence at Soto Cano Base Is Not Critical, document number NSIAD-95-39, (Washington: GAO, February 8, 1995): 12 <http://frwebgate.access.gpo.gov/cgi-bin/useftp.cgi?IPaddress=waisback.access.gpo.gov&filename=ns95039.txt&directory=/disk b/wais/data/gao>,
Adobe Acrobat (.pdf) format <http://frwebgate.access.gpo.gov/cgi-bin/useftp.cgi?IPaddress=waisback.access.gpo.gov&filename=ns95039.pdf&directory=/dis kb/wais/data/gao>.

[4] General Accounting Office, Continuing U.S. Military Presence 12.

[5] United States, General Accounting Office, 1996 DOD Budget: Potential Reductions to Operation and Maintenance Program, document number NSIAD-95-200BR, (Washington: GAO, September 1995): 19 <http://frwebgate.access.gpo.gov/cgi-bin/useftp.cgi?IPaddress=wais.access.gpo.gov&filename=ns95200b.txt&directory=/diskb/wais/d ata/gao>,

Adobe Acrobat (.pdf) format <http://frwebgate.access.gpo.gov/cgi-bin/useftp.cgi?IPaddress=wais.access.gpo.gov&filename=ns95200b.pdf&directory=/diskb/wais/data/gao>.

Guantánamo Bay Naval Station, Cuba:

1 U.S. Naval Station Guantánamo Bay, Cuba, April 1998, <http://www-nmimc.med.navy.mil/gitmo/NAVBASE/navbase1.htm>.

2 U.S. Naval Station Guantánamo Bay, Cuba.

3 United States, Department of Defense, "Active Duty Military Personnel Strengths by Regional Area and by Country, September 30, 1997," Defense Department Fact Sheet, November 1997, April 1998,
Adobe Acrobat (.pdf) format <http://web1.whs.osd.mil/mmid/military/hst0997.pdf>, index of military strength fact sheets <http://www.defenselink.mil/news/indexpages/fact.html>.

Operation Laser Strike:

[1] William W. Mendel and Murl D. Munger, "The Drug Threat: Getting Priorities Straight," Parameters XXVII:2 (Carlisle, PA: U.S. Army War College, Summer 1997): 110-24 <http://carlisle-www.army.mil/usawc/Parameters/97summer/munger.htm>.

[2] United States, Defense Department, Kenneth H. Bacon, Assistant Secretary of Defense, Public Affairs, News Briefing, Tuesday, June 25, 1996, 2:30 p.m. <http://www.defenselink.mil/news/Jun1996/t062596_t0625asd.html>.

[3] United States, Executive Office of the President, Office of National Drug Control Policy, The National Drug Control Strategy: Budget Summary, Washington, February 1998: 57-8 <http://www.whitehousedrugpolicy.gov/pdf/sum_pt1.pdf>.

[4] United States Southern Command, Statement of General Charles E. Wilhelm, USMC, Commander in Chief, before the Committee on Government Reform and Oversight, Subcommittee on National Security, International Affairs, and Criminal Justice, House of Representatives, March 12, 1998: 18.

[5] United States, Bureau for International Narcotics and Law Enforcement Affairs, Department of State, International Narcotics Control Strategy Report, Washington, March 1998, March 2, 1998 <http://www.state.gov/www/global/narcotics_law/1997_narc_report/index.html>.

[6] Department of State, International Narcotics Control Strategy Report.

[7] United States, Executive Office of the President, Office of National Drug Control Policy, Statement by General Barry R. McCaffrey, director, before the Committee on Government Reform and Oversight, Subcommittee on National Security, International Affairs, and Criminal Justice, U.S. House of Representatives. October 1, 1996, April 1998 <http://www.whitehousedrugpolicy.gov/news/testimony/narrativ.html>.

[8] Richard K. Kolb, "Tracking the Traffic. U.S. Southcom Counters Cocaine at the Source," Dialogo: The military forum of the Americas. (U.S. Southern Command: July-September 1997) <http://www.allenwayne.com/dialogo/julsep97/frames/article.htm>.

[9] Wilhelm 7.

[10] United States, Department of State. Enhanced Multilateral Drug Control Cooperation: A Counternarcotics Alliance for the Hemisphere. (Washington: Department of State, September 1997): 8 <http://www.whitehousedrugpolicy.gov/enforce/rpttocong/rpttoc.html> Adobe Acrobat (.pdf) format <http://www.whitehousedrugpolicy.gov/enforce/rpttocong/report.pdf>.

[11] Kolb.

[12] Kolb.

U.S. Support Group - Haiti:

[1] United States Southern Command, Statement of General Charles E. Wilhelm, USMC, Commander in Chief, before the Committee on Government Reform and Oversight, Subcommittee on National Security, International Affairs, and Criminal Justice, House of Representatives, March 12, 1998.

United States, Department of Defense, "Active Duty Military Personnel Strengths by Regional Area and by Country, September 30, 1997." Fact Sheet, October 1997, April 1998 <http://web1.whs.osd.mil/mmid/military/hst0997.pdf>.

[2] Wilhelm.

[3] Wilhelm.

[4] Wilhelm.

[5] Wilhelm.

Operation Safe Border:

[1] Gen. Henry H. Shelton, USA, commander in chief, U.S. Special Operations Command, Department of Defense, "Special Operations Forces: Key Role in Preventive Defense," Defense Issues 12:12 (Washington: American Forces Information Service, 1997) March 1998 <http://www.defenselink.mil/pubc/di97/di1212.html>.

[2] Shelton.

[3] "U.S. Army Training and Operations Update," Armylink News (Washington: U.S. Army, March 4, 1998) April 1998 <http://www.dtic.mil/armylink/news/Mar1998/r19980305_update.html>.

[4] "U.S. Army Training and Operations Update," Armylink News (Washington: U.S. Army, March 4, 1998) April 1998 <http://www.dtic.mil/armylink/news/Jan1998/r19980108update.html>.

[5] United States Southern Command, Statement of General Charles E. Wilhelm, USMC, Commander in Chief, before the Committee on Government Reform and Oversight, Subcommittee on National Security, International Affairs, and Criminal Justice, House of Representatives, March 12, 1998: 9.

Demining in Central America:

[1] United States Southern Command, Statement of General Charles E. Wilhelm, USMC, Commander in Chief, before the Committee on Government Reform and Oversight, Subcommittee on National Security, International Affairs, and Criminal Justice, House of Representatives, March 12, 1998: 15.

[2] Wilhelm 16.